Communications
in Computer and Information Science   1838

Rationale

The CCIS series is devoted to the publication of proceedings of computer science conferences. Its aim is to efficiently disseminate original research results in informatics in printed and electronic form. While the focus is on publication of peer-reviewed full papers presenting mature work, inclusion of reviewed short papers reporting on work in progress is welcome, too. Besides globally relevant meetings with internationally representative program committees guaranteeing a strict peer-reviewing and paper selection process, conferences run by societies or of high regional or national relevance are also considered for publication.

Topics

The topical scope of CCIS spans the entire spectrum of informatics ranging from foundational topics in the theory of computing to information and communications science and technology and a broad variety of interdisciplinary application fields.

Information for Volume Editors and Authors

Publication in CCIS is free of charge. No royalties are paid, however, we offer registered conference participants temporary free access to the online version of the conference proceedings on SpringerLink (http://link.springer.com) by means of an http referrer from the conference website and/or a number of complimentary printed copies, as specified in the official acceptance email of the event.

CCIS proceedings can be published in time for distribution at conferences or as post-proceedings, and delivered in the form of printed books and/or electronically as USBs and/or e-content licenses for accessing proceedings at SpringerLink. Furthermore, CCIS proceedings are included in the CCIS electronic book series hosted in the SpringerLink digital library at http://link.springer.com/bookseries/7899. Conferences publishing in CCIS are allowed to use Online Conference Service (OCS) for managing the whole proceedings lifecycle (from submission and reviewing to preparing for publication) free of charge.

Publication process

The language of publication is exclusively English. Authors publishing in CCIS have to sign the Springer CCIS copyright transfer form, however, they are free to use their material published in CCIS for substantially changed, more elaborate subsequent publications elsewhere. For the preparation of the camera-ready papers/files, authors have to strictly adhere to the Springer CCIS Authors' Instructions and are strongly encouraged to use the CCIS LaTeX style files or templates.

Abstracting/Indexing

CCIS is abstracted/indexed in DBLP, Google Scholar, EI-Compendex, Mathematical Reviews, SCImago, Scopus. CCIS volumes are also submitted for the inclusion in ISI Proceedings.

How to start

To start the evaluation of your proposal for inclusion in the CCIS series, please send an e-mail to ccis@springer.com.

Dalila Durães · Alfonso González-Briones ·
Marin Lujak · Alia El Bolock · João Carneiro
Editors

Highlights in Practical Applications of Agents, Multi-Agent Systems, and Cognitive Mimetics

The PAAMS Collection

International Workshops of PAAMS 2023
Guimaraes, Portugal, July 12–14, 2023
Proceedings

 Springer

Editors
Dalila Durães 🆔
University of Minho
Braga, Portugal

Alfonso González-Briones 🆔
University of Salamanca
Salamanca, Spain

Marin Lujak 🆔
University Rey Juan Carlos
Mostoles, Spain

Alia El Bolock
German International University
Cairo, Egypt

João Carneiro 🆔
ISEP/GECAD
Porto, Portugal

ISSN 1865-0929   ISSN 1865-0937 (electronic)
Communications in Computer and Information Science
ISBN 978-3-031-37592-7   ISBN 978-3-031-37593-4 (eBook)
https://doi.org/10.1007/978-3-031-37593-4

This Springer imprint is published by the registered company Springer Nature Switzerland AG
The registered company address is: Gewerbestrasse 11, 6330 Cham, Switzerland

Preface

The PAAMS Workshops complemented the regular program with new or emerging trends of particular interest connected to multi-agent systems. PAAMS, the International Conference on Practical Applications of Agents and Multi-Agent Systems, is an evolution of the International Workshop on Practical Applications of Agents and Multi-Agent Systems. PAAMS is an international yearly setting for presenting, discussing, and disseminating the latest developments and the most important outcomes related to real-world applications. It provides a unique opportunity to bring multi-disciplinary experts, academics, and practitioners together to exchange their experience in the development of agents and multi-agent systems.

This volume presents the papers that were accepted in the workshops during the 2023 edition of PAAMS: the Workshop on Adaptive Smart areaS and Intelligent Agents (ASSIA), the Workshop on Character Computing (C2), and the Workshop on Decision Support, Recommendation, and Persuasion in Artificial Intelligence (DeRePAI). Each paper submitted to PAAMS went through a stringent single-blind peer review by three members of the international committee of each track. From the 26 submissions received, 14 were selected for presentation at the conference.

The conference was organized by the LASI and Centro Algoritmi of the University of Minho (Portugal). We would like to thank all the contributing authors, the members of the Program Committee, the sponsors (AIR Institute, and Câmara Municipal de Guimarães) and the Organizing Committee for their hard and highly valuable work. We are grateful for the funding supporting the project "*XAI: Sistemas inteligentes auto-explicativos creados con modelos de mezcla de expertos*" (Id. SA082P20), funded by the Regional Government of Castilla y León and FEDER funds.

Thanks for your help – PAAMS 2023 would not exist without your contribution.

July 2023

Dalila Durães
Alfonso González-Briones
Marin Lujak
Alia El Bolock
João Carneiro

Organization

General Co-chairs

Philippe Mathieu   University of Lille, France
Frank Dignum   Umeå University, Sweden
Paulo Novais   University of Minho, Portugal
Fernando De la Prieta   University of Salamanca, Spain

Workshop Chairs

Dalila Durães   University of Minho, Portugal
Alfonso González Briones University of Salamanca, Spain

Advisory Board

Bo An   Nanyang Technological University, Singapore
Paul Davidsson   Malmö University, Sweden
Keith Decker   University of Delaware, USA
Yves Demazeau   Centre National de la Recherche Scientifique,
                     France
Tom Holvoet   KU Leuven, Belgium
Toru Ishida   Kyoto University, Japan
Takayuki Ito   Nagoya Institute of Technology, Japan
Eric Matson   Purdue University, USA
Jörg P. Müller   Clausthal Technical University, Germany
Michal Pěchouček   Technical University in Prague, Czech Republic
Franco Zambonelli University of Modena and Reggio Emilia, Italy

Local Organizing Committee

Paulo Novais (Chair)   University of Minho, Portugal
José Manuel Machado (Co-chair)   University of Minho, Portugal
Hugo Peixoto   University of Minho, Portugal
Regina Sousa   University of Minho, Portugal
Pedro José Oliveira   University of Minho, Portugal

Francisco Marcondes   University of Minho, Portugal
Manuel Rodrigues   University of Minho, Portugal
Filipe Gonçalves   University of Minho, Portugal
Dalila Durães   University of Minho, Portugal
Sérgio Gonçalves   University of Minho, Portugal

Organizing Committee

Juan M. Corchado Rodríguez   University of Salamanca and AIR Institute, Spain
Fernando De la Prieta   University of Salamanca, Spain
Sara Rodríguez González   University of Salamanca, Spain
Javier Prieto Tejedor   University of Salamanca and AIR Institute, Spain
Ricardo S. Alonso Rincón   AIR Institute, Spain
Alfonso González Briones   University of Salamanca, Spain
Pablo Chamoso Santos   University of Salamanca, Spain
Javier Parra   University of Salamanca, Spain
Liliana Durón   University of Salamanca, Spain
Marta Plaza Hernández   University of Salamanca, Spain
Belén Pérez Lancho   University of Salamanca, Spain
Ana Belén Gil González   University of Salamanca, Spain
Ana de Luis Reboredo   University of Salamanca, Spain
Angélica González Arrieta   University of Salamanca, Spain
Angel Luis Sánchez Lázaro   University of Salamanca, Spain
Emilio S. Corchado Rodríguez   University of Salamanca, Spain
Raúl López   University of Salamanca, Spain
Beatriz Bellido   University of Salamanca, Spain
María Alonso   University of Salamanca, Spain
Yeray Mezquita Martín   AIR Institute, Spain
Sergio Márquez   AIR Institute, Spain
Andrea Gil   University of Salamanca, Spain
Albano Carrera González   AIR Institute, Spain

PAAMS 2023 Organizers and Sponsors

Contents

Workshop on Adaptive Smart areaS and Intelligent Agents (ASSIA)

Workshop on Adaptive Smart areaS and Intelligent Agents (ASSIA)

In this workshop, we discussed technological solutions for Adaptive Smart Areas, geo-positioned locations with a high need for sensorization, which facilitates their adaptation to significant changes in environmental conditions. Proposed solutions should facilitate decision-making of independent entities, fostering collaboration and coordination among them to improve available resources or increase their efficiency in a specific area (cities, buildings, villages, farms, forests, etc). Adaptive Smart Areas represent a new way of thinking about any kind of space by shaping a model that integrates aspects like energy efficiency, sustainable mobility, protection of the environment, and economic sustainability. These areas provide potentially unlimited settings for intelligent agents to display their ability to react, act proactively, interact between themselves, or otherwise plan, learn, etc., in an intelligent, or somewhat human, manner.

Therefore, this workshop aimed to discuss the use of agent technology for Adaptive Smart Areas to provide intelligence to any of these areas. We welcomed any paper about experiences on the use of agents in Adaptive Smart Areas tackling issues related to smart architectures, simulations, intelligent infrastructure, smart transport, robotics, open data, etc. We also intended to address specific methodological and technological issues raised by the real deployment of agents in Adaptive Smart Areas.

Topics that were relevant for the workshop included especially applications, but also theoretical approaches, based on (but not limited to):

- Smart city modeling
- Smart city simulation
- Precision agriculture
- Smart farming
- Intelligent infrastructures
- Sensors and actuators
- ML-enabled predictive and analytic solutions
- Intelligence applications and crop monitoring
- Smart health and emergency management
- Smart environments
- Smart education
- Smart health
- Smart mobility and transportation
- Intelligent vehicles
- Ethical and legal issues in Adaptive Smart Areas
- Cloud and edge assisted applications
- Agricultural robotics
- Data sharing and privacy
- Cost-efficient wireless sensor nodes, network architecture, and implementation
- New environment sensor technologies

Organization

Organizing Committee

Vicente Julián	Universitat Politècnica de València, Spain
Adriana Giret	Universitat Politècnica de València, Spain
Carlos Carrascosa	Universitat Politècnica de València, Spain
Juan Manuel Corchado	Universidad de Salamanca, Spain
Sara Rodríguez	Universidad de Salamanca, Spain
Fernando De la Prieta	Universidad de Salamanca, Spain
Alberto Fernández	Universidad Rey Juan Carlos, Spain
Holger Billhardt	Universidad Rey Juan Carlos, Spain
Marin Lujak	Universidad Rey Juan Carlos, Spain

Program Committee

Alfonso González Briones	University of Salamanca, Spain
Ana Belén Gil González	University of Salamanca, Spain
Gonçalo Marques	Polytechnic Institute of Coimbra, Portugal
Jaume Jordán	Universitat Politècnica de València, Spain
Javier Parra	University of Salamanca, Spain
Joao Carneiro	ISEP/GECAD, Portugal
José Machado	University of Minho, Portugal
Juan M. Alberola	Universitat Politècnica de València, Spain
Jürgen Dunkel	Hochschule Hannover, Germany
Marian Cristian Mihaescu	University of Craiova, Romania
Pasqual Martí	Universitat Politècnica de València, Spain
Radu-Casian Mihailescu	Malmö University, Sweden
Ralf Bruns	Hochschule Hannover, Germany
Ramon Hermoso	University of Zaragoza, Spain
Stella Heras	Universitat Politècnica de València, Spain
Victor Sanchez-Anguix	Universitat Politècnica de València, Spain
Iván Bernabé	Rey Juan Carlos University, Spain
Marcelo Karanik	Rey Juan Carlos University, Spain
Cedric Marco Detchart	Universitat Politècnica de València, Spain
Jaime Rincón Arango	Universitat Politècnica de València, Spain

Agrobots Architecture and Agrobots-Sim Simulator for Dynamic Agri-Robot Coordination

Jorge Gutiérrez-Cejudo[iD], Marin Lujak[✉][iD], and Alberto Fernández[iD]

CETINIA, University Rey Juan Carlos, Madrid, Spain
{jorge.gutierrez,marin.lujak,alberto.fernandez}@urjc.es

Abstract. In this paper, we present a distributed multi-agent architecture, Agrobots architecture, for dynamic agriculture robot fleet coordination as well as a software package, Agrobots-SIM, developed for efficient modelling and simulation of dynamic multi-robot task allocation and vehicle routing problem in agriculture robot (agrobot) fleets. In contrast to other multi-robot applications, an agrobot fleet may be composed of specialized robots for a certain task and of generic robots requiring a specific detachable tool (implement) for different tasks. The proposed package extends the existing package Patrolling_SIM [15] made for multi-robot patrolling and accommodates for dynamic multi-robot task allocation and vehicle routing problem considering robot battery autonomy as well as contingencies by dynamic updates during simulation of the data related with environment, tasks, and robots. Moreover, Agrobots-SIM accommodates different inter-robot communication strategies to simulate real-world communication conditions. The developed package is implemented in the Robot Operating System with distributed controllers that allow both off-line and on-line distributed control. We show the functioning of the simulator in several use-case experiments.

Keywords: Distributed MAS · Stage · ROS · multi-robot task allocation · multi-robot routing · multi-robot simulation

1 Introduction

In this paper, we propose distributed multi-agent architecture, Agrobots architecture, and the Agrobot-SIM package for autonomous and distributed coordination of agriculture robot (agrobot) fleets. The proposed architecture accommodates distributed vehicle routing (VRP) and multi-robot task allocation (MRTA) problems in agriculture. The proposed Agrobot-SIM package extends Patrolling_SIM for multi-robot patrolling and is a stand-alone application for mobile robot simulation implemented in the Stage simulator, running in Robot Operating System (ROS). ROS is becoming a standard software implementation tool in robotics, mechatronics and wider.

D. Durães et al. (Eds.): PAAMS 2023, CCIS 1838, pp. 5–17, 2023.
https://doi.org/10.1007/978-3-031-37593-4_1

In addition to the features already present in Patrolling_SIM, the developed package disposes of the following features: MRTA and VRP in the agriculture context considering robot battery autonomy and battery recharging deposits and, in case of contingencies, dynamic updates of parameters and variables related both with the robots and the tasks. Moreover, the proposed software package disposes of different strategies for inter-robot communication to simulate the contingencies and communication conditions that may appear in the field. The developed package is implemented with distributed controllers that allow both off-line predefined control laws and on-line distributed and predictive control. The implementation in Stage and ROS allows for the straightforward implementation of controllers into real physical systems. We show the functioning of the simulator in several use-case experiments available in the GitHub repository[1].

The paper is organised as follows. In Sect. 2, we give preliminaries and describe state-of-the-art in fleet simulation in general and the simulation of fleets of agriculture robots in particular. Section 3 presents the distributed Agrobots architecture for agri-robot task allocation and routing, and discusses implementation choices considering real world conditions and relevant communication challenges. In Sect. 4.1, we present the requirements for the Agrobots-SIM simulator. Section 4 presents the proposed simulator architecture based on the Patrolling_SIM package. We present the main developments and the package extensions performed in Sect. 4.3. We give a use-case example in Sect. 5. The conclusions and lines of future work in Sect. 6 close the paper.

2   Preliminaries and State of the Art

Vehicle fleet simulation is a well-researched topic necessary for efficient implementation of fleet coordination solutions in the real world for, e.g., ambulance fleets [1,11], bike fleets [6] and taxi fleets [2,3]. Contrary to these, service robotics has specific requirements, such as hardware abstraction, device drivers, and communication between processes over multiple machines. All of these resulted in the development of ROS [8], a meta-operating system between an operating system and middleware. ROS functions as a full operating system for service robotics composed of a set of free open-source software libraries as a base for the development of robotics applications [16].

In agriculture robotics, there are robots specialised for certain task (e.g., irrigation, ploughing, harvesting, etc.), as well as generic robotic platforms that use detachable heterogeneous implements to perform different tasks. Thus, it is necessary to create simulation tools that will represent the physical robot actuation with high fidelity for both types of robots and, by doing so, decrease the cost of deployment in the real world. In [18], different robot simulation tools were compared in agriculture. The mobile robot simulation environment in [5] allows for the performance analysis, cooperation and interaction of a set of autonomous robots moving in a three-dimensional (3D) world. Moreover, FroboMind platform

---

[1] https://github.com/JorgeGutierrezCejudo/AgroRobotSimulator.git.

[7] evaluates the task performance in precision agriculture, while the architecture in [14] controls a group of robots in charge of maintenance tasks in agriculture.

ROS libraries for task allocation and planning are ROS Plan Library and the Task and Motion Planning (TAMP) library. However, ROS Plan uses the unscalable PDDL (Planning Domain Definition Language), while TAMP library uses a hierarchical task network (HTN) planner for task decomposition. None of these can efficiently and effectively model the VRP and the MRTA problem in agriculture, the subject of the Agrobots architecture. However, patrolling and vehicle routing are both problems that involve determining the most efficient and effective routes for a set of vehicles to follow to achieve a specific objective. In patrolling, the objective is to monitor and secure a particular area or route, while in the MRTA and VRP, the objective is to assign a set of tasks to a set of agents and deliver or pickup items to/from a set of locations through vehicle routing, respectively. Both problems require the agents to visit these locations, while optimising their cost, travel time and/or other resources.

Patrolling_SIM[2] is a package for multi-robot patrolling [19] that may be implemented in Stage or Gazebo. Stage [19] and Gazebo [9] are multi-robot simulators based on ROS or ROS2 [10]. Stage is a 2D robot simulator that provides a simple, lightweight platform for testing basic robot behaviours in a simulated environment, while Gazebo is a more advanced 3D robot simulator that allows for complex simulation of robots and environments.

The objective of Patrolling_SIM is to test algorithms for patrolling a set of tasks by a robot team. In a given scenario, a graph representation is used, where nodes represent locations to visit while the arcs represent physical links between adjacent nodes. Each robot is given a task (next node to be visited). Once a robot reaches a node, it chooses its next task (node) according to some decision strategy. Eleven patrolling algorithms are available in the Patrolling_SIM package for which the key performance indicator is the node idleness, i.e. the average time between visits by any robot. Even though patrolling, task assignment and vehicle routing are distinct problems, they share several similarities in terms of the objectives, constraints, and optimisation techniques involved, sufficient for adaptation of this package to the MRTA and VRP problem in the agri-robot context. This is why, in this paper, we study and extend this package.

3   Multi-agent Based Agrobots Architecture

In this section, we propose a distributed multi-agent architecture for dynamic coordination of agrobot fleets, and, in particular, for dynamic MRTA and VRP, as seen in Fig. 1. This architecture is inspired by the distributed architecture for real-time evacuation guidance in large smart buildings in [12]. Agrobots architecture is composed of agriculture robots (autonomous vehicles) designed as autonomous collaborative agents that may communicate with each other and interact in the environment. The changes in the environment are detected by the

---

[2] https://github.com/davidbsp/patrolling_sim

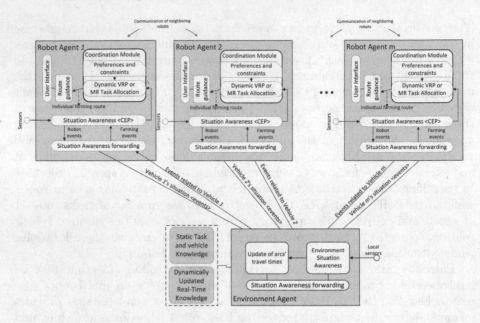

Fig. 1. Multi-agent architecture for agrirobot team task allocation and routing.

Environment Agent that keeps, updates, and transmits the information related with the tasks and the robots in the environment.

Each *robot agent* is composed of the following modules (Fig. 1): *user interface*, *route guidance*, *coordination*, *situation awareness*, and *situation awareness forwarding*. *User interface* is used for visualisation of the data the robot disposes of. Through *route guidance*, the robot navigates autonomously through the environment. The *coordination module* takes user's preferences and context constraints for selecting the best dynamic VRP or MRTA algorithm based on the sensors readings. These are managed in the *situation awareness module* that uses Complex Event Processing and updates relevant environment information. The *situation awareness forwarding* exchanges information with the robots in its communication range and with the environment. Locally available information is read by a robot's sensors. Each agent updates its own location and the information about the locations of other communicating agents together with the tasks' states as it moves through the field and communicates with others.

Each robot operates independently and is responsible for assigning its tasks and finding the best route in collaboration with the robots in its communication range through real-time inter-robot local information exchange and cooperation based on vicinity in the *Coordination Module*. The tasks could include harvesting, ploughing, or irrigation, monitoring certain locations, or responding to specific events. Overall, the choice between applying the MRTA or VRP coordination algorithm depends on the specific requirements of the system and the problem being solved. The coordination module considers these factors and finds the approach that best meets the actual requirements of the system. Both task assignment and vehicle routing may be done through any suitable efficient and robust multi-robot task allocation or vehicle routing algorithm [4,17].

Communication is achieved using a decentralised messaging system, such as a peer-to-peer network or a distributed hash table, which enables the agents to exchange messages and data without a central server. ROS provides several mechanisms to implement the communication protocol, e.g., topics, services, and actions. Moreover, ROS provides several communication protocols to allow information exchange (e.g., location, sensor readings, task assignments and states), including the Publisher-Subscriber and the Client-Server patterns.

The communication in ROS is performed between nodes, the basic unit of work in ROS and can be thought of as small, modular programs that perform specific tasks. For example, a node is responsible for reading data from a sensor, processing or publishing it to another node or topic. Topics allow nodes to send and receive messages asynchronously, while services provide a synchronous request-response communication. Actions are similar to services but allow for the possibility of feedback messages and the ability to cancel the request.

Such a multi-agent system is scalable, has fewer levels of authority, and does not suffer from the "single point of failure" problem seen in centralized systems. Among other constraints, task assignment and vehicle routing consider constraints on limited robot autonomy and the assignment to the service stations that are most appropriate in respect to a predefined fleet objective. Dynamic task assignment problem and dynamic vehicle routing problem consider' congestion and may consider other possible contingencies.

4 Agrobots-SIM

In this Section, we first describe the requirements of the simulator for agrobot applications; then we present the basis of the proposed Agrobots-SIM package, Patrolling_SIM, and, at the end, we explain the extensions done to respond to the requirements for agrorobot application.

4.1 Simulator Requirements for Agrorobot Applications

In this section, we describe the key simulator requirements for the Agrobots architecture proposed in Sect. 3:

- **Multi-robot support:** The simulator should be able to simulate multiple robots working together in a team. It should enable their mutual coordination and communication of, e.g., their location, task status, and battery levels.
- **Autonomy support:** The simulator should support asynchronous and distributed decision making and should be able to simulate robots that are autonomous, meaning that they are able to make their own decisions without human intervention, independently or collaboratively with other robots.
- **Battery life support:** Robots are supplied by limited energy supply through batteries. To support battery recharge in continuous robot missions, the simulator should consider battery recharging points when calculating routes.

– **Efficiency support:** The simulator should be able to evaluate the efficiency of the robots in completing their tasks. This includes the time taken to complete a task, the amount of energy used, and the resources consumed. With this aim, the simulator should consider optimization in a graph with weighted arcs, nodes or both.

– **Dynamic task performance:** The simulator should be capable of taking into account the dynamic nature of the scenarios and contingencies related to the execution in real time. This means that the tasks can change over time, and the robots should be able to adapt to these changes.

– **Tool-based task performance:** The simulator should be able to simulate tasks that require the use of a detachable tool, such as a plow or a harvester.

Agriculture fleet vehicle routing problem considers task assignment and vehicle routing, and is explained in [13]. Overall, a good simulator for multi-robot agriculture MRTA and VRP should be able to simulate a wide range of scenarios, and should be flexible enough to adapt to changes.

4.2   Patrolling_SIM

The base of the proposed Agrobots-SIM package is Patrolling_SIM package. Patrolling_SIM is a set of simulation tools and algorithms designed to model and evaluate patrolling strategies for robots composed by the Patrolling_SIM architecture (see Fig. 2):

1. Environment: If we compare the environment to a theater play, the simulation environment is the instance where the stage, the actors and the play to be performed will be defined. In our case, the stage will be the *map*; the actors will be the *robots* and the play will be the *graph*.

2. Algorithm: The role of decision-making algorithms is to calculate the next task for each robot based on the given problem definition. There are eleven patrolling algorithms included in the simulator.

3. Simulate engine: Patrolling_SIM follows an event-based approach, as the system conditions change when an event occurs. In addition, this simulator allows for event creation.

4. Visualisation: This module allows for real-time visualisation of robot behaviour following a given routing or task assignment algorithm. In addition, it can serve as a filter to evaluate whether the high-fidelity simulation considering robotic dynamics reflects the expected behaviour of the algorithm. Among the options offered by the visualisation module, one can visualise the range of the robot's sensors (Fig. 3a), follow a specific robot or even observe the simulation from a robot's point of view (Fig. 3b).

5. Data analysis: Once a patrolling cycle is complete, a file with the results is created. A patrol cycle is completed when all points are visited twice. We need to remember that this package was initially created for patrolling, so the main feature to compare different algorithms is the time between each visit or *idleness*, i.e., the duration between two robot visits to a task.

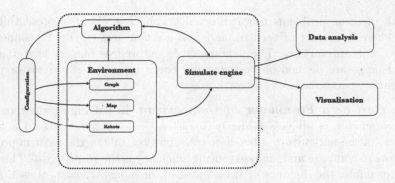

Fig. 2. Patrolling_SIM architecture

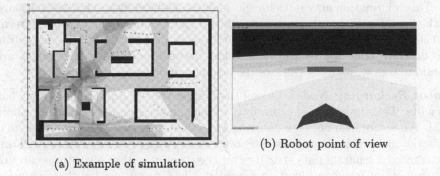

(a) Example of simulation

(b) Robot point of view

Fig. 3. Visualization of the simulation

4.3 Agrobots-SIM: An Extension and Modification of Patrolling_SIM

Next, we discuss how we extended and modified the Patrolling_SIM package to accommodate for agricultural robot fleet coordination. Patrolling, task assignment and the vehicle routing problem are optimization problems with a similar structure, which is why we decided to reuse Patrolling_Sim package rather than to create a new package from scratch. Thus, we reused the similar parts and extended the package with the elements unique to dynamic MRTA and VRP in agriculture robot fleets. Below, we present the different aspects developed to adapt the package to our fleet coordination problem.

Both of these problems use a directed graph $G = (V, E)$ representing the fields, where V is a set of vertices, and E is a set or arcs $(i, j) \in V$, connecting any two adjacent vertices. The pending tasks, as well as battery charging and tool exchange are defined on vertices, and edges represent the roads or paths that connect two adjacent vertices.

Route Cost as a Parameter of Comparison. In patrolling, the most relevant parameter is idleness (time between two consecutive visits to a task). However, in the agriculture robot fleet coordination, one of the most important indicators to compare and analyse routing efficiency is the route's cost. This may be, for example, the distance or time travelled, or monetary cost, of each robot and the cost of the fleet as a whole. This is why we modified the data analysis module to include the route cost as a parameter of comparison.

This information may serve for the analysis of efficiency and fairness measures of the fleet. For this purpose, we used the previously built topic *position* in terms of the (x, y) coordinates of each robot in each period of time. By measuring the distance travelled by the same robot between two consecutive steps, and accumulating it, we keep track of the accumulated cost of the route.

Robot Recharging Nodes. One of the biggest robots' limitations is their battery life. This limitation is taken into account in the development of Agrobots-SIM. We distinguish between *charging vertices* $V_r \in V$ (where robots must go to recharge their battery) and *task vertices* $V_t \in V$ (with pending tasks to perform). We created a separate data structure for these nodes so that algorithms can take this constraint into consideration if needed. The structure of the charging nodes consists of the identifier, the coordinates of the node, the cost to reach the node, and an indicator of whether the node is in use or not. By taking into account the cost of reaching the charging nodes from a momentary position, a robot must be able to complete the assigned tasks and reach the charging point that is reachable by the remaining battery autonomy. In addition, usually, charging points are limited in number, so we incorporate the usage indicator (*idle, occupied*), and in this way, we dynamically consider the time necessary to charge the battery. In this way, we may better represent in simulation real-world task assignment considering contingencies.

Tools Implementation. In agriculture robotics, robots have to use different tools for different tasks. Tasks may differ in the tool requirements, while robots may differ in tool compatibility. From this perspective, we distinguish two cases: (i) a robot with an inseparable tool that is specialised for certain task, where compatibility is considered only between a robot and a task, and (ii) a robot requires a specific detachable tool to perform a task.

The exchange of the tools (implements) is defined on the set of vertices $v \in V_e$. A robot may detach its mounted tool and, if necessary, attach a new one available on the location of these vertices that have a sufficient infrastructure to deposit the tools. These vertices may overlap with the task vertices $v \in V_t$, where $V_t \subset V$.

At the beginning of the simulation, the user is required to define each robot and its tool requirements (if any). Tools may be attached and detached on the graph nodes assigned for that. In terms of the data to be designated for the tool graph, we must establish which tools are available, which robots are able to use these tools and which tasks they can perform. We must also establish the coordinates of each task, as well as the neighbours of these tasks and their orientation and the cost of reaching them, i.e. the same information as the graph that does not take into account the assignment of the tools.

Dynamic Graph Update. A dynamic task is a task that appears or changes at a certain time during the simulation. The original Patrolling_SIM architecture does not permit this kind of updates because the simulation engine loads the coordinates of the tasks at the start of the simulation from the graph file, and they do not change throughout the simulation. To solve this problem, we used event creation. With these new events, we can load at any moment a new graph file. The *all tasks completed* event is triggered when a robot completes a given set of tasks. At this moment the graph of the robot may be changed to a new one so it may continue pursuing new tasks. We must keep in mind that the graph change will only occur locally in the robot that has visited these tasks, and not globally (the other robots will continue to perform tasks, each one on its own (compatible) version of the graph).

The second event created is called *patrol cycle complete*. In this case, the graph is changed on all robots at the same time. This happens when a patrol cycle is finished. This can be done on an ongoing basis, switching from one graph to another when each patrol cycle is over. However, in order to make this constant change of graphs, they must be balanced, i.e. they must have the same number of tasks. Thus, the changes can be made after a certain number of periods of time, so that the appearance of dynamic tasks may be simulated. To simulate a robot breakdown, a robot may be stopped in the simulation through the update of its graph to the one with only one isolated node representing its actual position.

Communication Means and Trust in Antagonistic Environments. We allowed for the creation of new messages, which facilitates addressing communication problems that were not possible previously. One of them is how algorithms can adapt to different types of communication, such as broadcast, multicast or one-on-one communication. In this way, we can analyse not only their adaptation but also their efficiency in managing the problem of routing agri-robot fleets.

Another possibility is the existence of one-on-one communication and multi-hop communication considering a communication range. Even though all robots may subscribe to a topic, restrictions can be created based on the actual position of the robots and their communication ranges so that only certain neighbouring robots can acquire this information. Another implementation is in the study of antagonistic algorithms, where two teams of robots are competing one against other in order to achieve the same goal. This may be used to compare different types of robots, in order to analyse their effectiveness and efficiency with the same algorithm, or even to create algorithms where the robots send false information to the opposing team.

RVIZ as Visualisation Module. Information display and options that can be configured in Stage are limited. Thus, we integrated RVIZ (short for "ROS visualisation") as a visualisation module. RVIZ is a 3D visualisation software tool for robots, sensors, and algorithms, simpler to use than Gazebo. It allows for visualising the robot's perception of its world (real or simulated) and displaying multiple pieces of information. Furthermore, RVIZ is up to date with the latest ROS distributions. It allows using markers, which are shapes that can be displayed at any moment. These markers open up new options for the study of algorithms since it is possible to simulate the appearance of dynamic obstacles and thus analyse the behaviour of the dynamic algorithms.

5   Simulation Use-Case

In this section, we look at some concrete simulations to show how the Agrobots-SIM package works. To adapt the simulator to our problem, a bitmap was created based on an agricultural field with several crops. We can see the process in Fig. 4. In the same way, we created the graph as seen in Fig. 5. This graph takes into

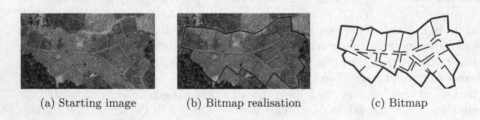

(a) Starting image   (b) Bitmap realisation   (c) Bitmap

Fig. 4. Bitmap realisation process

consideration charging points nodes and task nodes. However, none of the tested algorithms takes into account this implementation.

First Simulation. We divide the graph file into two different scenarios, remembering the fact that the graphs must be balanced. This way when a robot had finished five tasks, *all tasks completed* appears and the graph of this robot changes to other assigned tasks (if any). As a result, we are able to create a first change in each of the individual robots.

Second Simulation: As we did before, we work with the split graph, so when a patrol cycle is completed, the scenario changes due to the **complete patrol cycle** event. Contrary to the first simulation, all robots change the graph at the same time.

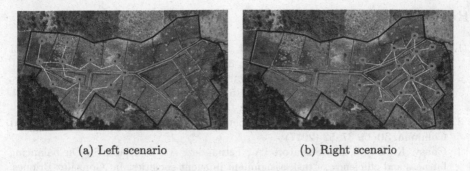

(a) Left scenario   (b) Right scenario

Fig. 5. The graph file divide in two scenarios

6 Conclusions and Future Work

In this paper, we proposed distributed multi-agent architecture, Agrobot architecture for agrorobot fleet coordination and the Agrobots-SIM extension of the Patrolling_SIM package for agriculture robot fleet simulation. We have added the following functionalities to the mentioned package: the requirements on heterogeneous detachable tools that are needed for the execution of tasks by robots, dynamic change of costs of a route for each vehicle, adaptation from the patrolling task to the multi-robot task allocation problem and the vehicle routing problem, where the simulation stops when the last task is visited. Moreover, we have introduced recharging nodes for battery recharging of robots and separated them from the nodes to visit. Moreover, the robots may mutually communicate with the neighbouring robots in a limited communication range to find a route for each one of them in a distributed way.

In future work, we plan to simulate the dynamic real-time coordination of random and real-world agriculture robot fleets with varying size by the usage of the Agrobots architecture and the Agrobots-SIM package in Stage and Gazebo. We plan to monitor the proposed solution to ensure that it is performing as expected and will address any issues or inefficiencies to optimise the performance of the system. Finally, we plan to deploy the proposed Agrobots architecture and the Agrobots-SIM package in a real-world agrirobotics scenario once they have been tested with real-world data and refined.

Acknowledgements. This work has been partially supported by grants PID2021 -123673OB-C32 and TED2021-131295B-C33 funded by MCIN/AEI/10.13039 /501100011033 and by "ERDF A way of making Europe" and the "European Union NextGenerationEU/PRTR", respectively; as well as AGROBOTS Project funded by the Community of Madrid, Spain.

References

1. Billhardt, H., Fernández, A., Lujak, M., Ossowski, S.: Agreement technologies for coordination in smart cities. Appl. Sci. **8**(5), 816 (2018)
2. Billhardt, H., et al.: Towards smart open dynamic fleets. In: Rovatsos, M., Vouros, G., Julian, V. (eds.) EUMAS/AT -2015. LNCS (LNAI), vol. 9571, pp. 410–424. Springer, Cham (2016). https://doi.org/10.1007/978-3-319-33509-4_32
3. Billhardt, H., et al.: Coordinating open fleets. A taxi assignment example. AI Commun. **30**(1), 37–52 (2017)
4. Cousy, K., Lujak, M., Salvatore, A., Fernández, A., Giordani, S.: On balancing fairness and efficiency of task assignment in agent societies. In: González-Briones, A., et al. (eds.) PAAMS 2022. CCIS, vol. 1678, pp. 95–107. Springer, Cham (2022). https://doi.org/10.1007/978-3-031-18697-4_8
5. Emmi, L., Paredes-Madrid, L., Ribeiro, A., Pajares, G., de Santos, P.G.: Fleets of robots for precision agriculture: a simulation environment. Ind. Robot Int. J. **40**(1), 41–58 (2013)
6. Fernández, A., Billhardt, H., Ossowski, S., Sánchez, Ó.: Bike3S: a tool for bike sharing systems simulation. J. Simul. **14**(4), 278–294 (2020)
7. Jensen, K., Larsen, M., Nielsen, S., Larsen, L., Olsen, K., Jørgensen, R.: Towards an open software platform for field robots in precision agriculture. Robotics **3**, 207–234 (2014)
8. Joseph, L.: Robot Operating System (ROS) for Absolute Beginners. Springer, Cham (2018). https://doi.org/10.1007/978-1-4842-3405-1
9. Koenig, N., Howard, A.: Design and use paradigms for gazebo, an open-source multi-robot simulator. In: 2004 IEEE/RSJ IROS (IEEE Cat. No. 04CH37566), vol. 3, pp. 2149–2154. IEEE (2004)
10. Koubaa, A.: Robot Operating System (ROS): The Complete Reference, vol. 3. Springer, Cham (2019). https://doi.org/10.1007/978-3-319-91590-6
11. Lujak, M., Billhardt, H.: Coordinating emergency medical assistance. In: Ossowski, S. (ed.) Agreement Technologies. LGTS, vol. 8, pp. 597–609. Springer, Dordrecht (2013). https://doi.org/10.1007/978-94-007-5583-3_35
12. Lujak, M., Billhardt, H., Dunkel, J., Fernández, A., Hermoso, R., Ossowski, S.: A distributed architecture for real-time evacuation guidance in large smart buildings. Comput. Sci. Inf. Syst. **14**(1), 257–282 (2017)
13. Lujak, M., Sklar, E., Semet, F.: Agriculture fleet vehicle routing: a decentralised and dynamic problem. AI Commun. **34**(1), 55–71 (2021)
14. Nebot, P., Torres-Sospedra, J., Martínez, R.: A new HLA-based distributed control architecture for agricultural teams of robots in hybrid applications with real and simulated devices or environments. Sensors **11**, 4385–400 (2011)
15. Portugal, D., Iocchi, L., Farinelli, A.: A ROS-based framework for simulation and benchmarking of multi-robot patrolling algorithms. In: Koubaa, A. (ed.) Robot Operating System (ROS). SCI, vol. 778, pp. 3–28. Springer, Cham (2019). https://doi.org/10.1007/978-3-319-91590-6_1
16. Quigley, M., Conley, K., Gerkey, B., et al.: ROS: an open-source robot operating system. In: ICRA Workshop on Open Source SW, vol. 3, no. 2, p. 5 (2009)
17. Sánchez, A.L., Lujak, M., Semet, F., Billhardt, H.: On balancing fairness and efficiency in routing of cooperative vehicle fleets. In: 12th International Workshop on Agents in Traffic and Transportation Co-Located with IJCAI-ECAI 2022, vol. 3173 (2022)

18. Shamshiri, R., Hameed, I., Pitonakova, L., et al.: Simulation software and virtual environments for acceleration of agricultural robotics: features highlights and performance comparison. Int. J. Agric. Biol. Eng. **11**(4), 15–31 (2018)
19. Vaughan, R.: Massively multi-robot simulation in stage. Swarm Intell. **2**, 189–208 (2008). https://doi.org/10.1007/s11721-008-0014-4

Improving Public Transportation Efficiency Through Accurate Bus Passenger Demand

Alejandro Ibáñez[1], Jaume Jordán[1]([✉]) [iD], and Vicente Julian[1,2] [iD]

[1] Valencian Research Institute for Artificial Intelligence (VRAIN), Universitat Politècnica de València, Camino de Vera s/n, 46022 Valencia, Spain
{jjordan,vinglada}@dsic.upv.es
[2] Valencian Graduate School and Research Network of Artificial Intelligence, Universitat Politècnica de València, Valencia, Spain

Abstract. This paper highlights the significance of efficient management of public transportation systems for providing high-quality service to passengers. The prediction of bus occupancy levels plays a critical role in optimizing bus routes, improving service reliability, and reducing passenger wait times. However, there is a lack of research in this area, and most existing studies focus on either real-time sensor data or historical bus occupancy data. This paper aims to establish a benchmark for bus and other public transport systems by using traditional and machine learning techniques to build models that can accurately predict bus occupancy levels. The main contribution of the study is to create an initial passenger demand with a specific environmental setup and evaluate the performance of the approach using a dataset collected from a real-world bus system. Through experimental simulations, the authors hope to identify long-term issues in the public transportation system and prevent possible problems, such as bottlenecks, shortages during rush hours, or wastage of resources. The paper emphasizes the importance of accurate bus passenger demand and highlights the need for further research in this area to enhance the efficiency and reliability of public transportation systems.

Keywords: Bus transportation · urban mobility · passenger prediction · data analysis · machine learning

1   Introduction

Public transportation, particularly buses, plays a critical role in ensuring smart cities are efficient, sustainable, and livable. With growing urbanization, traffic congestion, and environmental concerns, it has become essential to promote the use of public transportation. Buses offer a cost-effective and eco-friendly alternative to private cars, reducing traffic congestion and greenhouse gas emissions. By investing in public transportation infrastructure, smart cities can also promote economic growth, job creation, and social mobility. Therefore, it is crucial to prioritize public transportation as a means of transportation to improve the quality of life for citizens and create more sustainable cities.

Transportation by bus is an essential need in many countries and cities around the world. According to statistics, 12% of the population[1] in the United States depends on public transport to commute daily, which is low compared to other countries like South Korea, where it reaches 40% of the total and it is expected to reach higher levels, making the efficient management of public transportation systems crucial for providing high-quality service to passengers. One important aspect of this is the prediction of bus occupancy levels, as it can help optimize bus routes, improve service reliability, and reduce passenger wait times. Accurately predicting bus occupancy levels can also enable the deployment of dynamic bus scheduling and real-time passenger information systems.

Despite the importance of bus occupancy prediction, there is a lack of research in this area. Most existing studies focus on either real-time sensor data or historical bus occupancy data, which we want to focus on. Historical data let us make long-term prediction studies in different situations in a process of "whatification" and detect possible problems in the public transportation system such as bottlenecks, shortages during rush hours, or wastage of resources, among others, which lets prevent those problems by enacting modifications over the route planning or resource assignment.

This paper is part of a larger study that aims to establish a benchmark for bus, underground or any other kind of public transport system through experimental simulation to observe the system's performance over different environments and highlight long-term issues. Therefore, the main contribution of this paper is to create an initial passenger demand with a particular environment setup. For this purpose, we use traditional and machine learning techniques to build models that can accurately predict bus occupancy levels and evaluate the performance of our approach using a dataset collected from a real-world bus system.

The rest of the paper is organized as follows: Sect. 2 describes the dataset and the given treatment. Section 3 reviews the literature on bus passenger flow prediction methodologies and presents the proposed methods. Then, we present and analyze the results of the models in Sect. 4. Finally, Sect. 5 presents some conclusions and future works.

2 Data

In recent years there have been countless efforts to improve public transport systems. In many cases, these efforts involve the generation and analysis of numerous data sources to identify patterns, trends and insights that can aid in decision-making processes. In this work, we have opted for the dataset of the Ames Transit Agency located in Ames, Iowa, since it has the most complete information that we have found about public bus transportation in cities.

---

[1] https://www.statista.com/chart/25129/gcs-how-the-world-commutes/.

2.1   Data Source

The bus occupancy data were obtained from multiple routes operated by Ames Transit Agency in Ames, Iowa, metropolitan area from October 2021 to June 2022 [11]. The data was collected through a system of automatic passenger counters (APCs) so that each database entry corresponds to the passenger boarding and alighting of each bus at each stop. In addition to this information, each individual details the route, the scheduled and actual arrival and departure times, and the capacity of the vehicle. There are a total of 9 circular routes, 3 linear routes; where the outward and inward journeys are marked as two different routes, and 1 hybrid route; which during the school year works as a linear route and as a circular route during summer. Of these routes, 4 show operational inconsistencies: 1 changes part of the journey on weekdays and weekends, 1 has limited service, causing periods of lack of data, and 2 do not operate or change the part of the journey during summer. There are a total of 5 bus types, depending on the capacity of passengers, which from order of usage are 60 (70.02%), 65 (23.16%), 90 (4.84%), 40 (1.63%), and 20 (0.35%).

2.2   Pre-processing

The dataset was first reduced by keeping the routes that did not show inconsistencies, having then 2 linear and 7 circular routes; linear routes have not been transformed into circular ones since the main requirement that having an outward journey means having a return one was rarely met. Furthermore, during the data collection period, the routes have undergone variations due to the elimination or addition of stops, for which the dataset has been adapted by eliminating the stops that no longer exist and ignoring the new ones. Further research showed that some routes had more than one pattern, as due to certain events, the route is temporarily altered; nevertheless, due to the timeliness of these cases, it was decided to omit them from the dataset.

Since the prediction aims to estimate the number of passengers that need the bus service around an area within a certain time range and the data is presented as records, they must be aggregated to create flows. For this process, firstly, the stops that will be grouped into sections and the time ranges must be defined. The criteria followed to determine the sections within a route was, in the first instance, dividing each route taking the neighborhoods of Ames as a basis and then subdividing those groups considering changes in the surroundings of a bus stop, such as transitioning from a residential to a commercial zone; always taking a minimum of three stops per section. The exact section division can be seen in Fig. 1. Regarding the time zones, the schedule of Iowa State University[2] was followed as a basis, creating 7 time periods to address the fluctuation of passenger occupancy. The time division can be seen in Table 1, where the time ranges night periods of the previous and current day have been aggregated into the '1_night' period since they represent, in fact, the same period. The aggregation is then

---

[2] https://www.event.iastate.edu/?sy=2023&sm=01&sd=26&featured=1&s=d.

done having the route as the first level, then the section, followed by the date and finally, the time range.

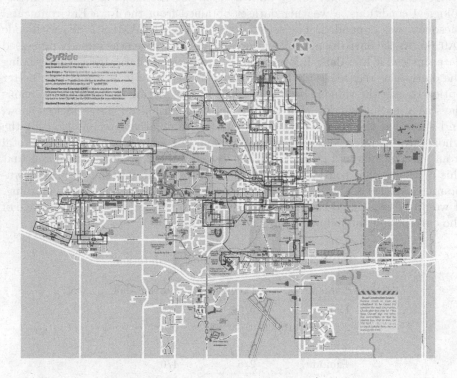

Fig. 1. Ames routes sections division

As the occupancy rate in public transportation follows weekly trends [6], two additional columns were created to keep that context: "ons_yesterday" and "ons_last_week". "ons_yesterday" stores the total onboardings during the previous day at the same route, section and hour range, whereas "ons_last_week" does the same, just not for the previous day, but for the previous week at the same

Table 1. Time periods division.

Time period	Starts	Ends
1_night	22:00 (previous day)	4:59
2_early_morning	5:00	8:59
3_morning	9:00	11:59
4_midday	12:00	14:59
5_afternoon	15:00	18:59
6_evening	19:00	21:59

weekday. With this, not only a general trend is procured, but also a particular trend for each weekday.

To enrich the quality of the data by studying the effect of different meteorological conditions, a weather dataset obtained from the Iowa Environmental Mesonet[3] was appended. The selected station was the AMES 5 SE, with code IA0203. As the data did not follow the same granularity as the already processed data, instead it had daily information, it was decided that, rather than keeping the daily value regardless of the hour range or a sixth of it, it would be a better option to infer the value in each hour range by considering the next and previous days as a moving window. For the precipitation variables (rain + melted snow, and snow), as the daily value represents the cumulative precipitation for the whole day, the inferred hour range value would be a sixth of the weighted total from the previous and current day; as seen in Table 2, as it is considered that this method would consider the precipitation trends and attenuate peak downpours. Nevertheless, as the snow depth value is taken first thing in the morning, it would be considered the melting of the snow by having a weighted average of the current and the following day; as seen in Table 3.

Table 2. Weighted window for precipitation.

Time period	Previous day	Current day
1_night	5/6	1/6
2_early_morning	4/6	2/6
3_morning	3/6	3/6
4_midday	2/6	4/6
5_afternoon	1/6	5/6
6_evening	0/6	6/6

Table 3. Weighted window for snow depth.

Time period	Current day	Following day
1_night	6/6	0/6
2_early_morning	5/6	1/6
3_morning	4/6	2/6
4_midday	3/6	3/6
5_afternoon	2/6	4/6
6_evening	1/6	5/6

The final dataset and the description of each field can be seen in Table 4.

[3] https://mesonet.agron.iastate.edu/request/coop/fe.phtml.

Table 4. Variable description

Variable	Description
hour	Time range. See Table 1
weekday	Day of the week
day	Day of the month. Kept only to order the dataset
month	Month of the year
year	Kept only to order the dataset
section	Stops aggregation in each route
route_name	Identifier of the different lanes in Ames' bus transport
ons_yesterday	Total onboarding during the previous day for a certain section within a certain route in a certain hour. Only for onboarding prediction
ons_last_week	Total onboarding during the previous week at the same weekday for a certain section within a certain route in a certain hour. Only for onboarding prediction
precip_mm	Inferred total rain and melted snow precipitation during the same hour range of the previous day
snow	Inferred total snow precipitation during the same hour range of the previous day
snow_d	Inferred inches of accumulated snow for the same hour range of the previous day
ons	Target variable. Accumulated quantity of individuals that get on the bus at any stop of a certain section

3 Methods

Bus passenger flow prediction has been a widely discussed topic in recent years. We can observe two categorizations of the approaches, depending on the time scope, real-time or atemporal prediction, and models themselves, traditional or deep learning methods, where the combination of real-time and deep learning is the clear favorite.

In the line of the last group, we can find Baghbani et al. [1], who used a graph representation of the stops of the bus routes with a convolutional layer for a Long Short-Term Memory (LSTM) model. Nagaraj et al. [9] use a combination of three deep learning techniques, a greedy-layer algorithm to prepare the data for prediction by fetching the numerical columns from the original dataset and relating it to each region; then an LSTM layer is used to filter the data batches by removing redundant data, which are the input of a Recurrent Neural Network (RNN) for prediction. Although our case is not a real-time forecasting system, we could observe that the LSTM technique is widely used, so treating our data as a series may be suitable.

Nevertheless, our case is closer to an atemporal prediction. In this area, we found Liyanage et al. [7], who use two different networks based on an LSTM layer, in one case uni-directional and bi-directional in the other, for passenger prediction within a time range. This inspired us to use an LSTM-based network, as we have the same data representation in aggregated time segments, with the exception of just employing uni-directional LSTM layers; since the bi-directional layers are not suitable for a real-world environment, as for a prediction at t + 1, the time-segments t + 2 and following are used as inputs.

Ming et al. [8] propose a multistep-ahead prediction hybrid system using an ARIMA-SVM model. The model consists of two stages, where an Autoregressive Integrated Moving Average (ARIMA) model is used to analyze the linear part of the problem, and a Support Vector Machine (SVM) model is developed to model the residuals from the ARIMA model, which contains information about the non-linearity. Two multistep-ahead forecasting strategies are employed, iterated, which predicts one sample at a time, and direct, which takes the dataset in groups of n sequential samples to be predicted in one go. Due to the similarity of the direct strategy to our case, apart from that in our case, the n sequential samples are grouped into one, we found it interesting to use an SVM technique applied for regression to fit non-linear data, as after the aggregation the data gains non-linearity.

Zhang et al. [12] use a Grey Prediction Model (GM), specifically the first order Grey Model GM(1, 1), as, due environment complexity, it is commonly used a single factor, which is the series itself. The main benefit of this model is that it distinguishes patterns within the days of the week and from week to week, that is, a Monday in the week t + 2 will be mainly influenced by the Mondays in weeks t + 1, t, and so, but also by the trend observed in the whole week t + 1. As aggregating the data may cause the loss of autocorrelation, a GM(1, 1) model is not the most suitable; nevertheless, this inspired us to use a variant of it, the GM(1, n). This model makes use of the serial variables to make the prediction to supply the lack of self-explicability.

3.1   Experiment Design

As our study uses a temporal segmentation of the data, we can consider two cases: whether the autocorrelation is kept or not, since we do not have the occupancy at each stop anymore, but an aggregation of the total occupancy within a period and sector. If the autocorrelation still exists in our data, treating it as a series problem will get appropriate results; we can do this since we still have a temporal order within the segmented data. On the other hand, if the autocorrelation is insufficient, we will opt for a more traditional approach treating each segment as individual to be predicted via regression.

For the regression approach, we have blocks of individuals independent of each other, as they do not have the context of previous time steps. Nevertheless, as in reality, the appearance of trends can happen, having a significant impact on the prediction capability of a given individual. The previous variables "ons_yesterday" and "ons_last_week" are used to guide the models giving the context of the normal and periodic trends, respectively.

We will consider the Random Forest (RF), Support Vector Machine for Regression (SVR) and Neural Network (NN) techniques for this approach. RF [3] combines multiple decision trees to create robust predictions, it has been chosen due to its capability to handle non-linear relationships and high-dimensional data, as in our case. SVR [4] creates a hyperplane that separates the individuals, as the RF, its capability to distinguish non-linear relationships and handle high-dimensional data has been of interest to us. Finally, the NN [2] learns the relationships among the variables to create its prediction, since it is highly customizable, we decided to iterate over multiple designs; the final one is a dense NN with 6 hidden layers of the following sizes: 64, 64, 32, 32, 16, 8, with a ReLU (rectified linear unit) activation function in the layers and a linear one for the output layer.

Regardless of the technique, we will create an independent model for each route. This decision requires less time for model convergence and prediction than other solutions, such as, e.g., a general model with a route variable decision-maker.

In the series approach, the dataset is structured in independent series for each section within a route, which means that we will create a separate model for each section. In this case, we would not use the variables "ons_yesterday" and "ons_last_week", since the main feature of the models of this type is to use the own target variable as a look-back for predicting a new value, and we are not interested in have repetitive data, which translates into heavier and slower to train models. As in the previous methods, we want to capture the normal and periodic trends, so the look-back range will cover the previous week for a given individual. Apart from the target variable, we will make use of the variables "precip_mm", "snow" and "snow_d", since, as they are numeric data, they are also serial data that can be used as input for the models.

The LSTM and GM models will be used for series prediction. LSTM [10] is a type of RNN particularly effective for time-series regression tasks; similarly to the NN, it is highly customizable; we created a sequential model composed of an LSTM layer of size 100 and a dense output layer with a linear activation function. GM [5] is a widely used technique for passenger flow prediction, since it focuses on finding the normal and periodic trends; in our case, we will use the variant GM(1, n) which uses other serial variables alongside the target one for predicting each new value.

4   Results

For the LSTM and GM models, the train-test split needs to be logical, which means that the test data must be the following time steps of the train data, this has been done in a proportion of an initial 80/20. After predicting a new time step, this value is introduced in the train split for predicting the following value.

On the other hand, the RF, SVR and NN models do not need that kind of split, but instead, it is preferable to perform a random split, since we will cover a wider variability of the data by considering a high variety of time steps. Performing a retraining at each time stop would also be interesting and have similar results, unfortunately, the temporary cost of it is enormous. The same 80/20 proportion will be considered for these models.

We want to compare how each model works for different routes to study their adaptability work regardless of the context of the route; nevertheless, each one has different magnitudes. The metric developed to assess that problem has been an R2 score calculated over the predicted values and the actual values of the test set. This metric calculates the similarity of two distributions. The range of this score covers from minus infinity to one, the closer to one, the better the model fits for that route. Higher R2 values indicate that the model explains a larger proportion of the variation in the data, suggesting a better fit. Nevertheless, the R2 score does not indicate the correctness or reliability of the model's predictions, and it can be influenced by the number of predictors in the model. Therefore, we combine its use with another metric.

To compare models between them is preferable to use an absolute metric over the results, for which the mean absolute error (MAE) has been chosen, which calculates the absolute error between every pair of predicted values and the actual ones and performs the mean of all the errors. In practice, the MAE provides an interpretation of the model's performance. It measures the average absolute difference between the predicted values and the actual values, which implies having a measure of the average error you may have for any predicted value.

4.1   Prediction Accuracy

The performance results are displayed in Table 5, where the green cells represent the best model for each route. We can see that the level of aggregation used has greatly eliminated the autocorrelation of the data, as the LSTM and GM, not only are not the best model for any route, but also the metrics for them are nowhere near the regression models; since LSTM averages a 43.97% for R2 score and 13.85 as MAE, and -35.06% and 43.93 respectively for GM. Therefore, the aggregation of data performed during the preprocessing has significantly reduced the autocorrelation of data, that is, the direct relation between near adjacent data points. This has provoked the LSTM and GM to perform worse.

Nevertheless, there is not a clear winner within the regression models, since, depending on the criteria used, the best model for each route differs. If both metrics agree on the model for a certain route, that should be the chosen model. That is the case of routes 1 Red West, 2 Green East, 2 Green West, 3 Blue, 5 Yellow, 7 Purple, 9 Plum and 23 Orange, which show values over 82% for the R2 score, except for 5 Yellow, which is 70.2%.

The rest of the routes show little difference in the metrics of the best-elected models, so the recommendation, in this case, is to always choose the model with a smaller MAE value. For routes 1 Red East and 14 Peach, the improvement in MAE is almost insignificant (0.001 and 0.021, respectively), but for 11 Cherry, the difference is 0.504.

According to the number of wins of each model, the RF technique results as the best model for both the R2 score and MAE, with 8 and 7 victories, respectively. In the second position comes the NN model, with 3 and 2, respectively. And finally, the SVR technique only results in the best model twice for the MAE metric.

Table 5. Metrics performance. Routes: (1E: 1 Red East, 1W: 1 Red West, 2E: 2 Green East, 2W: 2 Green West, 3: 3 Blue, 5: 5 Yellow, 7: 7 Purple, 9: 9 Plum, 11: 11 Cherry, 14: 14 Peach, 23: 23 Orange)

Route	NN		RF		SVR		LSTM		GM	
	R2	MAE	R2	MAE	R2	MAE	R2	MAE	R2	MAE
1E	0.831	5.216	0.856	4.818	0.833	4.817	0.381	6.482	-0.024	7.259
1W	0.930	4.452	0.919	4.489	0.856	5.373	0.355	7.192	-1.453	14.766
2E	0.830	2.479	0.872	2.311	0.853	2.350	0.354	3.393	-0.180	3.564
2W	0.846	2.137	0.861	2.035	0.849	2.212	0.375	5.101	-0.665	7.078
3	0.927	12.112	0.912	12.196	0.902	14.098	0.543	14.984	-0.228	17.349
5	0.588	2.137	0.702	1.789	0.691	1.846	0.365	2.097	-0.194	2.137
7	0.777	3.544	0.820	3.268	0.813	3.666	0.445	4.035	-0.152	4.432
9	0.810	12.145	0.822	11.913	0.784	13.326	0.403	13.540	-0.316	54.321
11	0.940	7.371	0.935	6.867	0.913	9.037	0.542	12.593	-0.035	15.742
14	0.451	1.381	0.625	1.153	0.593	1.132	0.237	1.502	-0.073	1.680
23	0.881	83.662	0.892	72.366	0.884	20.201	0.837	81.472	-0.537	354.865
Wins	3	2	8	7	0	2	0	0	0	0

From the results shown in Table 5, routes 5 Yellow and 14 Plum are notable for their low R2 score but also low MAE. The opposite happens with route 23 Orange, with an R2 score very close to one but a high MAE value.

Figures 2a and 2b show that the predictions fall within a small range. As the R2 score focuses on the similarity of the prediction distribution to the actual one, small errors within a narrow range translate into dissimilarity. Nevertheless, as our final focus is to assign buses according to the estimated passenger flow, any deviation within these ranges would not lead to significant resource shifts.

On the other hand, Fig. 2c shows that the nature of this route is to have high variability; this distribution has been correctly captured according to the R2 score. Nevertheless, it still happens that any minor deviation in a prediction may cause major bus rescheduling since, as seen in Table 5, the average error for the best case, RF model, is around 72, which is over a single bus capacity.

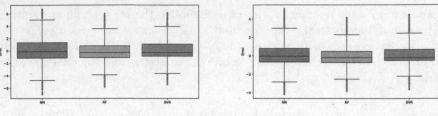

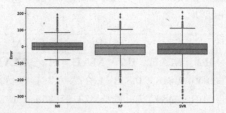

(a) Boxplot model comparison for route 5 Yellow   (b) Boxplot model comparison for route 14 Peach

(c) Boxplot model comparison for route 23 Orange

Fig. 2. Box plots of different routes.

5 Conclusions

In conclusion, this paper emphasizes the importance of effective management of public transportation systems to provide passengers with high-quality service. One key factor in achieving this goal is the accurate prediction of bus occupancy levels, which can help optimize bus routes, increase service reliability, and decrease passenger wait times. However, there is a limited amount of research in this area, with most existing studies focusing on either real-time sensor data or historical bus occupancy data. Therefore, this study aimed to set a benchmark for bus and other public transport systems by using both traditional and machine learning techniques to develop models that can predict bus occupancy levels with high accuracy. The main contribution of the study is the creation of an initial passenger demand with a specific environmental setup, and the evaluation of the proposed approach using a dataset collected from a real-world bus system.

In this sense, two different approaches have been explored, from which treating the problem as a series has clearly proved not to be suitable. This is because, by creating time segments during the preprocessing, the capability of self-explanation in the series has been lost. Nevertheless, we cannot assume that regardless of the level of aggregation used, the phenomenon remains the same. This is not part of our scope as using smaller aggregation ranges is not useful for our final purpose.

Based on the data achieved from the bus network of Ames, Iowa, it has been observed that, among the proposed, there is not a regression model that is above the rest; since, depending on the particularities of each route, each requires a customized study to optimize the system.

This work is part of a greater study that aims to establish a benchmark for bus, underground or any other kind of public transport system through experimental simulation. Therefore, this procedure is used to create an initial passenger demand with a particular environment setup. Furthermore, it is more beneficial for our purpose to use regression instead of series techniques since the first methods let us, with the given data, create any environment with few experimental data, while it is needed to continue the series up to the experimental point to recreate the conditions wanted in the second case.

Acknowledgements. This work is partially supported by grant PID2021-123673OBC31 funded by MCIN/AEI/ 10.13039/501100011033 and by "ERDF A way of making Europe". Jaume Jordán is supported by grant IJC2020-045683-I funded by MCIN/AEI/ 10.13039/501100011033 and by "European Union NextGenerationEU/PRTR".

References

1. Baghbani, A., Bouguila, N., Patterson, Z.: Short-term passenger flow prediction using a bus network graph convolutional long short-term memory neural network model. Transp. Res. Rec. **2677**(2), 1331–1340 (2023)
2. Bishop, C.: Neural Networks for Pattern Recognition. Oxford University Press, Oxford (1995)
3. Breiman, L.: Random forests. Mach. Learn. **45**, 5–32 (2001). https://doi.org/10.1023/A:1010933404324
4. Cortes, C., Vapnik, V.: Support-vector networks. Mach. Learn. **20**, 273–297 (1995). https://doi.org/10.1007/BF00994018
5. Julong, D.: Introduction to grey system theory. J. Grey Syst. **1**, 1–24 (1997)
6. Liu, Y., Liu, Z., Jia, R.: DeepPF: a deep learning based architecture for metro passenger flow prediction. Transp. Res. Part C Emerg. Technol. **101**, 18–34 (2019)
7. Liyanage, S., Abduljabbar, R., Dia, H., Tsai, P.: AI-based neural network models for bus passenger demand forecasting using smart card data. J. Urban Manag. **11**, 365–380 (2022)
8. Ming, W., Bao, Y., Hu, Z., Xiong, T.: Multistep-ahead air passengers traffic prediction with hybrid ARIMA-SVMs models. Sci. World J. **2014**, 567246 (2014)
9. Nagaraj, N., Gururaj, H.L., Swathi, B.H., Hu, Y.-C.: Passenger flow prediction in bus transportation system using deep learning. Multimedia Tools Appl. **81**(9), 12519–12542 (2022). https://doi.org/10.1007/s11042-022-12306-3
10. Schmidhuber, J., Hochreiter, S.: Long short-term memory. Neural Comput. **9**, 1735–1780 (1997)
11. Wilbur, K.: CyRide Automatic Passenger Counter Data, October 2021–June 2022 (2022)
12. Zhang, Z., Xu, X., Wang, Z.: Application of grey prediction model to short-time passenger flow forecast. In: AIP Conference Proceedings, vol. 1839 (2017)

Pre-processing Techniques and Model Aggregation for Plant Disease Prevention

C. Marco-Detchart[1]([envelope]) [iD], J. A. Rincon[1,2] [iD], V. Julian[1,2] [iD],
and C. Carrascosa[1] [iD]

[1] Valencian Research Institute for Artificial Intelligence (VRAIN), Universitat
Politècnica de València (UPV), Camino de Vera s/n, 46022 Valencia, Spain
{cedmarde,vjulian}@upv.es, {jrincon,carrasco}@dsic.upv.es
[2] Valencian Graduate School and Research Network of Artificial Intelligence
(VALGRAI), Universitat Politècnica de València (UPV), Camí de Vera s/n, 46022
Valencia, Spain

Abstract. Image processing techniques have become increasingly popular in plant disease classification. However, one of the major challenges in this field is accurately identifying and classifying different diseases based on plant images. Pre-processing techniques such as smoothing and sharpening can play a crucial role in improving the accuracy of disease classification. These techniques can enhance the quality of the images and reduce noise, making it easier for machine learning algorithms to extract meaningful features from the images. In this context, these techniques can significantly improve the overall accuracy of plant disease classification systems. This paper aims to explore the potential of preprocessing techniques such as smoothing and sharpening in enhancing the quality of plant images for disease classification.

Keywords: Decision-making · Consensus · Classification · Aggregation

1 Introduction

Plant diseases pose a significant threat to global food security, causing crop yield losses and reducing the quality and quantity of agricultural products. Early detection and accurate classification of plant diseases are crucial to effective disease management and mitigation [8]. In recent years, advancements in computer vision and image processing techniques have facilitated the development of automated plant disease detection and classification systems [7,20]. Image classification has emerged as a critical task in various fields, including remote sensing [10,18] or biomedical imaging [21]. Image classification aims to categorize images into particular classes based on their visual features. However, the quality of the images and noise levels can pose significant challenges to producing accurate classification results. Therefore, preprocessing techniques play an essential role in image classification by extracting relevant information and removing unwanted noise from images.

D. Durães et al. (Eds.): PAAMS 2023, CCIS 1838, pp. 30–40, 2023.
https://doi.org/10.1007/978-3-031-37593-4_3

One of the most usual preprocessing techniques used is image normalization [19]. Normalization involves converting the pixel values of an image to a common scale. This helps remove any variation in the intensity of images due to different lighting conditions. Normalization can be performed using various techniques such as histogram equalization, contrast stretching, and logarithmic transformation. Another preprocessing technique used in plant disease classification is cropping. Cropping involves removing the background of an image and keeping only the region of interest. This can help in reducing the amount of noise in the image and improve the accuracy of disease classification. Preprocessing techniques, such as smoothing or sharpening, are used to enhance the quality of images. Smoothing techniques aim to reduce image roughness and enhance the image quality (*e.g.* removing noise, blur or artifacts), while sharpening techniques, on the other hand, enhance the image details and edges. Regarding smoothing, one of the most common techniques used in plant disease classification is the Gaussian filter. The Gaussian filter is a low-pass filter that smooths the image by removing high-frequency components. This helps reduce noise in the image and improve the accuracy of disease classification. Finally, the Laplacian filter is a sharpening technique used in plant disease classification. The Laplacian filter is a high-pass filter that enhances the edges in an image. This can help improve the accuracy of disease classification by making distinguishing between healthy and diseased plants easier.

Preprocessing techniques such as smoothing and sharpening can improve image classification accuracy by enhancing image features [14], reducing noise, and extracting essential information. Smoothing techniques work by averaging the pixel values over a defined area, reducing noise, and removing irrelevant information. On the other hand, sharpening techniques increase the contrast between adjacent pixels making edges more distinct and improving the classification accuracy.

The use of preprocessing techniques in image classification is particularly crucial in the context of plant disease detection, which requires high accuracy and precision to prevent plagues and avoid unnecessary chemical use. The early detection of plant diseases can potentially reduce the spread of the disease, thereby minimizing the use of chemical treatments, ultimately improving crop yields and reducing the adverse effects on the environment.

Context-aware smoothing is an efficient technique for preprocessing images in the context of plant disease detection. This technique works by preserving edges while adapting the image smoothing by measuring and filtering pixel intensities based on the surrounding context. Approaches like Bilateral [23] and Mean shift [5] filtering are examples of widely used techniques for context-aware smoothing. More recent approaches, such as Gravitational smoothing [16], present promising results in this area.

Satellite and aerial imaging are also valuable resources in precision agriculture for monitoring crop health and detecting disease symptoms [4,17]. With the increasing availability of satellite and aerial imaging, the need for efficient preprocessing techniques to improve classification accuracy becomes even more significant. Efficient preprocessing can help simplify and speed up the classification process, making it scalable to large datasets.

On the other hand, strategies exist to increase classification performance by combining multiple models [6], helping to reduce the uncertainty and ambiguity associated with the classification process. These alternatives permit incorporating variety into the final model, where each model is trained and fused. For this fusion step, aggregation functions play a crucial role in fusing information in order to obtain consensual decisions, as it is shown for edge detection [15].

The usefulness of aggregation functions lies in their ability to fuse the classification results from multiple classifiers, thereby increasing the accuracy of the classification process. Aggregation functions reduce the effect of outliers and noise in the classification process by filtering out irrelevant information. This increases the robustness of the classification result, making it more reliable.

Different types of aggregation functions are used in the literature, including maximum, minimum, average, and weighted average [3]. Each function has its advantages and is suitable for specific situations. For example, the maximum function is useful when the classification result is required to be conservative, while the minimum function is suitable when the classification result is required to be optimistic.

According to all of this, this work presents an aggregation framework to fuse a collection of classification models for plant disease detection. In this framework, we propose to use in a first step preprocessing techniques to train an initial model in addition to the raw input and a second step where various aggregation functions are put to the test. The results obtained suggest that the combined use of image preprocessing techniques and model fusion help improve classification performance for automatic plant disease detection.

The rest of the paper is structured as follows. Section 2 is devoted to describing the proposed approach for classification and model fusion, Sect. 3 describes the experiments conducted to evaluate our proposal, and finally, conclusions are presented in Sect. 4.

2   System Description

In this section, we expose the framework used for plant disease prevention based on a classification system able to run on low-cost edge devices.

The consensus classification system proposed in this work is based on MobileNetV2 network. This is deep learning model has an architecture that is specifically designed for mobile and low-power devices. The architecture incorporates a number of novel features and optimizations which allow it to achieve state-of-the-art accuracy on a variety of image classification tasks while still maintaining a small model size and computational efficiency.

The MobileNetV2 architecture consists of a series of convolutional layers, each with a common structure known as a *bottleneck block*. This block comprises a 1×1 convolution layer, a depthwise separable convolution layer, and another 1×1 convolution layer. By using this structure, the model is able to dramatically reduce the number of parameters required while still maintaining a high degree of accuracy.

One important aspect of the MobileNetV2 architecture is the use of *inverted residual* blocks, which are designed to preserve information and gradients across multiple layers. These blocks include a shortcut connection that preserves the input information in case it is needed again later in the model.

Additionally, in order to help reduce the amount of training data and improve accuracy, transfer learning can be used, introducing the weights of the pre-trained model as a starting point. Another important technique to improve the generalization ability of the model and reduce overfitting is data augmentation, which creates additional training data by making transformations (such as rotation or flipping) over the input dataset.

Our proposal consists of training three MobileNetV2 models with the original dataset and over two modified ones by applying smoothing and sharpening to the images. Then the classifiers are fused using an aggregation function which permits to obtain a consensus result between the set of classifiers.

The fusion process plays a crucial role in the final decision step of each model, where the computation of probabilities for each class takes place. Rather than simply selecting the maximum response from a single model, we employ a comprehensive approach that involves calculating probabilities for each class in three different models: the original, smoothed, and sharpened models. These probabilities are then fused using various aggregation functions, resulting in 38×3 probabilities. By combining the outputs of the three models, we obtain a final set of 38 probabilities, from which we select the maximum response as our ultimate decision. This multifaceted fusion process enhances the accuracy and robustness of our model, allowing for more reliable and confident predictions.

Table 1. Hyperparameters used to configure the neural net used in the experiments.

#	Net Type	Epochs	Learning Rate	Transfer Learning	Data Augmentation
S_1	MobilenetV2	7	0.001	✗	✗
S_2	MobilenetV2	7	0.001	✓	✗
S_3	MobilenetV2	7	0.001	✗	✓
S_4	MobilenetV2	7	0.001	✓	✓

3   Experimental Setup

This section presents the neural networks used for the experiments and the two approaches used as a preprocessing step before the neural net execution. The schema for the model fusion and the different aggregation function alternatives are also exposed (Fig. 1).

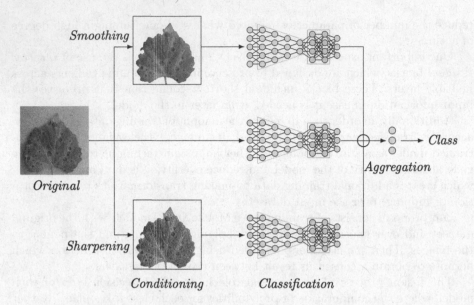

Fig. 1. Schematic representation process from the image input/capture to its classification, with the different models trained with the preprocessing alternatives.

3.1 Preprocessing

One of the fundamental phases in computer vision tasks is data preprocessing. In this experiment, we stick to the conditioning phase as described in the Bezdek Breakdown Structure (BBS) [2] for edge detection. Conditioning consists in applying some sort of transformation to an image so that it is enhanced to ease its processing in further steps. The most common treatment done to images is for noise reduction, data simplification or normalization.

One of the most common conditioning operations is image smoothing, which can be of two types. On the one hand, non-context-aware *e.g.* mean filtering, Gaussian filter [11] where usually the filtering is done through a kernel that is the same for every element of the image, and that does not adapt to the data; on the other hand, context-aware *e.g.* Mean-shift [5], Bilateral [23] or Gravitational filtering [16].

In this experiment, we focus on context-aware approaches, particularly the Gravitational one. The Gravitational Smoothing (GS) approach interprets an image as a set of particles with a spatial-tonal descriptor. That is, it represents each of the pixels (p) of the image as a 5-D structure $p = (x, y, r, g, b)$ where (x, y) are the spatial coordinates in the image and (r, g, b) the colour intensity in each of the RGB space. In this sense, each pixel in the image is treated as if it were a point mass subject to gravitational attraction from neighbouring pixels.

The basic idea is to consider each pixel in the image as a particle with mass equal to one and then calculate the gravitational force (attractive or repulsive) between each pixel and its neighbouring pixels. The strength of the force is determined by the distance between each pixel and its neighbours. The resulting gravitational forces cause the pixels to move towards each other, which leads to a smoothing effect on the image. Moreover, this approach permits us to invert the sense of the forces, allowing us to apply smoothing or sharpening to the image to remove details and texture of the image or enhance defects.

The process is performed iteratively, each iteration calculating the gravitational forces and moving the pixels accordingly in the colour space, keeping the spatial position fixed. The number of iterations and the strength of the gravitational forces can be adjusted to control the degree of smoothing. The parameters of the GS have to be carefully selected as they can lead to loss of detail and blurring of edges.

For the experiments of this work, we use GS with 10 iterations with a spatial neighbourhood of radius 4, a colour factor of 0.9, a spatial factor of 0.1 and a G constant of 0.04.

3.2   Classification Fusion

In order to perform the data fusion from the different classifiers trained with each of the images, both conditioned and original, we expose some basic aggregation concepts.

Definition 1 [1,3]. *A mapping $M : [0,1]^n \to [0,1]$ is an aggregation function if it is monotone non-decreasing in each of its components and satisfies $M(\mathbf{0}) = 0$ and $M(\mathbf{1}) = 1$.*

An aggregation function M is an averaging or mean if

$$\min(x_1,\ldots,x_n) \leq M(x_1,\ldots,x_n) \leq \max(x_1,\ldots,x_n).$$

A relevant type of aggregation function are the Ordered Weighted Averaging (OWA) operators presented by Yager [25].

Definition 2. *An OWA operator of dimension n is a mapping $\Phi : [0,1]^n \to [0,1]$ such that it exists a weighting vector $\boldsymbol{w} = (w_1,\ldots,w_n) \in [0,1]^n$ with $\sum_{i=1}^{n} w_i = 1$, and such that*

$$\Phi(x_1,\ldots,x_n) = \sum_{i=1}^{n} w_i \cdot x_{\sigma(i)},$$

where $\mathbf{x}_\sigma = (x_{\sigma(1)},\ldots,x_{\sigma(n)})$ is a decreasing permutation on the input $\boldsymbol{x}$.

In [24] a way to compute the weighting vector is presented:

$$w_i = Q\left(\frac{i}{n}\right) - Q\left(\frac{i-1}{n}\right),$$

where Q is a fuzzy linguistic quantifier as, for instance,

$$Q(r) = \begin{cases} 0 & \text{if } 0 \leq r < a, \\ \frac{r-a}{b-a} & \text{if } a \leq r \leq b, \\ 1 & \text{if } b < r \leq 1, \end{cases} \qquad (1)$$

with $a, b, r \in [0, 1]$.

For this experiment, we use the OWA operator that represents the linguistic label constructed using the parameters in Table 2.

Table 2. OWA operators representing linguistic labels along with their construction parameters

#	a	b	Linguistic label
OWA^1	0.3	0.8	*the majority of*
OWA^2	0	0.5	*at least half of*

Definition 3. *A function* $\mathsf{m} : 2^N \rightarrow [0, 1]$ *is a fuzzy measure if, for all* $X, Y \subseteq N$, *it satisfies the following properties:*

1. *Increasingness: if* $X \subseteq Y$, *then* $\mathsf{m}(X) \leq \mathsf{m}(Y)$;
2. *Boundary conditions:* $\mathsf{m}(\emptyset) = 0$ *and* $\mathsf{m}(N) = 1$.

An example of a commonly used fuzzy measure is the power measure, which we use in this work:

$$\mathsf{m}_q(X) = \left(\frac{|X|}{n}\right)^q, \text{ with } q > 0, \qquad (2)$$

where $|X|$ is the number of elements to be aggregated, n the total number of elements and $q > 0$. We have selected this measure due to the performance obtained in terms of accuracy in classification problems [12, 13].

Definition 4 [22]. *The discrete Sugeno integral is defined with respect to a fuzzy measure* m *by:*

$$Su_{\mathsf{m}}(\boldsymbol{x}) = \bigvee_{i=1}^{n} \left(x_{(i)} \wedge \mathsf{m}(A_{(i)})\right)$$

where (i) *is a permutation on* 2^N *such that* $x_{(i-1)} \leq x_{(i)}$ *for all* $i = 1, \ldots, n$, *with* $x_{(0)} = 0$ *and* $A_{(i)} = \{(1), \ldots, (i)\}$.

3.3   Experiment Results

In this section, we present the outcomes obtained with various configurations listed in Table 1 with original raw images (R_{1-4}), preprocessed with gravitational smoothing (Sm_{1-4}) and sharpening (Sh_{1-4}) and fusing with the Sugeno integral

(S_{1-4}) and two OWA alternatives ($OWA_{1-4}^{1,2}$). Quantitative results are shown in Table 3.

For the experiments, we utilized the PlantVillage dataset [9] consisting of 87,000 RGB images of healthy and diseased crop leaves, categorized into 38 distinct classes. For effective training of our model, we partitioned the dataset into three subsets, maintaining an 80/20 ratio, with 80% of the data allocated for training, 10% for testing, and the remaining 10% reserved for validation purposes.

The classification evaluation is done by constructing a confusion matrix where True Positive (TP), True Negative (TN), False Positive (FP) and False Negative (FN) are extracted. Then, to quantify the results the following well-known Precision (PREC), Recall (REC) and F_β measures are considered:

$$\mathrm{PREC} = \frac{\mathrm{TP}}{\mathrm{TP} + \mathrm{FP}}, \quad \mathrm{REC} = \frac{\mathrm{TP}}{\mathrm{TP} + \mathrm{FN}}, \quad F_\alpha = \frac{\mathrm{PREC} \cdot \mathrm{REC}}{\beta^2 \cdot \mathrm{PREC} + \mathrm{REC}}.$$

We select the values of $\beta = 0.5$ and $\beta = 1$ as the most commonly used in the literature.

Table 3 shows the performance of different approaches for plant disease classification using raw images (R), smoothing (Sm), sharpening (Sh), and fusion approaches with Sugeno integral (S) and two OWA alternatives (OWA^1, OWA^2).

For raw images, the R_1 and R_3 approaches performed the best with F_1 scores of 0.886 and 0.883, respectively.

When applying smoothing to the original raw images prior to the model training, the Sm_1 and Sm_3 approaches had the best performance with F_1 scores of 0.951 and 0.935, respectively. These performance scores show how applying a preprocessing technique where spurious information is removed while keeping edges has its benefits.

On the contrary, when using sharpening, the Sh_2 approach had the best performance with an F_1 score of 0.942 and the Sh_1 approach had a slightly lower F_1 score of 0.932, being the second best performer. Even tough sharpening images before training the model increase the model performance but not as much as the smoothing alternative.

In order to benefit from the strengths and weaknesses of each of the models, we evaluate the performance of the fusion of the different models in three different ways. For the model fusion approaches, the S_1 approach had the best performance with an F_1 score of 0.966, having a performance increase with respect to its individual alternatives.

Finally, in the case of the two OWA alternatives, OWA^1 and OWA^2, had similar performance with the OWA_2^1 and OWA_2^2 approaches having the best performance with F_1 scores of 0.970 and 0.969, respectively. And close to them OWA_1^1 with 0.970.

In general, it can be observed that the preprocessing techniques improved the performance of the raw image approaches, with smoothing having a more significant impact. The model fusion approaches showed promising results withhigh

Table 3. Resulting test performance of the different approaches trained with the parameters in Table 1 with raw images and preprocessed ones (using smoothing and sharpening) and model fusion with the Sugeno integral and two OWA alternatives over the PlantVillage dataset. Results are shown in terms of *Prec*, *Rec*, $F_{0.5}$ and F_1.

#	PREC	REC	$F_{0.5}$	F_1
R_1	.881	.904	.882	.886
R_2	.829	.852	.813	.807
R_3	.881	.897	.881	.883
R_4	.852	.862	.836	.831
Sm_1	.957	.947	.954	.951
Sm_2	.851	.802	.814	.792
Sm_3	.940	.935	.937	.935
Sm_4	.952	.926	.941	.932
Sh_1	.933	.939	.932	.932
Sh_2	.962	.934	.952	.942
Sh_3	.904	.899	.900	.897
Sh_4	.868	.846	.839	.823
S_1	.967	.967	.966	.966
S_2	.931	.942	.930	.931
S_3	.954	.956	.954	.954
S_4	.942	.943	.939	.938
OWA_1^1	.973	.970	.971	.970
OWA_2^1	.974	.975	.974	**.974**
OWA_3^1	.961	.961	.960	.960
OWA_4^1	.961	.955	.958	.955
OWA_1^2	.972	.969	.971	.969
OWA_2^2	.974	.974	.974	**.974**
OWA_3^2	.960	.961	.960	.959
OWA_4^2	.958	.952	.954	.952

precision, recall, and F_1 scores. The OWA alternatives showed similar performance, but the OWA^1 approach tended to perform slightly better. Overall, a combination of preprocessing techniques and model fusion approaches show a promising direction for improving plant disease classification performance.

4   Conclusions and Future Work

The findings of this study demonstrate that employing image preprocessing and model fusion techniques can significantly enhance the classification performance of plant diseases. Specifically, model fusion using aggregation functions such as

Sugeno Integral and OWA have been investigated. Our results reveal that the use of OWA function outperformed other techniques, indicating its suitability for plant disease classification applications.

Furthermore, the proposed approach not only improves the classification accuracy but also enables the use of simpler classification models, which are less computationally expensive to train. The ability to achieve superior performance using simpler models is highly desirable for practical applications in precision agriculture, where resources such as computing power and data storage are often limited.

Overall, the combination of image preprocessing and model fusion using OWA aggregation function offers a promising approach for improving the classification accuracy of plant diseases. This approach can potentially be deployed in real-world agricultural settings, contributing to the early detection and mitigation of plant diseases, leading to higher crop yields and sustainable agriculture.

In forthcoming studies, our aim is to incorporate advanced imagery, such as satellite, drone-level and multi-spectral images, as an adjunct to acquire an initial classification of potential issues in cropland and, subsequently, concentrate on specific land sectors. Furthermore, a plausible extension could entail integrating visual data with various sensor modalities, such as location, temperature, humidity, and soil composition, to extract potential markers that may reveal the onset of diseases before visible symptoms manifest.

Acknowledgements. This work was partially supported with grant PID2021-123673OB-C31 funded by MCIN/AEI/10.13039/501100011033 and by "ERDF A way of making Europe", Consellería d'Innovació, Universitats, Ciencia i Societat Digital from Comunitat Valenciana (APOSTD/2021/227) through the European Social Fund (Investing In Your Future) and grant from the Research Services of Universitat Politècnica de València (PAID-PD-22).

References

1. Beliakov, G., Pradera, A., Calvo, T.: Aggregation Functions: A Guide for Practitioners, vol. 18 (2007)
2. Bezdek, J., Chandrasekhar, R., Attikouzel, Y.: A geometric approach to edge detection. IEEE Trans. Fuzzy Syst. **6**(1), 52–75 (1998)
3. Calvo, T., Kolesárová, A., Komorníková, M., Mesiar, R.: Aggregation operators: properties, classes and construction methods. In: Aggregation Operators. Studies in Fuzziness and Soft Computing, vol. 97, no. 1, pp. 3–104 (2002)
4. de Castro Megías, A.I., et al.: Applications of sensing for disease detection. In: Kerry, R., Escolà, A. (eds.) Sensing Approaches for Precision Agriculture. PPA, pp. 369–398. Springer, Cham (2021). https://doi.org/10.1007/978-3-030-78431-7_13
5. Comaniciu, D., Meer, P.: Mean shift: a robust approach toward feature space analysis. IEEE Trans. Pattern Anal. Mach. Intell. **24**(5), 603–619 (2002). ISBN: 0162-8828
6. Dietterich, T.G.: An experimental comparison of three methods for constructing ensembles of decision trees: bagging, boosting, and randomization. Mach. Learn. **40**, 139–157 (2000). https://doi.org/10.1023/A:1007607513941

7. Ferentinos, K.P.: Deep learning models for plant disease detection and diagnosis. Comput. Electron. Agric. **145**, 311–318 (2018)
8. Gavhale, K.R., Gawande, U., et al.: An overview of the research on plant leaves disease detection using image processing techniques. IOSR J. Comput. Eng. (IOSR-JCE) **16**(1), 10–16 (2014)
9. Hughes, D., Salathé, M., et al.: An open access repository of images on plant health to enable the development of mobile disease diagnostics. arXiv preprint arXiv:1511.08060 (2015)
10. Kussul, N., Lavreniuk, M., Skakun, S., Shelestov, A.: Deep learning classification of land cover and crop types using remote sensing data. IEEE Geosci. Remote Sens. Lett. **14**(5), 778–782 (2017)
11. Lindeberg, T.: Scale-space for discrete signals. IEEE Trans. Pattern Anal. Mach. Intell. **12**(3), 234–254 (1990)
12. Lucca, G., et al.: Preaggregation functions: construction and an application. IEEE Trans. Fuzzy Syst. **24**(2), 260–272 (2016)
13. Lucca, G., Sanz, J.A., Dimuro, G.P., Bedregal, B., Bustince, H., Mesiar, R.: CF-integrals: a new family of pre-aggregation functions with application to fuzzy rule-based classification systems. Inf. Sci. **435**, 94–110 (2018)
14. Madrid, N., Lopez-Molina, C., Hurtik, P.: Non-linear scale-space based on fuzzy contrast enhancement: theoretical results. Fuzzy Sets Syst. **421**, 133–157 (2021)
15. Marco-Detchart, C., et al.: Ordered directional monotonicity in the construction of edge detectors. Fuzzy Sets Syst. **421**, 111–132 (2021)
16. Marco-Detchart, C., Lopez-Molina, C., Fernandez, J., Bustince, H.: A gravitational approach to image smoothing. In: Kacprzyk, J., Szmidt, E., Zadrożny, S., Atanassov, K.T., Krawczak, M. (eds.) IWIFSGN/EUSFLAT -2017. AISC, vol. 642, pp. 468–479. Springer, Cham (2018). https://doi.org/10.1007/978-3-319-66824-6_41
17. Mazzia, V., Comba, L., Khaliq, A., Chiaberge, M., Gay, P.: UAV and machine learning based refinement of a satellite-driven vegetation index for precision agriculture. Sensors **20**(9), 2530 (2020)
18. Melgani, F., Bruzzone, L.: Classification of hyperspectral remote sensing images with support vector machines. IEEE Trans. Geosci. Remote Sens. **42**(8), 1778–1790 (2004)
19. Petrellis, N.: Plant disease diagnosis with color normalization. In: 2019 8th International Conference on Modern Circuits and Systems Technologies (MOCAST), pp. 1–4. IEEE (2019)
20. Shruthi, U., Nagaveni, V., Raghavendra, B.: A review on machine learning classification techniques for plant disease detection. In: 2019 5th International Conference on Advanced Computing & Communication Systems (ICACCS), pp. 281–284. IEEE (2019)
21. Sudharshan, P., Petitjean, C., Spanhol, F., Oliveira, L.E., Heutte, L., Honeine, P.: Multiple instance learning for histopathological breast cancer image classification. Expert Syst. Appl. **117**, 103–111 (2019)
22. Sugeno, M.: Theory of fuzzy integrals and its applications. Ph.D. thesis, Tokyo Institute of Technology, Tokyo (1974)
23. Tomasi, C., Manduchi, R.: Bilateral filtering for gray and color images, pp. 839–846 (1998). ISBN: 81-7319-221-9
24. Yager, R.: Quantifier guided aggregation using OWA operators. Int. J. Intell. Syst. **11**(1), 49–73 (1996)
25. Yager, R.R.: On ordered weighted averaging aggregation operators in multicriteria decisionmaking. IEEE Trans. Syst. Man Cybern. **18**(1), 183–190 (1988)

A SPADE Multi-agent Application for Outdoor CO_2 Monitoring

Sergio Márquez-Sánchez[1,2](✉) iD, Sara Rodríguez-González[1],
Sergio Alonso Rollán[1], Javier Palanca Cámara[3], Andrés Terrasa Barrena[3],
and Fernando De la Prieta[1]

[1] BISITE Research Group, University of Salamanca, Edificio Multiusos I+D+i, Calle
Espejo s/n, 37007 Salamanca, Spain
{smarquez,srg,sergio.alro,fer}@usal.es
[2] Air Institute, IoT Digital Innovation Hub (Spain), 37188 Salamanca, Spain
[3] Valencian Research Institute for Artificial Intelligence (VRAIN), Universitat
Politècnica de València, Cno. de Vera s/n, 46022 València, Spain
{jpalanca,aterrasa}@dsic.upv.es

Abstract. The Internet of Things (IoT) has emerged as a powerful computation environment that interconnects diverse devices to decentralized systems and which can be deployed in numerous domains. Multi-Agent Systems (MAS) have been identified as a promising paradigm for the development of smart applications, including IoT devices. In this context, this paper introduces an air quality monitoring and prediction application which uses a multi-agent platform called SPADE. SPADE has recently incorporated an extension that allows for the seamless integration of IoT devices into multi-agent systems, called SPADE Artifact, which conforms with the theoretical A&A (Agents and Artifacts) Meta-Model. Furthermore, gas sensing, particularly measuring CO_2 concentration as an indicator of air quality. Outdoor air quality is a critical factor to consider for ensuring the health and safety of individuals in urban and suburban environments. By utilizing IoT artifacts to integrate gas sensing devices into MAS, it becomes feasible to accurately monitor and manage outdoor air quality, enabling decision-making on measures such as reducing traffic or controlling industrial emissions to improve air quality. This paper highlights the significance of integrating gas-sensing devices in IoT artifacts within MAS for effective monitoring and management of outdoor air quality in the era of IoT.

Keywords: Air Quality · Intelligent Agent · Artifacts

1 Introduction

The Internet of Things (IoT) has ushered in a transformative era of global connectivity, revolutionizing industries and daily life with thousands of different "smart objects" that can communicate with each other. However, despite the tremendous potential of IoT, many IoT devices, such as sensors, actuators, and wearables, often lack intrinsic intelligence due to limitations in their

D. Durães et al. (Eds.): PAAMS 2023, CCIS 1838, pp. 41–52, 2023.
https://doi.org/10.1007/978-3-031-37593-4_4

hardware and software capabilities. This deficiency hampers the development of comprehensive solutions that can effectively integrate diverse artificial intelligence techniques in the IoT ecosystem. To overcome this challenge, Multi-Agent Systems (MAS) and Agent-Based Computing (ABC) have emerged as promising paradigms, capable of facilitating the incorporation of IoT devices into such solutions [9]. MAS and ABC provide a framework that allows IoT devices to be seamlessly integrated in distributed and intelligent systems, enabling them to communicate, coordinate, and participate in the global decision-making. By leveraging the collective intelligence of interconnected agents and IoT devices, MAS and ABC enable the development of innovative IoT solutions in domains such as smart cities, industrial automation, healthcare, and transportation, leading to enhanced efficiency, safety, and sustainability.

Gas sensing has seen significant advancements in recent years, with various types of sensors offering different properties such as sensitivity, selectivity, response time, and production costs. As there is no one-size-fits-all solution, the choice of sensor depends on the specific circumstances and the intended use of the obtained data. Measuring air quality in indoor spaces, smart cities, environmental monitoring, wearables, and industrial environments are some of the contexts where gas sensing can be implemented.

In recent times, outdoor air quality monitoring has become increasingly important. The monitoring of outdoor air quality is crucial in determining the level of air pollution and its potential impact on human health. High levels of pollutants such as PM2.5, ozone, and nitrogen dioxide can cause respiratory problems, heart disease, and other health issues. By monitoring the levels of these pollutants in the air, outdoor air quality monitoring can help prevent risks to public health by alerting individuals to avoid certain areas or take appropriate measures such as wearing masks or staying indoors. Additionally, outdoor air quality monitoring can provide valuable data for policymakers to develop strategies for the improvement of air quality and protection of public health.

In this paper, we present a case study where CO_2 concentration values are measured and analyzed in detail, as it serves as the primary indicator of air quality in the area under investigation. By leveraging MAS and ABC paradigms, we aim to develop an intelligent and distributed system for gas sensing in outdoor environments, with the potential to predict and mitigate risks associated with poor air quality.

2   State of Art

The state of the art in indoor gas sensing, specifically in terms of CO_2 concentration, has been extensively studied due to the health risks associated with high concentrations. This section provides an overview of gas sensing technology, with a focus on indoor gas and CO_2 sensing, as well as insights from related studies in fields such as industry and smart cities.

Several projects have been developed in the field of smart cities, aiming to predict gas concentrations in different areas of the city by combining weather forecasting with gas concentration measurements [1]. Another approach is the development of Internet of Things (IoT)-based environment monitoring systems for tracking environmental parameters, such as air quality, in urban areas [2]. Additionally, opportunistic mobile sensing systems have been implemented in public transport to measure gas concentrations in small cities [3]. In the field of industry, numerous studies have been conducted to measure gas concentrations emitted from industrial activities that may pose health risks. For example, sensing technologies have been implemented in poultry production to measure air temperature, relative humidity, and air quality, among other parameters [4]. Studies have also been conducted at workshops supporting offshore oil stations in Norway to measure CO_2 concentration [5]. Indoor air quality assessment in the refinery industry, including measurements of RSP and different gases such as CO and CO_2, has also been explored [6]. Indoor air quality (OAQ) management in healthcare units is crucial for sustainability performance, as it impacts patient safety, occupational health and safety, and energy consumption. A study in Portugal analyzed IAQ in two hospitals and a primary care center, measuring temperature, relative humidity, CO_2 concentrations, bacteria, and fungi [7]. The results revealed that the exclusive use of natural ventilation is insufficient when occupancy is high, but effective when occupancy is low. The study also found a correlation between CO_2 concentration and bacterial load, and that low humidity reduces the concentration of fungi. The wide variety of sensors available today presents different properties and suitability for various circumstances. Electrochemical sensors, including those with conductive polymers, metal oxides, and carbon nanomaterials, are commonly used, along with other technologies such as photoacoustic effect, NDIR, TDLAS, and catalytic sensors [8].

Regarding multi-agent systems (MAS), in recent years, open MAS have gained significant attention in the scientific community for their potential in implementing virtual organizations. MAS are defined as open systems consisting of heterogeneous entities with a separation between form and function that defines their behavior [9]. Research has been conducted on modeling MAS and their implementation in complex scenarios [10–12]. With the emergence of the IoT, MAS-based technology has enabled the connection of small devices to open distributed intelligent systems, allowing for real-time exchange and transmission of knowledge [13]. However, current IoT networks often lack cooperative strategies that enable them to act as ubiquitous and intelligent systems, and the heterogeneity of devices in the IoT poses challenges in modeling large-scale systems [14]. Efforts have been made to extend the capabilities of IoT networks, such as equipping MAS with swarm intelligence [15], however, there is still a lack of effective mechanisms to deal with the heterogeneity of devices in multi-agent systems [16].

3   SPADE and SPADE Artifact Extension

SPADE is a flexible and open multi-agent system platform based on the XMPP standard communication protocol that allows for easy implementation of agents [18]. By using XMPP, SPADE agents are provided with both a message exchange and a presence notification mechanism in a native way. In addition, SPADE offers several facilities for agent development, including the use of Python as the main (but not the only) programming language, an asynchronous programming model to optimize performance and responsiveness, the use of plugins as a convenient way for the community to incorporate new functionalities (extensions), and a flexible agent model based on behaviors. In this model, each agent is internally structured in one or more behaviors, which are independent executable tasks following a particular execution pattern (such as cyclic, one-shot, or finite-state machine). Recently, a new type of behavior supporting the BDI (Belief-Desire-Intention) paradigm has been incorporated into SPADE, enabling agents to define behaviors with BDI reasoning capabilities.

In IoT domains, multi-agent systems typically interact with the environment by means of small IoT devices with limited resources. To develop MAS applications in such environments, SPADE has also adopted the A&A (Agents and Artifacts) Meta-Model [19], which has resulted in an extension called SPADE Artifact[1]. This extension maintains the expressiveness of the theoretical model while considering the typical characteristics of IoT devices, as it is now explained.

The A&A model proposes the environment to be a fundamental aspect in the process of designing and implementing a multi-agent system and, to do so, it incorporates the following abstractions: agents, artifacts, workspaces, and the environment. Agents represent the intelligent and autonomous parts of the system. Compared with agents, artifacts are simpler entities that model the elements that the system uses to interact with the environment. In particular, the model considers an artifact to be internally defined by its observable properties (aspects of the environment that the artifact can perceive), operations (actions that the artifact can perform in the environment), signals (asynchronous events which are triggered by conditions detected by the artifact), and a link interface by which artifacts can be interconnected to compose more complex ones. Workspaces are topological places composed of artifacts, and the environment corresponds to the set of all workspaces available to the multi-agent system.

In SPADE, artifacts have been incorporated as a new abstraction, however, they have been integrated as much as possible within the existing facilities and considering IoT devices' typical characteristics and limitations. First, observable properties have been implemented through the PubSub (Publish-Subscribe) mechanism, a well-known extension of XMPP already present in SPADE. Thus, agents interested in a particular artifact simply have to subscribe to it, and then every new perception of the artifact's properties is automatically sent to these agents. In addition, every artifact incorporates a default property called presence, by which it can communicate its status. Second, operations are implemented by adopting another XMPP extension implementing the XML-RPC standard. As a result, agents can send standard request messages to remotely perform any of the registered operations made available by the artifact. Thirdly, SPADE allows agents (and artifacts) to be implemented in different programming languages as long as they interact with the system in XMPP terms. As a result, small,

---

[1] https://github.com/javipalanca/spade_artifact.

embedded devices with very low hardware capabilities can be incorporated as artifacts in SPADE by using an appropriate language, such as C.

4 Application to Case Study: CO_2 PROJECT

The CO_2 PROJECT, a collaboration between the Air Institute and the University of Salamanca, focuses on studying and monitoring air quality, particularly carbon dioxide (CO_2), to identify environments that may promote the spread of respiratory diseases, such as COVID-19. The project has developed a device called Deep Air Control 4.0, equipped with sensors to monitor parameters such as temperature, atmospheric pressure, humidity, and CO_2 levels. It also has the potential to measure other parameters, such as volatile organic compounds (VOCs). The device is compact, low-power, and capable of monitoring air quality in public spaces to detect environments with poor ventilation that may contribute to respiratory disease transmission.

The main components of Deep Air Control 4.0 include an ESP32 WiFi microcontroller for processing and connectivity, an MH-Z19C infrared CO_2 sensor for gas detection, a BME680 sensor for temperature, atmospheric pressure, and humidity, a micro USB connector for power, a status LED for connection status visualization, and optional elements such as a buzzer or warning LED for audible or visual alerts on air quality (Fig. 1). The project utilizes a layered approach commonly found in Internet of Things (IoT) systems, with two main layers: the edge layer and the cloud layer. The edge layer, located at the edge of the system, consists of IoT devices and internet connectivity. The cloud layer encompasses data ingestion, data storage, analysis, and application layers. Users interact with both layers, configuring and manipulating physical devices, receiving visual and audible alerts, and accessing a web application to visualize collected data and set device configurations. The system is potentially scalable, with the ability to replicate layers in different environments.

The IoT devices developed for the project are responsible for sensing environmental parameters in indoor and outdoor spaces. The devices consist of a printed circuit board (PCB) with several components, including an ESP32 microcontroller for executing the project's firmware and communicating with the cloud environment. The microcontroller is selected from Espressif and supports WiFi, Bluetooth 4.2, and Bluetooth Low Energy (LE), with low power consumption and wide temperature range suitability. The devices also include a CO_2 sensor for measuring CO_2 levels, a BME680 sensor for measuring temperature, atmospheric pressure, and humidity, and a USB connector for powering the device. Status and power LEDs are included for the notification of users regarding device status. Figure 2 shows a final image of the manufactured device with the communications module, the microcontroller, the PCB with integrated sensors, as well as the protective case.

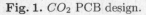

Fig. 1. CO_2 PCB design.

Fig. 2. Real device integrating the PCB and sensors.

The project has also designed an outdoor version of the device with the same features, but with a different design that includes an umbrella for weather protection. This outdoor device provides reference data on outdoor air quality, allowing for comparison with outdoor air quality and evaluation of the impact on historical heritage of cities. Motivated by the need to quickly and effectively understand how, where, and why diseases such as COVID-19 are transmitted, the project focuses on CO_2 as a vital parameter for preventing transmission and respiratory difficulties. The outdoor model of the device also extends the measurement to assess the impact on historical heritage of cities, considering the negative effects of CO_2 as a greenhouse gas. The data acquisition system of Deep Air Control includes sensing modules for measuring environmental parameters such as temperature, atmospheric pressure, humidity, and CO_2 levels. These measurements are accessible to users through a web interface that allows for real-time visualization and historical data analysis. The device can generate low air quality alerts, which can be either audible or visual on the device itself, or visual on the web platform. Users also have the option to configure email alerts or receive daily summaries/reports on the monitored room's air quality. Figure 3 shows a final image of the manufactured outdoor device.

5   Multi-agent System for CO_2 Concentration Monitoring

For this project, a multi-agent system has been developed using the SPADE platform and the SPADE Artifact extension described earlier in this paper. In short, the developed system consists of several components which belong to three main types: sensor artifacts, zone agents, and a dashboard agent. Figure 4 presents a general view of the application architecture, while these component types are further explained in the subsections that follow.

Fig. 3. Outdoor device case.

5.1 Sensor Artifacts

The sensor artifacts are SPADE artifacts connected to the physical outdoor CO_2 sensors deployed along the city. In this case study, the application has used some sensors deployed in Salamanca (Spain). These artifacts do not provide any kind of intelligent deliberation. Their only purpose is to read the values from their corresponding sensor and publish them in real-time on any other interested party (component) in the application. As explained above in Sect. 3, artifacts do that through the use of the *PubSub* protocol provided by SPADE.

5.2 Zone Agents

The zone agents represent different areas of the city, and their main purpose is collecting and processing the CO_2 concentration data from the sensors located in their respective areas. To do so, each zone agent focuses on the artifacts situated in its particular zone by subscribing to their *PubSub* events. Thus, as the physical sensors perform their CO_2 readings, they are sent to the corresponding zone agents in real time. Then, the zone agents combine the data collected by the artifacts in their respective areas and analyze it to detect abnormal values indicating high concentrations of CO_2, in some predefined ranges. If any zone agent detects a high concentration according to these ranges, it triggers an alarm and sends it to the dashboard agent for further action (see below). Figure 5 shows an example of how the status of each zone's alarm is depicted in the application's graphical user interface (GUI). In each zone, the current CO_2 value for the area is displayed, and the alarm status is represented by a color code (from green indicating a safe concentration to red indicating a dangerous one).

The zone agents also compute the forecasting of CO_2 concentration data in their respective zones and send it to the dashboard agent to be displayed in the application's GUI. These agents use time-series forecasting techniques to

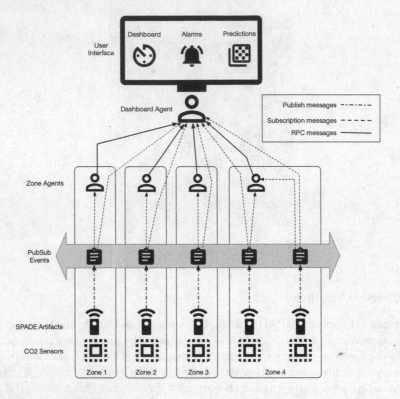

Fig. 4. Multi-agent system architecture

predict each zone's future CO_2 concentration levels. In this case, the application calculates a forecast for the next 7 days. The predicted values are then sent to the dashboard agent for display in the GUI. An example of how this forecasting is presented in the GUI is shown in Fig. 6.

5.3   Dashboard Agent

The dashboard agent is mainly responsible for displaying the application's GUI, shown in Fig. 8, which is a compilation of some of the features described above. For this purpose, this agent receives multiple types of data from the rest of the application's components. First, this agent subscribes to the artifacts in all the zones, in order to receive the CO_2 readings in real time. With this raw data, it computes and draws an interpolation map of CO_2 concentration, which is shown in Fig. 7.

Secondly, the dashboard agent also receives and displays the information generated by the zone agents, including both the alarm statuses and the forecast (predictions) of CO_2 concentration for the different city areas. Regarding the forecast, this agent is also responsible for calculating the aggregated values and predictions for the entire city and including them in the prediction chart.

610.5	801.0	855.0	1413.0
Zone 01	Zone 02	Zone 03	Zone 04
See data ➔	See data ➔	See data ➔	See data ➔

Fig. 5. Example of alarm values for the 4 CO_2 zones delimited in Salamanca.

5.4 Scalability and Adaptation of Application

This application has been built and tested for a case study located in Salamanca, where five sensors were deployed along the city. Since this is a small number of sensors, four different areas or zones were defined based on the location of the sensors. As shown in Fig. 4, Zones 1, 2, and 3 included a single sensor, while Zone 4 included two sensors since they were close enough to belong to the same zone.

Both the characteristics of SPADE and the system architecture allow to scale the application as the number of available CO_2 sensors increases, either by adding more artifacts to the existing zones or by adding new zones to the city. In fact, this would be a design decision depending on the areas of interest in the city by the application user, since SPADE could efficiently handle the data distribution with any configuration of zones (and of artifacts within a zone) with the minimum communication cost.

The application is also flexible and adaptable to different situations and domains. The alarm thresholds for the zone agents are configurable since the warning or danger levels could be different depending on the city or case study. Also, the time granularity for the forecast and the number of predicted values are also configurable. In this case study, the application computes one value a day (per zone) for seven days. However, depending on the domain this could be changed, for example, to compute an hourly forecast.

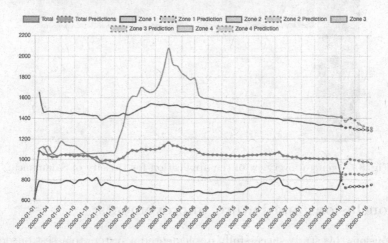

Fig. 6. Collected data (solid lines) and predicted data (dashed lines) for each of the zones and the total aggregation of all zones.

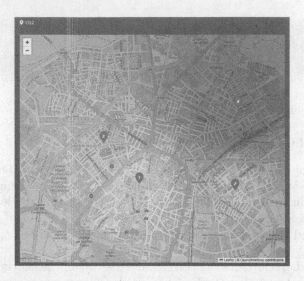

Fig. 7. An interpolated map of the CO_2 concentration in the city of Salamanca.

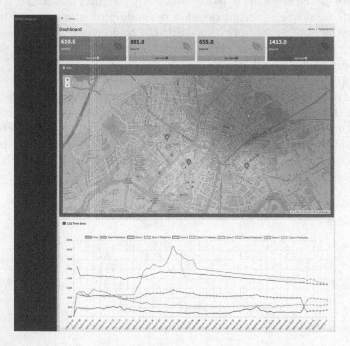

Fig. 8. A general overview of the application for the city of Salamanca.

6 Conclusions and Future Improvements

In conclusion, this study successfully implemented a system to assess outdoor air quality, utilizing various parameters such as CO_2 concentration, pressure, temperature, and humidity. The obtained measurements were analyzed to determine compliance with relevant legislation, with the aim of eliminating health risks associated with poor air quality and improving the health of individuals exposed to outdoor air pollution. Outdoor air quality monitoring is essential to ensure that air pollution levels are within safe limits and to identify pollution sources that may be contributing to poor air quality. By continuously monitoring outdoor air quality, appropriate measures can be taken to mitigate the impact of air pollution on human health and the environment.

Nowadays, the presence of IoT devices has become ubiquitous in several domains, from industry to smart cities or domotics. In such contexts, multi-agent system technologies have been proven to provide valid infrastructures to effectively integrate IoT devices in intelligent, dynamic, and flexible systems. This paper has presented a case study of a multi-agent application for air quality monitoring and prediction in the city of Salamanca. The application has been developed through the use of the SPADE multi-agent platform, and particularly, its extension for interacting with IoT devices, called SPADE Artifact. The extension conforms with the theoretical A&A Meta-Model, however, it has been adapted to the characteristics of typical IoT devices, while also taking advantage of several of the SPADE features.

The application has effectively integrated IoT devices (in this case, CO_2 sensors) into a multi-agent system that is able to collect, analyze and predict air quality conditions in some zones of interest within a city, around the locations where the sensors are physically deployed. The application is highly scalable and it is configurable in various aspects, such as the number and location of zones, the number of sensors/artifacts per zone, the time granularity of the air quality forecast, etc. The use of SPADE as the application's platform has had two principal benefits: first, an easy design and implementation of all the application components (artifacts, agents, the GUI, etc.). Second, the use of very efficient and convenient communication mechanisms (such as *PubSub*) is especially useful in the context of IoT environments, where the interaction among the smart objects and the rest of the application components is key.

Acknowledgements. This research has been supported by the project "COordinated intelligent Services for Adaptive Smart areaS (COSASS), Reference: PID2021-123673OB-C33, financed by MCIN/AEI/10.13039/501100011033/FEDER, UE.

References

1. Viqueira, J.R., et al.: Proyecto TRAFAIR: Generación y publicación de datos de calidad del aire en las ciudades de Zaragoza y Santiago de Compostela. Actas de las Jornadas de Ingeniería del Software y Bases de Datos (JISBD) (2019)
2. Shah, J., Mishra, B.: IoT enabled environmental monitoring system for smart cities. In: 2016 International Conference on Internet of Things and Applications (IOTA), pp. 383–388. IEEE (2016)
3. Diéguez, D.C., et al.: Monitorización de contaminación urbana mediante sensorización móvil oportunista en transporte público. Estudios de construcción y transportes (111), 7–21 (2009)

4. Corkery, G., Ward, S., Kenny, C., Hemmingway, P.: Incorporating smart sensing technologies into the poultry industry. J. World's Poultry Res. **3**(4), 106–128 (2013)
5. Molka-Danielsen, J., Engelseth, P., Wang, H.: Large scale integration of wireless sensor network technologies for air quality monitoring at a logistics shipping base. J. Ind. Inf. Integr. **10**, 20–28 (2018)
6. Abdullah, S., et al.: The assessment of indoor air quality (IAQ) at refinery industry. Int. J. Civ. Eng. Technol. **9**, 925–932 (2018)
7. Fonseca, A., Abreu, I., Guerreiro, M.J., Abreu, C., Silva, R., Barros, N.: Indoor air quality and sustainability management-case study in three Portuguese healthcare units. Sustainability **11**(1), 101 (2019)
8. Feng, S., et al.: Review on smart gas sensing technology. Sensors **19**(17), 3760 (2019)
9. Savaglio, C., Ganzha, M., Paprzycki, M., Bădică, C., Ivanović, M., Fortino, G.: Agent-based internet of things: state-of-the-art and research challenges. Futur. Gener. Comput. Syst. **102**, 1038–1053 (2020)
10. Foster, I., Kesselman, C., Tuecke, S.: The anatomy of the grid: enabling scalable virtual organizations. Int. J. High Perform. Comput. Appl. **15**(3), 200–222 (2001)
11. Bajo, J., et al.: An execution time planner for the ARTIS agent architecture. Eng. Appl. Artif. Intell. **21**(5), 769–784 (2008)
12. Costa, A., Rincon, J.A., Carrascosa, C., Julian, V., Novais, P.: Emotions detection on an ambient intelligent system using wearable devices. Futur. Gener. Comput. Syst. **92**, 479–489 (2019)
13. Leitao, P., Karnouskos, S., Ribeiro, L., Lee, J., Strasser, T., Colombo, A.W.: Smart agents in industrial cyber-physical systems. Proc. IEEE **104**(5), 1086–1101 (2016)
14. Wang, S., Wan, J., Zhang, D., Li, D., Zhang, C.: Towards smart factory for industry 4.0: a self-organized multi-agent system with big data based feedback and coordination. Comput. Netw. **101**, 158–168 (2016)
15. Rose, K., Eldridge, S., Chapin, L.: The internet of things: an overview. The Internet Society (ISOC) (2015)
16. Atzori, L., Iera, A., Morabito, G.: The internet of things: a survey. Comput. Netw. **54**(15), 2787–2805 (2010)
17. Palanca, J., Rincon, J.A., Julián, V., Carrascosa, C., Terrasa, A.: IoT artifacts: incorporating artifacts into the SPADE platform. In: Novais, P., Carneiro, J., Chamoso, P. (eds.) Ambient Intelligence-Software and Applications, pp. 69–79. Springer, Cham (2022). https://doi.org/10.1007/978-3-031-06894-2_7
18. Palanca, J., Terrasa, A., Julian, V., Carrascosa, C.: SPADE 3: supporting the new generation of multi-agent systems. IEEE Access **8**, 182537–182549 (2020). https://doi.org/10.1109/ACCESS.2020.3027357
19. Weyns, D., Omicini, A., Odell, J.: Environment as a first class abstraction in multiagent systems. Auton. Agents Multi-Agent Syst. **14**, 5–30 (2007)

Blockchain-Enabled Reward System for Sustainable Last-Mile Delivery in Urban Logistics: A Case Study on SimFleet Platform

Yeray Mezquita[1]([⊠])(iD), Sara Rodríguez[1](iD), Javier Palanca[2](iD),
and Javier Prieto[1](iD)

[1] BISITE Research Group, University of Salamanca, Salamanca, Spain
{yeraymm,srg,javierp}@usal.es
[2] Institut Valencià d'Investigació en Intel·ligència Artificial (VRAIN),
Universitat Politècnica de València, Valencia, Spain
jpalanca@dsic.upv.es

Abstract. To promote green transportation within cities, the concept of active mobility has gained attraction in the research community. In that sense, the use of IoT sensors along with open fleets, sharing vehicles, and pay-per-use mobility services, allow the development and deployment of new platforms that have the potential to offer active transportation to the citizens. On the other hand, the extreme dependence on the data generated by the sensors, and the need to share information between public and private companies, have arisen challenges in the traceability of the information generated, along with the security of the communications between devices. In that sense, the incorporation of blockchain technology seems the key aspect to allow the real implementation of these systems in the real world, protecting the communications between machines from external attacks, while implementing a service for the trackability of the information generated within the platform. This paper makes use of a tool developed by the authors to simulate a scenario in which the model proposed allows the optimization of last-mile delivery. Besides, the use of blockchain technology in these systems, also increases the transparency in the platform and trust of the users by being able to track the source of the information for the decision-making algorithm.

Keywords: Urban delivery · Active mobility · Blockchain

1 Introduction

Urban delivery platforms have become an essential part of modern urban logistics. The growth of e-commerce and the demand for fast and reliable last-mile delivery has made these platforms indispensable for businesses and consumers alike [15]. To optimize the efficiency of these platforms, MultiAgent Systems (MAS) have emerged as a promising solution. These systems can simulate the interactions and decision-making processes of multiple agents involved in the delivery process, from the retailers to the customers, and can help improve the overall performance of the platform [16].

In the mentioned context, the paper "An agent-based simulation framework for the study of urban delivery" [13] presents a new simulation framework called SimFleet, which is designed to study and improve urban logistics. The SimFleet platform is based on agent-based modeling and simulation techniques, and it incorporates real-world data to model the behavior of delivery vehicles, customers, and other actors in the urban delivery system. The paper highlights the importance of studying and improving urban logistics, given the increasing demand for e-commerce and last-mile delivery services and the associated challenges of traffic congestion, air pollution, and other environmental issues.

While the SimFleet simulation framework offers a powerful tool for studying and improving urban logistics, there are still challenges in ensuring the security and transparency of the platform. To address these challenges, this paper proposes the use of blockchain technology in SimFleet to enhance the platform's functionality. By implementing blockchain, SimFleet gains decentralized identity management, ensuring secure communication by preventing identity theft or impersonation. Additionally, the use of blockchain technology provides transparency and improves user trust, which can add value to the platform's services. This paper further proposes the use of blockchain-based green token-based reward system to promote active mobility, which can reduce the carbon footprint associated with traditional delivery methods.

The research on the SimFleet platform and the integration of blockchain technology is of significant importance to various stakeholders involved in the urban logistics sector. Firstly, it is relevant to companies operating in the delivery industry who can benefit from the improved efficiency and sustainability of their operations through the implementation of this platform. Additionally, policymakers and urban planners can use the results and insights generated from the simulations to design more effective urban delivery policies and infrastructure. Moreover, the research also addresses the environmental concerns associated with urban logistics, which is crucial to environmentalists and other stakeholders working towards sustainable development. Finally, researchers and academics studying multi-agent systems, simulation, and blockchain technology will find this paper valuable as it demonstrates the practical applications of these fields in a simulated real-world scenario.

This manuscript is structured in four other sections. Section 2 provides a background on what has been done regarding the implementation of blockchain technology in urban delivery platforms. The next section, Sect. 3, describes the proposed framework, which implements blockchain technology and showcases the requirements and characteristics of the modified framework. It is also described the reward system that incentivizes sustainable delivery behavior within the platform. Section 4 discusses the implementation of blockchain technology in the proposed framework. Finally, the paper concludes in Sect. 5 by highlighting the potential of blockchain technology to improve urban logistics and suggesting future directions for research in this area.

2 Background

Blockchain technology is a decentralized, digital ledger that records transactions in a secure and transparent manner. Each transaction is encrypted and stored across a network of computers, making it virtually tamper-proof and resistant to hacking. This technology is increasingly being explored and integrated into existing platforms and systems related to urban delivery and logistics [10]. Some of the ways in which blockchain is being used in this context include:

- Tracking and tracing: Blockchain can be used to provide end-to-end tracking and tracing of packages, from the point of dispatch to the point of delivery [6]. This can help reduce the risk of fraud and theft, and improve overall supply chain efficiency [8]. For example, the logistics provider DHL has partnered with Accenture to develop a blockchain-based system for supply chain visibility and product tracking [1].
- Smart contracts: Blockchain can be used to automate and enforce contracts between parties in the urban delivery industry [14]. For example, smart contracts can be used to automate the payment process between shippers and carriers, reducing costs and improving trust between parties [11]. In addition, smart contracts can be used to enforce delivery time windows and other contractual obligations, helping to improve customer satisfaction [10].
- Decentralized marketplaces: Blockchain can be used to create decentralized marketplaces for urban delivery services. These marketplaces can provide a secure and transparent platform for customers to access a range of delivery options from multiple providers [13]. In the case of the startup OpenPort, it is using blockchain to create a decentralized marketplace for road freight in Asia [7].
- Environmental sustainability: Blockchain can be used to incentivize and reward sustainable practices [4]. For example, the startup Urban Tech is using blockchain to create a rewards system for eco-friendly delivery practices, such as the use of electric vehicles and bikes [2].

Overall, the use of blockchain technology in existing platforms and systems related to urban delivery has the potential to improve supply chain transparency, reduce costs, enhance security, and promote sustainable practices [10,11]. However, there are also challenges and limitations to the adoption of blockchain technology in this context, including regulatory hurdles, technical complexity, and interoperability issues [3,9,12].

3 Proposed Framework

In this section, we will describe the key features and components of the proposed MAS platform and explain how it leverages blockchain technology to address the challenges of urban delivery. It is built upon the framework presented in the Sim-Fleet platform proposed in the paper "An agent-based simulation framework for the study of urban delivery" [13]. This framework is designed to simulate the urban delivery process and study the behavior of different agents, such as shippers, carriers, and customers. Building on this framework, we have developed a MAS that incorporates blockchain technology to provide greater security, transparency, and efficiency in the urban delivery process.

One of the main goals of incorporating blockchain technology into the proposed MAS is to create a reward system based on green tokens. These tokens will be used to incentivize and promote active mobility in urban areas, such as walking, cycling, and the use of public transportation. By using blockchain technology, we can ensure the transparency and security of the reward system, and enable users to earn and redeem tokens for their sustainable transportation choices. This not only promotes sustainable practices, but also helps to reduce traffic congestion, air pollution, and carbon emissions in urban areas. In the following sections, we will describe in detail how our platform design incorporates blockchain technology to allow the implementation of this reward system and the mechanisms that underpin it.

3.1   SimFleet Platform

SimFleet [13] is an application designed to simulate fleet management and coordination scenarios. Its architecture consists of four layers: the simulator, the fleet, the agents, and the coordination and negotiation strategies. These layers are designed to separate the functionality of the tool and to make it easy to adapt it to particular fleet and/or negotiation scenarios.

The first layer, the simulator, is the agent controlling the simulation process and serving the GUI. It is responsible for creating the rest of the application agents in the simulation, including the supporting agents like the Route Planner agent and the Directory agent. The Route Planner agent is responsible for calculating valid routes on city streets for the vehicles traveling from one point to another within the city. The Directory agent provides a directory service where agents providing services can register to be located by other agents during the simulation.

The second layer contains the fleets required in any given simulation. Each fleet includes the Transporter agent, which represents a vehicle and its driver, and the Fleet Manager agent, which is in charge of receiving requests from customers and making decisions about how to coordinate the transport process of the fleet's vehicles. The Fleet Manager agents use the Directory agent to register their respective fleet services, allowing the Transporters and the Customers to locate these services.

The third layer consists of the agents developed to control the workflow of the platform. It includes an agent for managing the fleets deployed, each Fleet Managers and all the Transporters of each fleet, and an agent for every Customer which may issue transport requests in the simulation. Customers may request transport services for any available fleet. This layer also allows for the case where the item to be transported is also the customer. Items to be transported are not represented as agents in SimFleet, since all the negotiation processes are carried out by the item's owner, the Customer agent, but as artifacts.

Finally, the fourth layer comprises the coordination and negotiation strategies that the simulation agents apply to request, select, organize, and coordinate transport services. Each agent incorporates its own strategy, implemented as a SPADE behavior, according to its role in the simulation environment and its own particular goals. The tool provides a basic default strategy for each of these three roles, but it is possible to define a particular strategy of each individual agent, hence allowing for much more sophisticated simulations. The tool uses the Strategy Pattern design pattern [5] in order to dynamically attach new, custom negotiation behaviors for the simulation agents at run time.

3.2 Blockchain Implementation

The implementation of the blockchain technology within the SimFleet platform is done transversal to the four layers of the framework, depicted in Subsect. 3.1, being a service from which each of the components of the platform could benefit. One of the first requirements for the implementation of this system is that each device and actor (as shown in Fig. 1) would be uniquely identified by their wallet address on the blockchain. This is called decentralized identity management, and, by using this approach, the system can ensure secure communications by preventing identity theft or impersonation between the actors and devices of the platform. In addition to decentralized identity management, it is crucial to implement auditability systems to ensure the wellbeing of the devices on the platform. These systems can help detect and prevent any unauthorized modifications or malicious activities, providing accountability and transparency for all actors involved. With the use of auditability systems, the SimFleet platform can ensure that the devices and actors operate within the expected parameters, maintaining the integrity and security of the platform.

As shown in Fig. 1, the new functions and characteristics of the platform can be listed as:

- The devices associated with each transporter (Transporter 1, Transporter 2) would send the information generated in each time window to their correspondent fleet manager (Manager Fleet 1, Manager Fleet 2). This process is depicted in the figure as "location structure" for simplification purposes. To ensure that the intermediary cannot modify the information received, this structure will be signed by the device that generates it and will have the hash of the information sent, in addition to the signature. This protects the information sent, so that even if it has not yet been added to the blockchain, intermediaries cannot modify it without being detected by the auditability systems and users. To determine who is responsible for modifying the information, each actor can store a temporary database to prove their good work on the platform to the auditors.
- Each stored data would be associated not only with the unique address of its creator but also with the unique identifier of the batch to which it should be grouped. Each lot of data will only group data from the same sensor, for example: if the sensor sends data every second, within a determined time

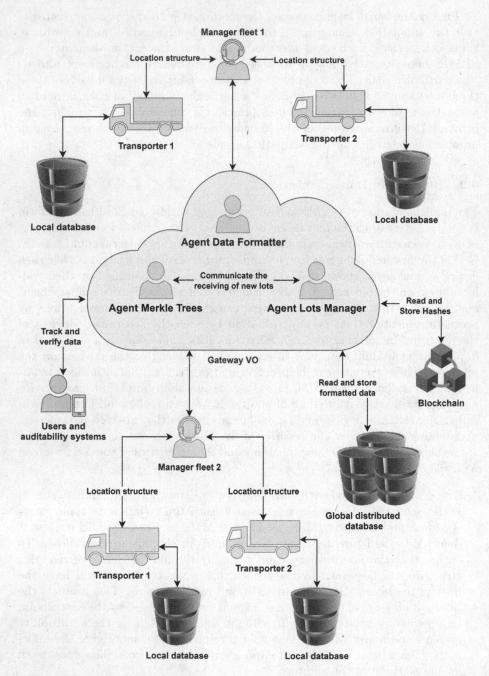

Fig. 1. This figure depicts the distribution of a common use case of the platform, where two different fleets are deployed within the platform, showcasing the interactions of the components.

window (5 min in our proposal), it will generate a batch of data with a size of 300 values. The Agent Lots Manager is the one responsible for creating the lots of data that will be sent to the Agent Merkle Trees.

- In the system, there should be a new agent that will perform a Merkle tree for each batch of data generated in every time window. The root of each tree will then be stored in the smart contract deployed on the blockchain network for later verification of the data. Each of these roots will contain data to identify them regarding the data batch and also store a boolean value indicating whether the referenced data is valid or not for further processing with the respective auditability systems used. The Agent Merkle Trees is the one who will create the Markle Tree form the lots of data received by the Agent Lots Manager.

In conclusion, thanks to the proposed platform, any actor on the platform can verify that the data lots stored come from the sensors that claim to be their authors. Furthermore, it can easily verify that the data batches used in the models have not been modified by third-party interests after they have been stored. This provides transparency to the system, improving user trust, while adding value to the platform's services.

3.3   Reward System

To encourage active mobility in last mile delivery activities, a green token-based reward system will be implemented in the platform. Users of the platform, such as delivery companies or individual couriers, will be awarded green tokens for each delivery completed using active mobility methods such as walking, cycling, or using electric vehicles.

The number of green tokens awarded will be based on the distance traveled, with a higher number of tokens given for longer distances. These tokens can be redeemed for various rewards, such as discounts on platform fees or access to premium features. Some examples of premium features that could be accessed using green tokens include:

- Redeeming tokens for cash: Users can convert their green tokens into cash or gift cards from partnering stores or brands.
- Premium access to analytics: Users can use their green tokens to unlock advanced analytics features such as real-time tracking of delivery performance, heat maps of delivery routes, and detailed reports on customer feedback.
- Specialized equipment: Users can use their green tokens to purchase specialized equipment such as high-quality backpacks, safety gear, or electric bicycles to improve their efficiency and safety while making deliveries.
- Discounts on eco-friendly products: Users can redeem their green tokens for discounts on eco-friendly products such as reusable bags, water bottles, or other sustainable products that align with the platform's mission of promoting environmental sustainability.

The use of a reward system based on green tokens will not only incentivize the use of active mobility methods, but it will also promote environmental sustainability and reduce carbon emissions associated with last mile delivery activities. Additionally, the reward system will enhance the user experience and improve the reputation and competitiveness of the platform in the market.

4   Discussion

The implementation of blockchain technology in urban delivery systems has the potential to revolutionize the industry, offering numerous benefits such as increased transparency, accountability, and security. One of the main advantages of implementing blockchain technology in the SimFleet platform is that it allows for decentralized identity management. This means that each device and actor involved in the platform can be uniquely identified by their wallet address on the blockchain, ensuring secure communications by preventing identity theft or impersonation. Additionally, the use of auditability systems can help detect and prevent any unauthorized modifications or malicious activities, providing accountability and transparency for all actors involved. By using these systems, the SimFleet platform can ensure that the devices and actors operate within the expected parameters, maintaining the integrity and security of the platform.

Another benefit of using blockchain technology in the SimFleet platform is that it provides transparency and improves user trust, which can add value to the platform's services. Users can easily verify that the data lots stored come from the sensors that claim to be their authors and that the data batches used in the models have not been modified by third-party interests after they have been stored. This can enhance the user experience and promote adoption of the platform by users.

Thanks to the use of blockchain technology in the SimFleet platform, it is possible to implement a green token-based reward system to promote active mobility of the users in urban delivery platforms. The use of this reward system in the SimFleet platform offers several benefits for the platform's users and the environment, like reducing the carbon footprint associated with traditional delivery methods thanks to the incentive program that encourages the use of active mobility methods for last-mile deliveries. Moreover, the reward system provides users with tangible benefits such as discounts on platform fees or access to premium features that enhance their experience and increase their loyalty to the platform, improving its network effect. The use of blockchain technology ensures the security and transparency of the reward system, preventing fraud or unauthorized access to the tokens. In general, the implementation of the green token-based incentive scheme represents a mutually beneficial solution for the SimFleet platform, its users, and the ecosystem, thereby aligning with the overarching mission of promoting environmental sustainability while enhancing the user experience.

5 Conclusion

In conclusion, this paper has presented the implementation of blockchain technology in the SimFleet platform, a novel agent-based simulation framework for urban delivery. The paper has demonstrated the potential of blockchain to introduce new features and functions to the platform, such as decentralized identity management, the need for auditability systems, and a green token-based reward system to incentivize active mobility. The benefits of these features are numerous, including increased transparency, accountability, and security, improved user trust, and enhanced environmental sustainability. The potential of blockchain to improve the efficiency and sustainability of urban logistics is substantial, and this paper serves as a call for further research and development in this area.

In terms of areas for further research and improvement, one potential path is to explore ways to optimize the use of blockchain technology in the SimFleet platform. For example, investigating ways to reduce the cost and complexity of implementation, or find ways to improve scalability while still maintaining the integrity and security of the platform. Additionally, further research could be done to explore the potential problems that could arise in the terms of privacy and data protection regulations for the users that interact with this kind of platforms.

Acknowledgements. This research has been supported by the project "COordinated intelligent Services for Adaptive Smart areaS (COSASS), Reference: PID2021-123673OB-C33, financed by MCIN/AEI/10.13039/501100011033/FEDER, UE.

References

1. Dhl and accenture unlock the power of blockchain in logistics. https://newsroom.accenture.com/news/dhl-and-accenture-unlock-the-power-of-blockchain-in-logistics.htm
2. Urban tech whitepaper. https://mastercardcontentexchange.com/news/media/kclf4qri/urban-tech-report-2022.pdf
3. Bernabe, J.B., Canovas, J.L., Hernandez-Ramos, J.L., Moreno, R.T., Skarmeta, A.: Privacy-preserving solutions for blockchain: review and challenges. IEEE Access **7**, 164908–164940 (2019)
4. França, A., Neto, J.A., Gonçalves, R., Almeida, C.: Proposing the use of blockchain to improve the solid waste management in small municipalities. J. Clean. Prod. **244**, 118529 (2020)
5. Gamma, E., Helm, R., Johnson, R., Johnson, R.E., Vlissides, J.: Design Patterns: Elements of Reusable Object-Oriented Software. Pearson Deutschland GmbH (1995)
6. Kouhizadeh, M., Sarkis, J.: Blockchain practices, potentials, and perspectives in greening supply chains. Sustainability **10**(10), 3652 (2018)
7. Lim, J., Noman, R.: Building the blockchain logistics protocol. https://openport.com/wp-content/uploads/2021/02/2018.01_OpenPort-Whitepaper_Blockchain-Logistics-Protocol-1.pdf

8. Liu, X., Barenji, A.V., Li, Z., Montreuil, B., Huang, G.Q.: Blockchain-based smart tracking and tracing platform for drug supply chain. Comput. Ind. Eng. **161**, 107669 (2021)
9. Mezquita, Y., Casado, R., Gonzalez-Briones, A., Prieto, J., Corchado, J.M., AETiC, A.: Blockchain technology in IoT systems: review of the challenges. Ann. Emerg. Technol. Comput. (AETiC) (2019). Print ISSN 2516-0281
10. Mezquita, Y., Casado-Vara, R., González Briones, A., Prieto, J., Corchado, J.M.: Blockchain-based architecture for the control of logistics activities: pharmaceutical utilities case study. Logic J. IGPL **29**(6), 974–985 (2021)
11. Mezquita, Y., Gil-González, A.B., Martín del Rey, A., Prieto, J., Corchado, J.M.: Towards a blockchain-based peer-to-peer energy marketplace. Energies **15**(9), 3046 (2022)
12. Mezquita, Y., Valdeolmillos, D., González-Briones, A., Prieto, J., Corchado, J.M.: Legal aspects and emerging risks in the use of smart contracts based on blockchain. In: Uden, L., Ting, I.-H., Corchado, J.M. (eds.) KMO 2019. CCIS, vol. 1027, pp. 525–535. Springer, Cham (2019). https://doi.org/10.1007/978-3-030-21451-7_45
13. Palanca, J., Terrasa, A., Rodriguez, S., Carrascosa, C., Julian, V.: An agent-based simulation framework for the study of urban delivery. Neurocomputing **423**, 679–688 (2021)
14. Srivastava, A., Dubey, V., Hazela, B.: Delivering green supply chain using blockchain technology for sustainable environment: a survey. In: Hassanien, A.E., Bhattacharyya, S., Chakrabati, S., Bhattacharya, A., Dutta, S. (eds.) Emerging Technologies in Data Mining and Information Security. AISC, vol. 1286, pp. 759–768. Springer, Singapore (2021). https://doi.org/10.1007/978-981-15-9927-9_74
15. Wang, X., et al.: How online food delivery platforms contributed to the resilience of the urban food system in china during the COVID-19 pandemic. Global Food Secur. 100658 (2022)
16. Wangapisit, O., Taniguchi, E., Teo, J.S., Qureshi, A.G.: Multi-agent systems modelling for evaluating joint delivery systems. Procedia Soc. Behav. Sci. **125**, 472–483 (2014)

Station Balancing System of a Bike Sharing System by Means of a Multi-agent System in Collaboration with the User's Decision

Belén Pérez-Lancho[1] , Alfonso González-Briones[1,2](✉) , Blanca Mellado Pinto[1],
and Sara Rodríguez[1,2]

[1] BISITE Research Group, University of Salamanca, Edificio Multiusos I+D+I, Calle Espejo
s/n, 37007 Salamanca, Spain
{lancho,alfonsogb,blancamellado,srg}@usal.es
[2] IoT Digital Innovation Hub (Spain), 37188 Salamanca, Spain

Abstract. On this work, we propose a balancing system for a bike sharing service,
based on the cooperation of the user in exchange for rewards. This system is
implemented as a multiagent system, using the JADE framework. The stations are
represented by agents and a server agent manages the consultations and loans of
the users. An advantage of this implementation is that it allows to add or remove
dynamically stations on run time. Another advantage is that it allows to distribute
the system in different machines. The urban mobility simulator SUMO was used
to test the effects of the use of the proposed system on the balancing of the bicycle
loan service of the city of Salamanca, "Salenbici". Different simulations were
run with varying levels of collaboration from the users. For this simulations, real
historical data from the use of the service was used.

Keywords: Multi-agent system · Balancing methods · SUMO · mobility
simulation · Bike Sharing System (BSS)

1 Introduction

Bicycle loan systems (BBS) are an alternative form of transportation in urban areas
that has recently become very popular, especially in large cities. Users have access to a
pool of bicycles distributed throughout the city. They can borrow them at any available
location and return them at another. In station-based BBSs, bicycles are distributed in a
group of fixed locations, called stations.

Many cities are implementing this type of shared transport because of its benefits
for the health of citizens, as well as for the environment and to reduce pollution levels
in urban centers. Despite all the advantages cited above, one factor that deters citizens
from using these systems is concern about the availability of bicycles at the stations they
wish to use.

Especially those users who use this service regularly and for specific daily trips (for
example, between home and work or school) need to ensure that the lack of bicycles or
spaces to leave them does not inconvenience or delay their day.

D. Durães et al. (Eds.): PAAMS 2023, CCIS 1838, pp. 63–73, 2023.
https://doi.org/10.1007/978-3-031-37593-4_6

Station balancing is the balanced distribution of bicycles among stations to prevent accumulation or shortages, and the measures taken to correct these. Typically, one or more employees manually move the bicycles. Efficient planning of station locations and distribution of bikes according to expected demand also help to maintain this balance.

In this paper, a different approach to the balancing problem of a BSS is explored by a system that uses users' own trips to dynamically relocate bikes among different stations.

In the proposed solution, the user gets a reward for choosing to use a station suggested by the system, instead of the nearest one. The station that is proposed as an alternative is chosen taking into account the priority of the station within the system (due to lack or excess of bicycles) and the additional distance to be traveled by the user.

The proposal makes use of a multi-agent system in which each station is re-presented by an agent that stores information about its status. The stations use messages to communicate this state and the user communicates with this system through a servletREST. A server agent within the multi-agent system handles requests and communication with the user and the stations.

To evaluate the performance of the system, a traffic simulation tool will be used, namely the SUMO (Simulation of Urban MObility) multimodal microscopic traffic simulator. First, the operation of the bicycle lending system will be simulated using real data as a base case. Then, several simulations will be performed using the proposed balancing system, each with a different degree of user collaboration. The results will be analyzed based on two parameters, the additional distance traveled by the user with respect to the base case and the improvement in the distribution of bicycles in the stations.

The paper is structured as follows, Sect. 2 reviews state-of-the-art proposals in this area. Section 3 presents the proposal and the Computer Vision techniques it generates to facilitate citizens detecting and correcting aspects in the design of smart city solutions, with special emphasis on aspects of inclusion. Section 4.2 describes the evaluation process and the key results. Finally, Sect. 5 draws some conclusions and future work.

2   State of Art

This paper addresses the problem of balancing a bicycle loan system, called Bike sharing Rebalancing Problem (BRP). By consulting the available literature, we find numerous examples of proposed solutions to this problem, all of them approaching the problem from different perspectives and employing different methods.

The most commonly used method to maintain balance in this type of system is to relocate, usually at night or at the end of the day, the bicycles between stations. This work can be carried out by BSS operators or by the use of trucks, especially in large cities with a high number of stations and bicycles. Efficient relocation and planning of the routes to be followed by the trucks to optimize the process is in itself an additional problem. In the paper (Gaspero, Rendl, & Urli, 2013), the authors propose a system that uses CP (Constraint Programming) and LNS (Large Neighborhood Search) to efficiently plan such routes. Another example is (Li, et al., 2021), which uses reinforced learning for the same purpose.

Another way to tackle the station balancing problem is to pre-plan station locations or the number of bicycles needed at each station, with the goal of meeting user demand, and reducing the need to move bicycles between stations.

The proposal by (Liu, et al., 2015) considers the mobility patterns of citizens, points of interest in the city, and the structure of the transportation network. These characteristics are used to find optimal station locations using artificial neural networks and genetic algorithms.

There are also systems that use historical user trip data, together with the current state of the system, to predict service trends. This is proposed by the following paper (Wang, He, Zhang, Liu, & H. Son, 2019), which presents eShare, a tool that uses past and present data from a BSS to infer future usage.

Finally, there are several examples of solutions that utilize users in a variety of ways to maintain the balance of a BSS. Some of them simply inform the user when there is no availability of bikes or free spaces at the station, or redirect them to a nearby station, as in the case of (Aeschbach, Zhang, Georghiou, & Lygeros, 2015). Others, following a method similar to the one used in this project, encourage users to collaborate in balancing the system, such as (Singla, Santoni, Bartók, Meenen, & Krause, 2015). Of great interest is the following work (Fernández, et al., 2019), in which different balancing strategies, scalable to large-city BSSs, some of which use user incentives, are proposed and compared. The different proposed strategies are evaluated using data from Madrid's BSS, BiciMAD, in the Bike 3S simulator, a tool that allows experimenting with BSS and evaluating different planning.

Regarding the use of multi-agent systems in balancing, the following work has been found for example (Luo, Du, Klemmer, Zhu, & Wen, 2022). In this case a hierarchical controller generates plans, which are evaluated in parallel using a multi-simulation environment. The results of these simulations are used to improve the controller by deep reinforcement learning.

3 Multi-agent System Architecture for Station Rebalancing of a Bike-Sharing System

The following is the system architecture showing the relationship between the agents that perform the balancing, user information ingestion and simulation tasks, which can be divided into two subsystems: (i) Multi-agent system for system balancing based on the Gaia methodology (Zambonelli, F., Jennings, N. R., & Wooldridge, M., 2005) to model the roles and communication between the agents; and (ii) Simulation of the system usage by means of SUMO (Fig. 1).

3.1 Balancing System

The balancing system maintains system status information, calculates the nearest and recommended stations, and returns the information to the user. Users query the system for information on the stations closest to their location. The system is a multi-agent system implemented in JADE, which includes a server agent and as many agents as stations in the BSS service. The system uses the FIPA and JADE Gateway agents for the management of messages, agents and service directory. The REST Servlet, implemented with Jersey, receives and processes the requests. The station agents store the necessary information for station operation and to collaborate in balancing the system, specifically

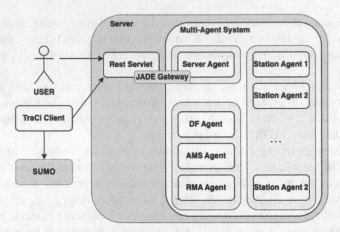

Fig. 1. System Architecutre.

the following data: station coordinates, maximum station capacity (number of locks), current number of bicycles, minimum number of bicycles that the station must have to function correctly, minimum number of available spaces that must be in the station for it to function correctly, daily demand prediction, default prediction if the daily prediction cannot be obtained. The agent executes two behaviors in parallel, a behavior (TickerBehaviour) that is executed by a timer once a day to obtain the number of loans and returns expected at the station and a cyclic behavior (CyclicBehaviour) that waits for the arrival of messages in a blocking manner. The agent can receive three types of messages from the server:

- **Metric request**: The server agent requests the distance and priority of a station in response to a metric request. The distance is calculated using the Haversine method, and the priority is calculated as the ratio between the number of bikes and the demand prediction. The station agent receives the request, calculates both metrics, and sends them back to the server agent.
- **Loan or return request**: The agent makes this request when a user has indicated that they want to borrow or return a bike at the station. Upon receiving the message, it is checked whether the action is possible. A loan cannot be made if there are no bikes available. If the loan is possible, the current number of bikes is modified.
- **Balanced information request**: The station agent responds to this request with information about the balancing status of the station. Since all stations have a different capacity, this value is calculated according to the following formula, which returns the normalized value between −1 and 1:

$$balanced = 2 * \frac{current\ number\ of\ bicycles}{maximum\ capacity\ of\ the\ station} - 1$$

When a request arrives from a user, the server agent evaluates the type of action to be performed and adds a simple behavior (or OneShotBehaviour in JADE), which performs the necessary action and finishes. These actions require communication with the station agents. The available actions are:

- **Station recommendation**: The agent receives coordinates from the user and requests metrics from nearby stations. It calculates the nearest station and recommends a station based on distances and station priorities. The priority varies between -20 and 20 depending on station occupancy, with priority 20 if the station is completely empty. For a loan, the lowest priority is sought. The response is sent in JSON format. The response contains the information about the nearest station and the recommended station, with the following fields for both (Table 1):

Table 1. Responses to requests for station suggestions

Station identifier	PUENTE_ROMANO
Coordinates	(40.959216404952215, −5.669309603365671)
Distance	0.32560276870601007
Priority	20
Current number of bicycles	0
Current number of spaces	11
Incentive	30

- **Loan request**: The agent requests the station agent to make a loan or return.
- **Balancing information request**: The agent asks all stations for their balancing information and returns it to the user.

For demand forecasting, the station agents of the BSS balancing system consult daily forecasts of the demand for bicycles and station spaces.

3.2 User System

It represents the user of the system, who is the person using the BSS. This is a fundamental element, as the balancing of the system requires their collaboration by accepting the proposed stations. Communication between the user and the system is based on REST requests and the JSON standard, which means that in the future this communication can be developed both from an application and from a web page or other systems.

3.3 Simulation System

To test the performance of the system, a simulation is carried out using SUMO. For this purpose, real historical data on BSS use is used.

- **TraCI client**: Module that makes requests to the balancing system pretending to be the users and connects to the SUMO simulation to recreate the actual trips.
- **SUMO**: TraCI connects to SUMO following a client-server scheme. SUMO receives messages from TraCI on port 8813.

4   Case Study

4.1   Experimental Set-Up

For the development of the solution, the Salamanca bicycle lending service, Salenbici (SalEnBici (2023) and the climatological information has used the API REST of the Agencia Estatal de Meteorología (AEMET OpenData (2023), has been taken as a specific use case. This service depends on the Salamanca City Council and has been in operation since 2010. Firstly, an analysis of the characteristics of the loan service has been carried out. A description of the dataset is shown in Table 2:

Table 2. Data provided by SalEnBici

Description of the data	Data on the use of the service by users. It collects the loans made, the date and time of the loan and the return, and the stations involved (origin and destination)
Data format	6 CSV files (data divided by year and semester)
Time scope collected	2017–2020
Number of stations represented	34 stations
Data confidentiality	Anonymised (user card number)

The dataset does not indicate the departure and arrival points desired by the users, but the stations used, assuming that they are the closest stations to the place of departure and arrival. For the simulation we are going to generate these points randomly at points close to the station. For this purpose, a maximum distance has been chosen and a point within the circle whose radius corresponds to the maximum distance has been randomly generated using a uniform distribution generation method. SUMO has been used to create the simulation environment to which the TraCi client will be connected by means of an XML configuration file, and a map of the streets and roads of Salamanca obtained by means of the OSMWizard tool is used.

4.2   Simulation Algorithm

The simulation algorithm is developed as follows:

- First, the script is connected to SUMO and the simulation is opened.
- The variables and tables described above are initialised.
- The script obtains information about the balancing of the stations, stores it and changes the colours of the station markers according to the value obtained for each station. To improve the performance of the simulation, this step is only executed at the beginning of the simulation to obtain the initial values and when any borrowing or return occurs.
- A TraCi function is used to check if there has been an arrival of any user at any station, obtaining the people who have finished a project in that step of the simulation. If there are any arrivals, they are managed.

- The first table is checked to see if there is a trip to be started in the next step of the simulation. If so, the trip is prepared and entered in the simulation.
- The next step of the simulation is executed.
- A check is made to see if all trips have been completed.
- If there are unfinished trips, the procedure is repeated.
- When all journeys have been completed, the statistics, both of the distance travelled by the users and of the system balancing during the simulation run, are collected and displayed graphically. The simulation is also closed.

When a user arrival occurs, the type of arrival is checked by means of the trip phase number in the table.

If it is an arrival at the origin station:

- A request is made to the balancing system to borrow the bike-cycle. In this way the system registers that there has been a change in the number of bicycles at the station.
- The bike route to the destination station is calculated using a TraCi function.
- The route is started in the simulation.
- The route information is updated. It is necessary to change the phase number in the tables.
- The calculated distance to be cycled is recorded.
- If it is an arrival at the destination station:
- A request is made to the balancing system to request the return of the bicycle.
- The walking route to the final destination is calculated using TraCi.
- The route is started in the simulation
- The route information is updated
- The walking distance to be travelled is recorded.

If the user has reached his final destination, his information is updated and the trip is added to the table of completed trips.

When it is detected that a new trip is to be started, the following algorithm is executed:

- A check is made to see if the balancing system for recommending stations is being used.
- If it is in use, it assesses whether the origin or destination station should be modified according to its suggestions.
- The coordinates of the arrival and departure points and stations are converted to positions on the simulation map, determined by the street and the position within the street closest to the coordinates. A TraCi function is used for this purpose.
- The trip is moved from the table of trips to be started to the table of started trips.
- The walking route to the origin station is calculated, using a TraCi function.
- The route to the origin station is started in the simulation.
- The walking distance to be travelled is recorded in the simulation statistics.

The following algorhythm, which takes into account whether the distance to the proposed station is less than the distance defined as maximum, is used to assess whether the system proposal is accepted. When the proposal is accepted, the information is replaced in the tables as it can be seen in Fig. 2.

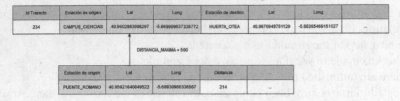

Id Trayecto	Estación de origen	Lat	Long	Estación de destino	Lat	Long	
234	CAMPUS_CIENCIAS	40.9602863098297	-5.669999637335772	HUERTA_OTEA	40.9676948751129	-5.68365469151027	...

DISTANCIA_MAXIMA = 500

Estación de origen	Lat	Long	Distancia	
PUENTE_ROMANO	40.95921640049522	-5.66930960336567	214	...

Fig. 2. Replacement of the original station by the proposed station.

4.3 Results

It has been observed that there is an impact of failed loans and returns on the system: when they occur, the results are not reliable. This is particularly noticeable in the third simulation, in which there were 7 failed returns. As the Salenbici service does not allow bicycles to be used at night, there were no changes in the balancing during these periods of time. The Fig. 3 shows the results of the balancing of the system. This result is calculated as the average of the balancing of all stations, using the absolute value and normalised between 0 and 1. The best result is 0, which would indicate perfect balancing at all stations. 1 is the worst result, indicating that all stations are either full or empty. As many of the stations are not used (borrowing tends to be concentrated at the same central stations), they remain in equilibrium and mitigate the effects on the value of the imbalance at the central stations. However, looking at the simulation, it can be seen that the use of the system contributes to greatly improve the balance of the system in the city centre.

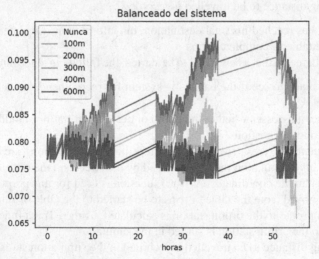

Fig. 3. System balancing results

The visual results of the simulations show more information about the balancing of the system. The Fig. 4 shows the status of the stations after the simulation without using the balancing system recommendations.

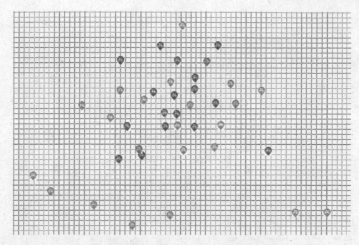

Fig. 4. Simulation without using the recommendations of the balancing system

We can compare this with the state of the system at the end of the simulation when the user accepts the suggestions if they are within 200 m. The change is remarkable (Fig. 5).

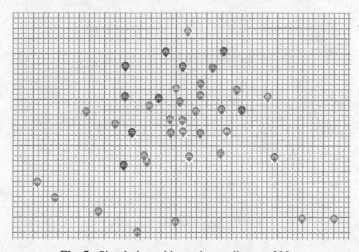

Fig. 5. Simulation with maximum distance 200 m

The state of the system when all requests are accepted is practically optimal. However, this situation is unrealistic, as it would require the full cooperation of all users, accepting very large distances (Fig. 6).

The simulation also allows to observe the balancing of each individual station at the end of the simulation (Fig. 7).

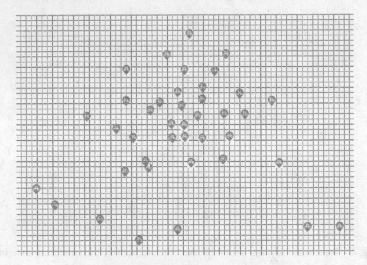

Fig. 6. Simulation with maximum distance 600 m

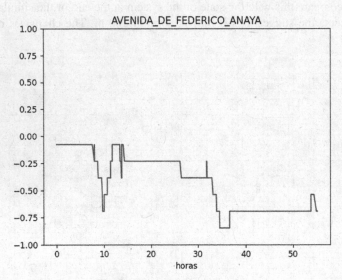

Fig. 7. Single-station balancing

5   Conclusions and Future Work

In conclusion, this work presents a complete system for the creation of a BSS station balancing system through user collaboration using agents, a method for predicting station demand and incorporating it into the balancing, and a tool for evaluating the performance of the system from real use cases. These components could be integrated into the management system of a BSS or used to evaluate different balancing algorithms.

As future work, it is proposed that the system will predict the predicted demand of the station for the current day, using machine learning methods. This information will be used in the system rebalancing system. In order to do this, it will be necessary to investigate different machine learning models that provide good results for this task.

Acknowledgments. This research has been supported by the project "Plataforma edge-iot basada en tecnologias dlt de alta eficiencia energetica para el intercambio de tokens digitales verdes mediante la ejecucion de contratos inteligentes, Reference: PDC2022-133161-C31, financed by MCIN /AEI/https://doi.org/10.13039/501100011033 and NextGeneration EU/PRTR, UE."

References

Aeschbach, P., Zhang, X., Georghiou, A., Lygeros, J.: Balancing bike sharing systems through customer cooperation - a case study on London's Barclays cycle hire. In: 2015 54th IEEE Conference on Decision and Control (CDC), pp. 4722–4727 (2015). https://doi.org/10.1109/CDC.2015.7402955

Fernández, A., Billhardt, H., Timón, S., Ruiz, C., Sánchez, Ó., Bernabé, I.: Balancing strategies for bike sharing systems. In: Lujak, M. (ed.) AT 2018. LNCS (LNAI), vol. 11327, pp. 208–222. Springer, Cham (2019). https://doi.org/10.1007/978-3-030-17294-7_16

Di Gaspero, L., Rendl, A., Urli, T.: Constraint-based approaches for balancing bike sharing systems. In: Schulte, C. (ed.) CP 2013. LNCS, vol. 8124, pp. 758–773. Springer, Heidelberg (2013). https://doi.org/10.1007/978-3-642-40627-0_56

Li, G., et al.: Towards smart transportation system: a case study on the rebalancing problem of bike sharing system based on reinforcement learning. J. Organ. End User Comput. **33**(3) (2021). https://doi.org/10.4018/JOEUC.20210501.oa3

Liu, J., et al.: Station site optimization in bike sharing systems. In: 2015 IEEE International Conference on Data Mining, pp. 883–888 (2015). https://doi.org/10.1109/ICDM.2015.99

Luo, M., Du, B., Klemmer, K., Zhu, H., Wen, H.: Deployment optimization for shared e-mobility systems with multi-agent deep neural search. IEEE Trans. Intell. Transp. Syst. **23**(3), 2549–2560 (2022). https://doi.org/10.1109/TITS.2021.3125745

Singla, A., Santoni, M., Bartók, G., Meenen, M., Krause, A.: Incentivizing users for balancing bike sharing systems. In: Twenty-Ninth AAAI Conference on Artificial Intelligence, pp. 723–729 (2015). https://www.aaai.org/ocs/index.php/AAAI/AAAI15/paper/view/9942/9319

Wang, S., He, T., Zhang, D., Liu, Y., H. Son, S.: Towards efficient sharing: a usage balancing mechanism for bike sharing systems. In: The World Wide Web Conference, San Francisco, CA, USA, pp. 2011–2021. Association for Computing Machinery (2019). https://doi.org/10.1145/3308558.3313441

Zambonelli, F., Jennings, N.R., Wooldridge, M.: Multi-agent systems as computational organizations: the Gaia methodology. In Agent-Oriented Methodologies, pp. 136–171. IGI Global (2005)

SalEnBici: Sistema de Préstamo de Bicicletas de Salamanca (2023). http://www.salamancasalenbici.com/. Accessed 27 Mar 2023

AEMET OpenData (2023). https://opendata.aemet.es/centrodedescargas/inicio. Accessed 27 Mar 2023

Workshop on Character Computing
(C2)

Workshop on Character Computing (C2)

The fifth consecutive workshop on Character Computing presented the emerging field and the opportunities and challenges it poses. Character Computing is any computing that incorporates the human character within its context (for more details see https://www.springer.com/gp/book/9783030159535 and https://en.wikipedia.org/wiki/Character_computing). The character includes stable traits (e.g., personality), variable affective, cognitive and motivational states, as well as history, morals, beliefs, skills, appearance and socio-cultural embeddings, to name a few. As the next step towards further putting humans at the center of technology, novel interdisciplinary approaches such as Character Computing are developing. The extension and fusion between the different computing approaches, e.g. Affective and Personality Computing, within Character Computing is based on well-controlled empirical and theoretical knowledge from Psychology. This is done by including the whole human character as a central part of any artificial interaction.

Character Computing has three main modules that can be investigated and leveraged separately or together: 1) character sensing and profiling, 2) character-aware adaptive systems, and 3) artificial characters.

The aim of the workshop is to inspire research into the foundations and applications of Character Computing by investigating novel approaches by both computer scientists and psychologists. C2 addresses applications, opportunities and challenges of sensing, predicting, adapting to, affecting or simulating human behavior and character.

This workshop seeks to promote Character Computing as design material for the creation of novel user experiences and applications by leveraging the evolving character of the user.

The main goal of this workshop is to:

- Provide a forum for computer science, technology, and psychology professionals to come together and network for possible future collaboration.
- Share experience obtained and lessons learned from past projects to understand the current state of the art of research conducted related to Character Computing.
- Identify challenges and opportunities the researchers faces to set up a current R&D agenda and community in this field.

C2 aims to bring together researchers and industry practitioners from both computational and psychology communities to share knowledge and resources, discuss new ideas and build foundations of possible future collaborations. The main aim is to further research into Character Computing by discussing potential ideas and challenges and sharing expertise among the participants. The workshop was held in a hybrid format like the conference, allowing registrants the choice to participate virtually or in-person in Guimarães (Portugal).

Organization

Organizing Committee

Alia El Bolock	German International University, Cairo, Egypt
Cornelia Herbert	Ulm University, Germany
Slim Abdennadher	German International University, Cairo, Egypt

Program Committee

Friedhelm Schwenker	Ulm University, Germany
Yomna Abdelrahman	Bundeswehr Universität München, Germany
Caroline Sabty	German International University, Cairo, Egypt
Dirk Reichardt	DHBW Stuttgart, Germany
Amr El Mougy	German International University, Cairo, Egypt
Walid El Hefny	German International University, Cairo, Egypt
Jailan Salah	German International University, Cairo, Egypt

Ethical Self-driving Cars: Resolving Conflicting Moral Decisions Among Groups of Vehicles

Khaled T. Aly[✉], Yasmin Mansy, Nourhan Ehab, and Amr El-Mougy

German University In Cairo, Cairo, Egypt
khaled.tamer@student.guc.edu.eg,
{yasmin.mansy,nourhan.ehab,amr.elmougy}@guc.edu.eg

Abstract. In unavoidable accident situations, self-driving cars (SDCs) find themselves to be the judge, and potentially the executioner, of a situation involving human and animal life. Equipping self-driving cars with ethical frameworks to be able to take a decision in such situations is not enough. Conflicts will inevitably occur on what should be done due to the different perceptions of each car and their potentially conflicting underlying moral codes. This paper describes an argumentation-based framework to allow cars in a group to engage in a human-like dialogue in order to resolve ethical conflicts in unavoidable accident scenarios. After a dialogue is completed, the decision with the strongest argument is chosen using traditional concepts of argumentation. Furthermore, due to the lack of absolute claims, a reasoning mechanism that deals with uncertainty, Dempster-Shafer Theory of Evidence (DST), is used to enhance the final decision. Results have shown the correctness of the proposed framework in accident scenarios using computer simulations.

Keywords: Argumentation · Conflict Resolution · Information Fusion · Autonomous Vehicles

1 Introduction

The technology of Self-driving Cars (SDCs) needs to prove that they are safer than the average human driver in order to resolve the public's concerns about their own safety [12]. Such concerns are rightfully motivated due various to real life accidents caused by SDCs that lead to the harm of pedestrians and drivers [13]. It is, thus, not surprising that surveys consistently reveal that people are cynical towards SDCs, going so far as preferring to be in control of their vehicles [12]. Thus, for this technology to be widely adopted, the public must trust that the vehicles will make morally acceptable decisions in any situation, particularly when an accident seems to be unavoidable and life is at stake. In these unavoidable accident situations, humans rely on their ethics, if they can. In SDCs, the artificial intelligence (AI) systems of the vehicle need to implement reasoning aspects of a human character that can make decisions based on socially acceptable moral codes. Having SDCs, with characters that are ethical and capable of

D. Durães et al. (Eds.): PAAMS 2023, CCIS 1838, pp. 79–91, 2023.
https://doi.org/10.1007/978-3-031-37593-4_7

having dialogues, decide their behaviors in high-risk situations, such as unavoidable accidents, is modeled as an instance of the Character Computing triad [8].

Fig. 1. An example of an unavoidable accident where a group of SDCs disagree on what should be done.

Figure 1 shows an example of such conflicting situations, where a group of SDCs, *Front-Car* (FC), *Back-Left-Car* (BLC), and *Back-Right-Car* (BRC), are faced with an unavoidable accident situation. *FC* and *BRC* would rather stay on the right lane as their moral code prefers saving the maximum number of people. However, *BLC* would rather swerve to the left as its moral code instructs it as such. If each car follows its own moral code without collaborating, then no one is spared. Our goal is to guide the cars to agree on a decision in such conflicting situations. It is important to note that it is not within the scope of this paper to determine what is morally right or wrong in such situations, as this is a topic that should be addressed by legislators and the general public.

To achieve this goal, we explore the use of argumentation-based dialogue between SDCs as a negotiative means of resolving any disagreements resulting from the moral reasoning and the sensor detection of the cars. Argumentation-based dialogue could be seen as a way to imitate human arguments about ethics. Therefore, it will allow intelligent agents to process ethics similarly to us. Thus, our objectives include: (1) Building a dialogue system powered by concepts of Argumentation Frameworks (AF), which is a method to represent conflicting information and reach conclusions from them, formalized in [3]. (2) Allowing reasoning with unreliable beliefs and installing a popular voting mechanism for beliefs using DST, a mathematical theory for reasoning with uncertainty [5]. (3) Testing the correctness of such system using the Carla simulator, a state-of-the-art simulator for SDCs [10].

The rest of this paper is organized as follows: Sect. 2 shows a language for agents. Next, Sect. 3 discusses an abstract architecture for the full process of determining which decision to take. Section 4 presents a validation of our system through a simulation. Section 5 is a review of related work, along with mentioning improvements on them used in this paper. Lastly, Sect. 6 concludes, while providing potential future work.

2 Building Blocks

2.1 Topic Language

We follow the technique of [11] by, first, introducing a *topic language*, or a list of propositions representing the words an agent knows, from which an argument can be created. The topic language is needed to carry the meaning of an argument and easy detection of an attack relation between arguments, which is a logical contradiction between the existence of two arguments at the same time. We use a propositional logic-based AF defined in [1] for simplicity.

As we are using descriptive proposition names, all propositions should be easily understood. Out of those propositions, an agent can create an argument which will have a value, representing the confidence levels of an agent in that proposition. Whether this value is coming directly from the sensors of the car or hard-coded does not affect its function or meaning. So, a proposition like *'more_people_on_left'* might be detected by the sensors with a confidence level of 50%. However, a goal like *'deontology_children'*, which means that the system is prohibited to kill children no matter the consequences, will intuitively have a value of 100%, as we will assume that the subjective moral belief of an agent can never be questioned or argued against.

2.2 Communication Language

Communication languages are locutions instantiated with an argument, created from the topic language, to produce a *speech act* [11]. In order for a receiver to know that an argument is, for example, a threat, it would require a language to contextualize said argument. This is done through speech acts which are shown in first column of Table 1, instantiated with an argument. Formally, for an agent with a knowledge base (KB) K, goals G, and opponent's goal GO, an *argument* is a pair $\langle S, h \rangle$ such that: (1) $S \subseteq K$, (2) $S \not\vdash \bot$, (3) $S \vdash h$, (4) S is a minimal set. S is then called the *support* of argument $\langle S, h \rangle$, while h is the *conclusion*. It could also be a triple $\langle S, g, go \rangle$ such that (1) $S \subseteq K$, (2) $g \in G$, (3) $go \in GO$. If a speech act is a threat, $S \cup \{\neg g\} \vdash \neg go$, if it is a reward, $S \cup \{g\} \vdash go$. [11]

Table 1. Possible Speech Acts With The Attack Relations Between Them

Speech Act	Possible Attackers
Request($\langle S,h \rangle$)	Reject($\langle S,h \rangle$)
Reject($\langle S,h \rangle$)	Threat($\langle S,g,go \rangle$),Reward($\langle S,g,go \rangle$)
Threat($\langle S,g,go \rangle$)	Counter-threat($\langle S,g,go \rangle$), Undercut($\langle S,h \rangle$)
Reward($\langle S,g,go \rangle$)	Undercut($\langle S,h \rangle$)
Counter-threat($\langle S,g,go \rangle$)	Counter-threat($\langle S,g,go \rangle$),Undercut($\langle S,h \rangle$), Threat($\langle S,g,go \rangle$), Reward($\langle S,g,go \rangle$)
Undercut($\langle S,h \rangle$), Rebuttal($\langle S,h \rangle$)	Undercut($\langle S,h \rangle$),Rebuttal($\langle S,h \rangle$),Threat($\langle S,g,go \rangle$), Reward($\langle S,g,go \rangle$)
Popular($\langle S,h \rangle$)	cannot be attacked, as the calculation must be true.
Concede(ϕ)	cannot be attacked, as it admits defeat on fact ϕ

For clarity, in a *Concede()*, once a group of agents surrenders a fact, it replaces the old beliefs in their *KB*. For a *Popular()* speech act, it represents that a certain proposition is shared by multiple agents, thus has more plausibility or weight against the logical negation of that fact. Suffice to say for now, this weight will be calculated by information fusion using DST. An attack between speech acts is determined by Table 1. The detailed table of all possible attacks, along with the specific conditions of the attack, is given in [11].

3   System Design

In abstract terms, the system we implemented accepts input from the object detection sensors of each car, then the output is simply the decision of the group, swerving left or right. A full representation of the system architecture is shown in Fig. 2.

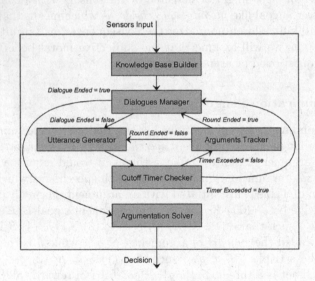

Fig. 2. Full Architecture.

First, we initialize the *KB* and beliefs of each agent using their sensor data, in addition to helping each car reach their initial preferred decision. That is the task of the *Knowledge Base Builder*. Second, we trigger the dialogue game with the *Dialogues Manager* supervising the process. Said process include generating an utterance, by the *Utterance Generator*, to reply back to a previous move, then memorizing the attack relations between all utterances, done by *Arguments Tracker*. Meanwhile, the *Cutoff Timer Checker* makes sure we do not exceed a deadline for argumentation. Finally, after the dialogue ends we determine a decision by the *Argumentation Solver* examining the completed dialogue.

3.1   Knowledge Base Builder

The *Knowledge Base Builder* is the very first module in the system. Its objective is to construct the *KB* and initially preferred decision for each car.

Sensors in SDCs implement an object detection algorithm which outputs the objects seen along with a degree of confidence in its detection. Due to the lack of absolute claims, a reasoning mechanism that deals with uncertainty must be used, thus we use the DST [9] for such application because it differentiates between lack of knowledge and uncertainty, unlike Probability Theory [5]. Normally, a SDC will have multiple sensors detecting the same context to have data redundancy. Thus, these readings must be unified to find the most accurate understanding of the situation. With m_i being a mass of belief, or sometimes called an evidence [5], of each source of evidence S_i [9], the approach to unify these readings on a proposition A for some sets B and C that support A would be, similar to [9], using the combination rule of DST, with each sensor treated as a different source of evidence:

$$[m_i \oplus m_j](A) = \frac{\sum_{B \cap C = A} m_i(B) m_j(C)}{1 - \sum_{B \cap C = \emptyset} m_i(B) m_j(C)} \tag{1}$$

After combination, we choose the reading with highest value as the true value of detection. Then we add to each agent's *KB*: their *facts*, *goals*, and *rules*.

Firstly, we initialize the facts an agent knows. This is a simple matter of checking conditions, for example, if an agent detects that there are 3 people on the right and 2 people on the left, it will add the facts *'more_people_on_right'* and *'¬more_people_on_left'* with their detection confidence levels, or strength, into its *KB*.

Secondly, an agent will figure out its goals by checking, given its moral preference and the facts it knows about the world, what would it prefer to do, swerve left or right, then such proposition,*'left'* or *'¬left'*, will be added to the *KB*. We will refer to this decision as the *subjective decision* of an agent.

Thirdly, the rules of the world are given to each agent's *KB*. As these logical implications are arbitrary for each application, a crude approach was followed of hard-coding each of them. An example of a rule would be: *'left ∧ more_people_on_left ∧ ¬more_people_on_right → ¬ prefer_more_people'*, which informally translates to 'if an agent swerves left, and the are more people on the left, then they would not be fulfilling a moral code of saving the most amount of people'.

The first car to detect an unavoidable accident, along with all other agents that agree with its decision, will be the proponents group, *PRO*, and all others as the opponents group, *OPP*. Note that this group assignment process, used in [6] to tackle *multiparty persuasion*, allows us to, similarly, tackle groups of any number of SDCs.

3.2   Dialogue Manager

This module triggers the dialogue between our two groups, *PRO* and *OPP*. In typical applications of dialogue protocols, a dialogue ends after one side concedes a fact, then a winner is determined. However, it might be the case that the loser is able to attack other arguments. A concession does not necessarily mean the end of the dialogue. *The dialogue manager* solves this issue. The idea is to run a dialogue until it ends in a concession. Then, in order to allow for other disagreements, we re-run the dialogue, or create a new *dialogue round*, with newly accepted facts. This will provide a chance for the group who conceded to re-argue their case. So, the task of the dialogue manager is keep track of the multiple dialogue rounds, while accumulating the results of all rounds into one coherent dialogue, then send it to the *Argumentation Solver* to determine a winner.

3.3   Utterance Generator and Arguments Tracker

The *utterance generator* and the *arguments tracker* form a loop that creates a dialogue round.

Utterance Generator   The *utterance generator*, first, gets the current group whose turn is it to play, *PRO* or *OPP*. Then for each agent in this group, the best possible utterance this agent can generate is appended to a list of possible replies. Next, one of these replies is selected to be played at random. To generate the best possible utterance an agent can make, a minmax-based algorithm, called M*, given in [14], is used. In abstract terms, this algorithm will (1) generate all possible utterances by the attacker agent to all previous moves in the dialogue and calculates their utility if played, (2) then, chooses the utterance with the highest utility. The utility of an utterance is calculated by sending the dialogue with the utterance itself to the *Argumentation Solver*. If the utterance allowed the agent who played it to win a dialogue, its utility is 100, a 0 if it is a draw, and -100 if it is a loss. The algorithm for generating all possible utterances for one move is shown below in Algorithm 1, note we use a backward chaining function, which is an a logical reasoning method that works backwards from a given goal to output a logical chain from an agent's *KB* to the goal [15].

The definitions of speech acts in this algorithm is defined by [11], thus our method involves agents using backward reasoning to look for such definitions. For instance, to create a *"Threat"* speech act, an agent should first construct a logical argument with its *KB*, along with the negation of some goal it has that concludes with the negation of an opposing agent's goal. Furthermore, as an argument will be made up of facts, the strength of that argument is equal the strength of the weakest fact used. This step is an application of Value-based AFs [4], which adds numerical values to each argument. In our application, this value will represent how strong an argument is. Moreover, Value-based AF needs a preference relation *valpref* describing the conditions for preferring a value over another [4]. In our case, the *valpref* function prefers stronger arguments, thus higher values.

Up until this point, all possible utterances are generated. However, not all of which are are valid or legal. Therefore, a filtering process is applied over this

---

Algorithm 1. generateAllPossibleReplies(move, agent, speechActsTable)

Require: move: a previous move generated by an opposing agent.
Require: agent: an agent trying to generate a reply to defeat "move".
Require: speechActsTable: Table 1 which defines the attackers of each speech act.
  attackerSpeechActs = getAttackersFromTable(move, speechActsTable)
  utterances = {}
  for all *speechAct* ∈ *attackerSpeechActs* **do**
    argument = {}
    if *speechAct* == *"Reject"or"Rebuttal"* **then**
      argument = backwardChaining(agent.KB, negate(move.conclusion))
    end if
    if *speechAct* == *"Undercut"* **then**
      argument = backwardChaining(agent.KB, negate(any of move.support))
    end if
    if *speechAct* == *"Threat"or"CounterThreat"* **then**
      argument = backwardChaining(agent.KB ∪ negate(agent.goal), negate(move.agent.goal))
    end if
    if *speechAct* == *"Reward"* **then**
      argument = backwardChaining(agent.KB ∪ agent.goal, move.agent.goal)
    end if
    strength = getValueOfWeakestFact(argument)
    utterances += makeSpeechAct(argument, speechAct, strength)   ▷ creates a speech act of specific, given type with some strength from a given argument
  end for
  return utterances

---

set. The filtering process is as follows: (1) Filtering all non-legal utterances, determined by calling the *legal-move function* [11], which ensures that: (a) *PRO* or *OPP* must play in their correct turn, (b) that a *Request()* must only be played as the very first move. (2) Removing all utterances that were uttered before. (3) Removing all utterances not satisfying *valprefs*.

If after the filtering process no possible utterance can be constructed, the agents to play will either concede, or try to construct a *Popular()* speech act.

Popular() Speech Act Consider the following scenario, if nine agents believe the fact *'more_people_on_left'* but none of their respective confidence levels are greater than one agent claiming *'¬more_people_on_left'*. It is unfair to immediately discredit nine agents. These weights must also be put into consideration. A *popular voting mechanism* is installed to calculate the cumulative confidence levels of one fact against the cumulative confidence levels of the negation of the fact. This would give agents a second chance to present the same fact but with proof that there are stronger reasons to believe them over others. Thus, we apply Equation (1) on that fact and its negation, with their confidence levels, from all agents, with each car being a source of evidence. If the combined confidence levels of P is greater than $\neg P$, it will create a *Popular()* speech act with an argument of S = { *popular_vote* , *popular_vote* → *P*}, h = *P*.

Arguments Tracker After generating a new utterance, *The arguments tracker* module will, now, give an ID number to that move while memorizing the ID number of the move it attacks. This module keeps record of all arguments presented, with the attack relations between them.

3.4 Argumentation Solver

This solver accepts the arguments and attack relations tracked in a completed dialogue and figures out its *grounded semantic*, a traditional concept in AF, of the given framework. A grounded semantics extension contains arguments which are either not attacked or defended by non-attacked arguments, it is always unique and exists [6]. After reaching the results, the solver checks which of the two moves are in the grounded semantics, *Request(A)* or *Reject(A)*, where A could be *left* or ¬*left*. If the former exists then the decision taken by the group is A, while if the latter the case, then the decision is ¬A.

3.5 Cutoff Timer Checker

A simple module developed for safety measures is the *cutoff timer checker*, triggered between generating an utterance and arguments tracking. Our scenario of an unavoidable accident, a critical situation where lives are at risk, demands some (user-defined) time limit for argumentation. Once this deadline is reached, a decision, with some justification, must be taken. A dynamic approach for determining a cutoff timer winner, would be giving the decision to the agent with the strongest facts supporting its *subjective decision*. All agents will base their *subjective decisions* on specific facts they detect, which could be referred to as *critical facts*, and the moral preference they have. if these *critical facts* are false, an agent has to reevaluate the decision in regards to its moral code. Therefore, a justifiable approach is to follow the car with the most confidence in its *critical facts*. Finding out the *critical facts* with highest belief value is, again, solved using information fusion using Equation (1). We then follow the owner of the those *critical facts*.

4   Evaluation

To test the correctness of the proposed system, unavoidable accident scenarios were created and visualized in the Carla Simulator to use its functionalities such as simulating SDCs with object detection sensors. To keep things simple, we evaluate the system on a small group of three cars. This allows us to highlight important insights gained from the use of our system, namely the benefits of DST. But as stated, the system should work for a situation of any number of cars. Amgoud *et al.*, in [2], formally defined the types of an *agreement* in AF-based dialogue protocols. We are interested in a particular type, an *optimal solution*. That is the outcome that would satisfy *all* agents [2], as no outcomes for concession exist in our studied scenarios. Thus, in our test case the *actual solution* will be compared to the *optimal solution* to test the correctness of our system, or to check whether our system reaches the *optimal solution* or not.

Our testing case is shown in Fig. 1, with *FC*, *BLC*, and *BRC*. The full context is shown in Table 2, with each context shown with its sensor detection levels.

Table 2. Context of Testing Case

Point of View	Left Context	Right Context	Moral Code	Subjective Decision	Objective Decision
Actual	1 male child & 1 male adult	1 male adult	-	-	-
Front-Car	1 male child & 1 male adult (51.4%)	1 male adult (51.4%) & 0 children (40.0%)	prefer_more _people	Right	Right
Back-Right-Car	1 male child & 1 male adult (35%)	0 people (35%)	prefer_more _people	Right	Right
Back-Left-Car	1 male adult (43%)	1 male child (43%)	deontology _children	Left	Right

Optimal Solution: Right. All cars should swerve right as it is objectively the correct decision to fulfil all their moral codes.

Note that each utterance in the dialogue will be accompanied with a quote for readability that is *not* part of our output which are the statements surrounded by '<' and '>'.

Once *FC* detects the situation, the dialogue will be as follows, with the action of the group shown in Fig. 3:

```
1.<PRO, 1, FC, Attacks:0, request(['-left'],-left),100>
FC: "I request we stay on the right."
--------------------------------------------------------------------
2.<OPP, 2, BLC, Attacks:1, reject(['-left'],-left),100>
BLC: "I reject we stay on the right."
--------------------------------------------------------------------
3.<PRO, 3, BRC, Attacks:2, reward(['-left & -there_is_children_on_left &
-there_is_children_on_right -> deontology_children', '-there_is_children
_on_left', '-there_is_children_on_right'],  -left, deontology_children),
35.19>
BRC: "If you stayed on the right and there is no children on either lane,
you'll fulfil your moral code of not harming children. I am sure by 35%."
--------------------------------------------------------------------
4.<OPP, 4, BLC, Attacks:3, undercut(['there_is_children_on_right'], there
_is_children_on_right), 43.3>
BLC: "There is a child on the right. I am sure by 43%."
--------------------------------------------------------------------
5.<PRO, 5, FC, Attacks:4, popularity(['popular_vote -> -there_is_children
_on_right', 'popular_vote'], -there_is_children_on_right), 61.12>
FC: "By a popular vote, there is more weight for the fact that there is
```

```
no children on the right. The cumulative belief in that fact is 61.12%"
--------------------------------------------------------------------------
6.<OPP, 6, BLC, Attacks:5, concede(['-there_is_children_on_right']),
61.12>
BLC: "I accept that there is no children on the right."
--------------------------------------------------------------------------
7.<PRO, 3, BRC, Attacks:2, reward(['-left & -there_is_children_on_left &
-there_is_children_on_right -> deontology_children', '-there_is_children
_on_left', '-there_is_children_on_right'], -left, deontology_children),
35.19>
BRC: "If you stayed on the right and there is no children on either lane,
your moral code of not harming children will be fulfilled. I'm sure
by 35%."
--------------------------------------------------------------------------
8.<OPP, 4, BLC, Attacks:3, concede(['-left']), 100>
BLC: "I accept we stay on the right."
--------------------------------------------------------------------------
Attack Relations: [('2', '1'), ('3', '2'), ('4', '3'), ('5', '4'),
('7', '2')]
Grounded Semantics: ['1', '3', '5', '7']

Output: Right
```

Fig. 3. Testing Case Output.

This case was an investigation of the value of adding the *Popular()* speech act using DST. The output decision correctly matched the optimal solution defined. As disallowing the popularity argument meant purely trusting the strongest fact, it is shown that it would lead to incorrect results, more specifically, *Pro* group would forced to concede that there is a child on the right. However, using DST as a popular vote argument added more depth to the definition of the strongest fact. Some limitations given our approach (for example, using the M* algorithm) is that one would expect performance to drop with bigger groups of SDCs. However, due to time constraints and our scope, the efficiency of the system has not been thoroughly explored. Furthermore, if there exists no optimal solution, meaning there are several objective decisions due to different moral frameworks deeming opposite decisions as moral, the output of the system would arbitrary, which is, arguably, the expected output for two opposite actions that are moral. Another potential limitation is that sensor data, the input of the system, are critical for the correctness of it.

To summarize, the findings of the simulation are as follows:

1. The proposed system is best used when all cars share the same moral code. If they do not, then at least the different moral codes should, given the same situation, output the same action as moral.
2. A popular speech act argument is useful when reaching the best picture possible, and leads to correct outcomes.

5   Related Work

The combinational use of AF and dialogue protocols have been used, by [7], in the imaginary context of agents escaping a burning building. The agents were exchanging arguments defending their theories on the location of the origin of the fire. However, their assumption of a perfect sensing agent will be relaxed in our paper. Each argument, or detection, will have a percentage value representing how accurate the detection is. Moreover, the advantages of information fusion, the process of merging different values into one, more comprehensive value, are gained by combining the readings of different sensors.

Another example is the work of [11], which provided the basis and inspiration for our system. Unlike them, however, our implementation will not depend on the length of the dialogue sequence to determine the winner. Instead, we will depend on the grounded semantics of AF to provide us a consistent set of arguments that survive together. Moreover, the proposed system will allow utterances to attack any previous utterance , not just the previous one. Additionally, we added a *Popular()* speech act to their suggested list in order to allow for reasoning with uncertainty.

Furthermore, our system can be extended to multi-agent systems of more than two agents, unlike both [2,11], This extension have been inspired by [6] but with the relaxing of their assumption that all agents will share the same argument set. Also, their protocol assumes choosing the first, or a random, argument to utter. This decision will be augmented by a version of M* algorithm, proposed by [14].

6   Conclusions and Future Work

The goal of this paper was mimicking humans' ethical reasoning and communication in SDCs, specifically the conflict resolution using argumentation-based dialogue of ethical decisions that cannot hold together in unavoidable accident scenarios where a group of SDCs is involved. First, a topic language and different classes of speech acts were detailed. Moreover, the implementation of the system was described. The results of such system are promising, proving that, assuming an *optimal solution* exists, the system will output the decision with the strongest justifications, and reach the *optimal solution*.

We propose to extend this work in several ways in the future: (1) extending the system to handle multi-lanes, not just left or right decisions, (2) a careful study of the case of equally strong arguments supporting opposite decisions, and (3) investigating an empirical study of the efficiency of this system.

References

1. Amgoud, L., Besnard, P.: A formal analysis of logic-based argumentation systems. In: Deshpande, A., Hunter, A. (eds.) SUM 2010. LNCS (LNAI), vol. 6379, pp. 42–55. Springer, Heidelberg (2010). https://doi.org/10.1007/978-3-642-15951-0_10
2. Amgoud, L., Dimopoulos, Y., Moraitis, P.: A unified and general framework for argumentation-based negotiation. In: Proceedings of the 6th International Joint Conference on Autonomous Agents And Multiagent Systems, pp. 1–8 (2007)
3. Baroni, P., Caminada, M., Giacomin, M.: Abstract argumentation frameworks and their semantics. Handb. Formal Argum. **1**, 157–234 (2018)
4. Bench-Capon, T.J.: Persuasion in practical argument using value-based argumentation frameworks. J. Log. Comput. **13**(3), 429–448 (2003)
5. Beynon, M., Curry, B., Morgan, P.: The dempster-Shafer theory of evidence: an alternative approach to multicriteria decision modelling. Omega **28**(1), 37–50 (2000)
6. Bonzon, E., Maudet, N.: On the outcomes of multiparty persuasion. In: McBurney, P., Parsons, S., Rahwan, I. (eds.) ArgMAS 2011. LNCS (LNAI), vol. 7543, pp. 86–101. Springer, Heidelberg (2012). https://doi.org/10.1007/978-3-642-33152-7_6
7. Bourgne, G., Hette, G., Maudet, N., Pinson, S.: Hypotheses refinement under topological communication constraints. In: Proceedings of the 6th International Joint Conference on Autonomous agents and Multiagent Systems, pp. 1–8 (2007)
8. El Bolock, A., Abdelrahman, Y., Abdennadher, S. (eds.): Character Computing. HIS, Springer, Cham (2020). https://doi.org/10.1007/978-3-030-15954-2
9. Huadong, W., Siegel, M., Stiefelhagen, R., Jie, Y.: Sensor fusion using dempster-Shafer theory [for context-aware HCI]. In: Instrumentation and Measurement Technology Conference, pp. 7–12 (2002)
10. Kaur, P., Taghavi, S., Tian, Z., Shi, W.: A survey on simulators for testing self-driving cars. In: 2021 Fourth International Conference on Connected and Autonomous Driving (MetroCAD), pp. 62–70. IEEE (2021)
11. Morveli-Espinoza, M., Possebom, A., Tacla, C.A.: A protocol for argumentation-based persuasive negotiation dialogues. In: Britto, A., Valdivia Delgado, K. (eds.) BRACIS 2021. LNCS (LNAI), vol. 13073, pp. 18–32. Springer, Cham (2021). https://doi.org/10.1007/978-3-030-91702-9_2
12. Nees, M.A.: Safer than the average human driver (who is less safe than me)? Examining a popular safety benchmark for self-driving cars. J. Safety Res. **69**, 61–68 (2019)
13. Nyholm, S.: The ethics of crashes with self-driving cars: a roadmap, i. Philos. Compass **13**(7), e12507 (2018)

14. Oren, N., Norman, T.J.: Arguing using opponent models. In: McBurney, P., Rahwan, I., Parsons, S., Maudet, N. (eds.) ArgMAS 2009. LNCS (LNAI), vol. 6057, pp. 160–174. Springer, Heidelberg (2010). https://doi.org/10.1007/978-3-642-12805-9_10
15. Russell, S., Norvig, P.: Artificial Intelligence: A Modern Approach (4th Edition), pp. 231–232. Pearson (2020)

Multi-modal Explainable Music Recommendation Based on the Relations Between Character and Music Listening Behavior

Fatma Elazab[1]([⊠]), Alia El Bolock[2], Cornelia Herbert[3], and Slim Abdennadher[2]

[1] German University in Cairo, Cairo, Egypt
`fatma.hossam@guc.edu.eg`
[2] German International University, Cairo, Egypt
`{alia.elbolock,slim.abdennadher}@giu-uni.de`
[3] Ulm University, Ulm, Germany
`cornelia.herbert@uni-ulm.de`

Abstract. Today's music scheme consists of a vast diverse collection of music and songs to be explored. Accordingly, most of the current music-playing and streaming services heavily rely on powerful recommendation techniques that help users explore different genres and aid in their decision-making. However, recommender systems should not treat all users the same by applying recommendation algorithms that do not include the user as the center of implementation as this may lead to an unpleasant user experience as each user has a different personality, taste, and different needs. The reasoning behind a recommendation should also be transparent to the users to adhere to recent requirements of the Ethical AI movement. In this work, we first study the effect of the person's personality, situation, and affect on music-listening behavior through data gathering. We use the extracted correlations as a basis for a character-based music recommendation system. To ensure transparency and increase the persuasiveness of the system, we use the proposed XReC framework to accompany our recommendations with multi-modal explanations. Explanation models are responsible for explaining to the user why a particular item is recommended. The results interpreted from the data gathered showed that not all character traits have a significant effect on music-listening behavior; however, only some traits showed correlations. The experiment conducted proved that including the character traits into the recommendation algorithm as well as adding explanations is promising, as participants preferred it over non-personalized, non-explained recommendations.

Keywords: Character Computing · Recommender Systems · Music · Explainable Recommendations · Personalization

1 Introduction

We are currently witnessing a global transformation of the music business. The music library became enormously big to the point that it is impossible for one

D. Durães et al. (Eds.): PAAMS 2023, CCIS 1838, pp. 92–103, 2023.
https://doi.org/10.1007/978-3-031-37593-4_8

individual to keep up with that evolution, highlighting the value of online streaming services with their sophisticated recommendation algorithms that guide users through various genres and assist in decision-making. Thus, recommendation systems are vital for e-commerce and multimedia platforms. However, recommender systems should not treat all users equally by implementing recommendation algorithms that do not put the user at the center of implementation, as each user has a unique personality, set of preferences, and set of needs. Therefore, personalization is necessary. According to [16, 22, 24], incorporating the user's personality into recommendation techniques outperforms state-of-the-art algorithms by improving recommendation accuracy and quality. Character Computing [1, 7] proposes that personality alone is insufficient. The whole character [6] (stable personality traits, socio-cultural embedding, and variable emotional and health states) of an individual should be used in personalization endeavors as human behavior is dictated by the character based on the situation. Accordingly, character-based recommender systems will surpass systems that consider one aspect of the human character, such as personality traits, emotional state, or demographic data. In this paper, we aim to find answers to the following research questions:

1. What is the effect of the person's personality, situation, and person's affect on music-listening behavior?
2. What is the effect of adding different character attributes to the recommendation process?
3. What is the effect of adding a personalized explanation to the recommendation?

Due to the lack of datasets that link the character with the listening behavior, we need to build our own that connects the user's personality, current affect, and situation with their preferred music to study the listening behavior. The results will then be incorporated into the XReC module that was proposed in [9]. An experiment was conducted to assess user feedback on the proposed personalized explainable recommendations.

The structure of this paper is as follows: The background and related work are in Sect. 2. In Sect. 3, our methodology is presented. Section 4 discusses the implementation of the application. The experimental design is presented in Sect. 5. Results and discussion are in Sect. 6. Finally, the conclusion and future work are presented in Sect. 7.

2   Background and Related Work

Recommender systems are considered a type of information filtering technique. It helps users in their decision-making. The overabundance of data available on the web in various domains, such as movies, songs, etc., creates a demand for powerful recommender systems. There are various techniques for how recommendation systems work. Some of the popular recommendation algorithms are collaborative filtering recommendation, content-based recommendation, a hybrid approach, demographic-based recommendation, and knowledge-based recommendation [13,14]. The choice of the recommendation algorithm is based on the domain, the available data, and the type of users. Collaborative filtering and content-based are two of the most famous techniques used. Collaborative filtering is also known as social filtering because the recommendation is based on the choices of other individuals who share similar interests [4]. The recommendation in content-based is based on item features. It suggests items that are similar to items that the user has previously liked [18,26].

Explainable recommendations are important as they ensure the credibility and transparency of the system, and they also increase persuasiveness. [28] provides an extensive review of explainable recommendation techniques and models in different domains. Explainability models can be applied to different recommendation applications such as entertainment, e-commerce, and e-learning. The research gap found is that the existing work done on achieving personalized recommender systems considers only one aspect of the human character. It could be the user's personality or emotional state. Thus, our goal is to incorporate all the dimensions that build the human character, such as personality traits, affective states, behavior, and situations.

The field of character computing advises taking into account the entire character rather than just one aspect of the person [6]. Personality traits, demographic information, and sociocultural embeddings make up the broad, stable factor of human character. On the other hand, emotion, mood, and behavior are considered the current factors [3,8]. Using character computing principles, a character-based chatbot with several n-dimensional traits based on human character components that the user can select from to create their desired character [10]. The authors in [2] aimed to develop a character-based meta-recommender system for movies that is adaptive in the way it recommends. According to [6], most existing research focuses on one aspect, such as affect or personality, and only takes the perspective of one field, such as psychology or computer science; in character computing, a joint perspective is followed while focusing on all relevant aspects that make up a human being. For each factor that contributes to building the human character, we need to find a way to define it so that we can embed it into our system. Getting the personality of the user is an essential part of our design, and it is one of the main components that make up the character. According to multiple studies in psychology [5,21,23,29], there are five primary personality traits. The five traits are the following: extraversion, agreeableness, conscientiousness, neuroticism, and openness to experience.

One of the most widely used tests is the Big Five Inventory [BFI] personality test. As its name suggests, it is a test that measures the five personality traits. It assigns a score to each trait. It is a self-report scale used to calculate scores for the five personality traits, and it has proven validity and reliability. There are multiple versions of the BFI test, such as BFI-10 [19] and BFI-44 [12]. The different versions differ in the number of questions given. The BFI-10, for example, is made up of ten questions; every two questions focus on a particular

trait. The BFI-44, on the other hand, is made up of 44 questions, and each trait
is calculated based on the answers to specific ones. Knowing the current mood
of the user is another essential part of our system. There are different tests that
are used to get the current mood from the answers to multiple questions. Some
of the popularly used tests are the Self Assessment Manikin [SAM] and the Positive Affect and Negative Affect Schedule [PANAS]. PANAS is one of the most
widely used scales to measure the emotion or mood of a person. It consists of 20
different words that describe the feeling, of which 10 are related to the positive
affect and the other 10 are related to the negative affect [15].

3   Methodology

Our goal is to investigate how the character affects music-listening behavior
and pinpoint the attributes that have a noticeable contribution so they may
be incorporated into recommender system models. In our approach, we have
followed the generic framework proposed in [9]. The framework suggested that
we can include character attributes such as personality traits, current affect,
and situation into a module named XReC that is responsible for character-
based recommendations and explanations. The process to identify the character
attributes that showed correlations with the listening behavior is shown in Fig. 1.

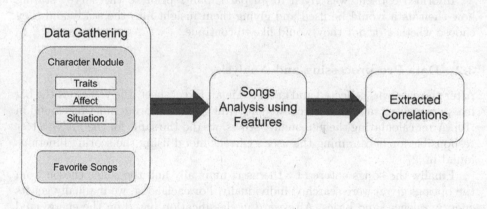

Fig. 1. The process for Finding Significant Character Attributes

3.1   Data Gathering

The limitation we have faced is the lack of an available dataset that connects people's personality traits, current mood, and situations with their music-listening
behavior. The data was collected through a survey that consists of the BFI-10
questionnaire, PANAS questionnaire, and a part for the user to enter his current
activity.

Finally, they had to answer the question *"Which song(s) would you choose from your playlist to listen to right now?"* where they enter the song name and the artist of one or more songs from their playlist to which they would choose to listen at the moment. An extra optional question was given consisting of four songs, and users had to choose the song that they would like to listen to. The four songs given were chosen based on a classification based on their energy and valence values. The valence of a song is a value ranging from 0 to 1 that measures the positivity of a song. In addition to valence, energy value measures how fast and energetic the song is. According to the emotional arousal-pleasure model [20], songs can be classified by their energy and valence features. The four categories are as follows: Happy/Slow: where the valence is high and the energy is low, Happy/Fast: where the valence and energy both have high values, Sad/Fast: when the valence has a low value and the energy has a high value, and finally, Sad/Slow where the valence and energy both have low values. For the survey, we intended to choose one song from each category. As a result, we manually checked the most well-known song's energy and valence values in each category. We included a link for each song to guide people to the song itself so they can listen to it and make a decision in case some participants were unfamiliar with the songs. The songs chosen are "Ben E. King - Stand By Me", "SAINt JHN - Roses (Imanbek Remix)", "The Weeknd - Blinding Lights", and "Billie Eilish - everything i wanted" in categories 1, 2, 3, and 4 respectively.

Informed consent was given to all participants prior to the survey stating how their data would be used and giving them insight into the study and they choose whether or not they would like to continue.

3.2   Data Pre-processing and Analysis

After the data was collected and gathered in an Excel sheet, the values for the big five personality traits were calculated according to the scoring functions found in [19]. After calculating the personality scores, we did the same for the PANAS test responsible for determining the user's current mood using the scoring functions found in [27].

Finally, the songs entered by the users manually and the songs chosen from the options given were searched individually. For each song, we manually get its energy, valence, and lyrics. Afterward, a classification based on the energy and valence values together is calculated for each song. According to [11], the songs are classified as follows: if the energy and valence are both greater than or equal to 0.5 then the music can be classified to **happy**. If the energy is greater than or equal to 0.5 and the valence is less than 0.5 then it is **angry**. The energy of less than 0.5 and valence greater than or equal to 0.5 would be classified as **relaxed**. And finally, if energy and valence are both less than 0.5 then it is **sad**.

In addition to the classification based on the energy and valence combined, we added two columns for classifying the songs based on their energy or valence individually so that we can study the effect on each feature separately as well as their combination. So if the energy is greater than or equals 0 and less than or equals 0.33 then it is considered a **slow-paced** song. If it is greater than 0.33 and less than or equals 0.66 then it is classified as **neutral** in terms of energy. And finally, if it is greater than 0.66 and less than or equals 1 then it is considered as **fast-paced** song. If the valence is greater than or equals 0 and less than or equals 0.33 then it is considered a **sad** song. If it is greater than 0.33 and less than or equals 0.66 then it is classified as **neutral** in terms of valence. And finally, if it is greater than 0.66 and less than or equals 1 then it is considered as **happy** song. Finally, the lyrics of each song need to be analyzed. The Python library used is the **VADER** sentiment analysis which is a model used for text sentiment analysis and is sensitive to both the polarity and intensity of the emotion.

The total number of individual users who took the survey was 152. However, some users took the survey more than once while doing a different activity with a different mood and chose different songs. Thus, we added those responses to the total number of entries which makes a total of 181 responses.

For the statistical analysis phase, we used **Multinomial Logistic Regression**; it predicts the likelihood that a category will fall under a dependent variable based on several independent variables. We wish to investigate how the character's various characteristics-including personality traits, current mood, and situation-affect music-listening behavior. To determine the impact of the various character traits both individually and collectively, a thorough analysis of the data is performed. Before we begin, we need to identify our dependent and independent variables. In our case, we have a total of four dependent variables which are:

1. Music classification based on the energy and valence values together with four levels (happy, sad, relaxed, and angry).
2. Classification based on the valence only with three levels (happy, sad, or neutral).
3. Classification based on the energy only with three levels (fast, slow, or neutral).
4. The sentiment of the lyrics with three levels (positive, negative, or neutral).

The independent variables in our case are the character attributes as follows: positive affect score, negative affect score, openness score, conscientiousness score, extraversion score, agreeableness score, neuroticism score, and the current activity. For each independent variable, we will check if we can predict the dependent variable or not using multinomial logistic regression.

After analyzing our data using multinomial logistic regression, we have found that not all the character attributes have a significant effect on the music-listening behavior. However, the results showed that the value of *conscientiousness* can be used to predict the sentiment of the lyrics whether positive, negative, or neutral. *Neuroticism* can be used to predict the energy type of the song whether it is fast-paced, slow-paced, or neutral. And finally, the user's current *activity* can be used to predict the valence of the song whether it is happy, sad, or neutral. These findings will be the foundation for the algorithm responsible for the recommendations and explanations.

4   Implementation

As a proof of concept, we implemented a web-based application by following the approach found in [9]. The aim of the application is to experiment the personalized recommendations and explanations after including the character in the process. As shown in Fig. 1 discussed in Sect. 3, after the data gathering process, we have done data analysis to find the character attributes that are correlated with the music listening behavior. The extracted correlations are the basis for the recommendations and explanations module [XReC] as well as the 5 personality traits, current mood, and current activity.

In the first part of our application, we needed to gather information about the user's character. Thus, in the beginning, the user signs up for the system by choosing a valid username and entering their email. Afterward, the users answer the personality questions using the BFI-10 test, followed by the emotions test using the PANAS test. Finally, it chooses one activity from a drop-down list of activities. The five personality traits score are considered stable factors, meaning that they are less likely to change in a short amount of time or in general. Thus, the user will only enter it once in our system. However, for the current affect and activity, the user has to answer them each time using the system because they are considered temporary variables that are more likely to be changed in a short amount of time.

The songs dataset is built from several datasets collected from **Spotify** that were available on **Kaggle**. For each song, valence and energy are considered in addition to the lyrics. We have only selected the English songs so that we could apply VADER to classify the songs based on the lyrical content as well.

The recommender algorithm is based on a hybrid approach between Collaborative Filtering and Content-based. Firstly, the collaborative filtering approach is based on the idea of finding similar users and then recommending what similar users like. Similar users in our system are the users that share the same character attributes. However, one drawback of this approach is that it can suffer from the cold start problem if there is not enough user data to be able to find similar ones. However, we overcame this problem by populating our database using the data collected. The collaborative filtering approach is based on the K-Means Clustering algorithm.

The attributes that will be fed to the algorithm are the features that we want to cluster the users upon it which in our case are the character attributes. However, after we collected the data as discussed in the previous Sect. 3, we found that not all character traits have a significant effect on our independent variables, thus there is no need to find the similarity between users using these traits. As a result, we only took the traits that showed significance which are conscientiousness, neuroticism, and the current activity. Thus, each time the user requests a recommendation, the recommender algorithm works as follows:

1. K-means clustering runs and the cluster containing the user is returned.
2. Find all the users in the cluster returned and identify the features of the songs preferred.

3. Apply a content-based approach to find all songs from the database with the returned features.
4. An explanation is provided to the user. The explanation is computed using the features that were used in the clustering phase in the form of "Because you scored relatively high/low scores in this domain, we think that you may like listening to this genre while doing this activity".
5. The playlist is presented to the user and the user can choose whether he liked the playlist provided or not. There exists a high probability that the user would not know the songs recommended. That is why we added a feature where it redirected the user to the song itself so that the user can listen and decide.

5 Experimental Design

In this section, we will discuss the experiment we have done using the implemented application discussed in the previous Sect. 4. The experiment conducted consists of three phases. In *phase 1*, the user had to choose between two playlists. The two playlists are personalized but they differ in the way they are personalized. To avoid overwhelming the users and for the benefit of the experimental timing, each playlist has only three songs chosen from the dataset based on the recommendation algorithm discussed earlier. In *phase 2*, we aim to answer our previously asked research question: "What is the effect of adding different character attributes in the recommendation process?" To be able to answer this question, we provided the users with two playlists. The first playlist consisted of songs suggested by our recommender algorithm which is a personalised one. For the second playlist, a non-personalized recommendation is presented to the user, and then the user has to choose one playlist out of the two. In *phase 3*, we tackled our third research question, which is: "What is the effect of adding a personalized explanation to the recommendation?". We presented the user with two playlists, and the user had to choose one. The two playlists are personalized based on K-means clustering; however, one playlist shows a personalized explanation, and the other playlist has no explanation. The explanation is computed using the features that were used in the recommendation process (in the clustering) in the form of "Because you scored relatively high or low scores in this domain, we think that you may like listening to this genre while doing this activity".

During the three phases, if the user selected a specific playlist, all of the songs in that playlist were added to the user's preferred song list that is saved in the database, which was later used by our algorithm. This also helps us populate our dataset, allowing us to make more accurate recommendations later on. Thus, our system always learns from the users. As a result, we added an extra option to the three phases, preventing users from selecting any playlist from the displayed playlists if they do not like the recommended songs. In this way, we have ensured that if a user picks a playlist, this means that the user likes the songs; thus, the response will be saved in our database and will be further used in the recommendation process for other users.

6   Results and Discussion

All participants are Egyptians with more than 90% of them within the "25–34" age group. 65.2% were females and 34.8% were males. Thus, gender and age will not be included in the analysis as the results could be biased because of the imbalance of the distribution. The results of phase 1 are as follows: it showed that 45.2% chose the first playlist. On the other hand, 54.8% chose the second playlist, where k-means clustering is used. The number of participants that chose the first playlist is actually close to the number of participants that chose the second playlist, with no significant finding. According to our analysis, the result is close because the two playlists consider the character but in different ways. Thus, the songs are quite similar in the two playlists presented to the users. In phase 2, the results showed that 54.8% chose the first playlist (the personalized playlist). On the other hand, 38.7% chose the second playlist (that does not take the character into consideration), and finally, 6.5% did not like either playlist. With more than 50% of the respondents picking our personalized playlist, this proves our point that taking the character into consideration in the recommender algorithm will outperform non-personalized recommendations. And it agrees with our findings from [17] that user-centric models are far more effective at suggesting accurate items. Finally, in phase 3, the results showed that 53.3% chose the first playlist (with the explanation). While 36.7% chose the second playlist (without explanation), and finally, 10% of the users did not like the two presented playlists. This proves that adding a personalized explanation to the recommendation has a positive effect, as it improves the trustworthiness, transparency, and persuasiveness of our algorithm as presented in [28].

After we found the results of the three phases, we wanted to explore our data further. Thus, for each of the four dependent variables discussed earlier, we computed the mean values for each character trait in addition to the user's current activity. The main findings observed that participants with a high mean value for positive affect prefer to listen to happy songs, which agrees with [25] justification that participants with higher values of positive affect are experiencing a positive mood while those with a lower mean value for positive affect prefer slow-paced songs. For the negative affect, we found that participants with a higher mean value listen to songs classified as sad, which means that they currently have feelings of sadness or nervousness; fast-paced songs are preferred by those with a lower mean value for the negative affect. Regarding the five personality traits: participants with a higher mean in the *openness to experience* trait listen to songs classified as happy with negative lyrics, while those with a lower mean tend to listen to slow-paced sad songs. For the *conscientiousness* trait, participants with a relatively higher mean preferred relaxed songs with positive lyrics; on the other hand, participants with a lower mean preferred angry songs with negative lyrics. participants with a relatively higher mean in *extraversion* trait tend to listen to angry songs with negative lyrics, while those with a relatively lower mean prefer songs classified as relaxed with positive lyrics. Higher mean values in the *agreeableness* trait preferred relaxed, slow-paced songs, but lower mean values preferred happy songs with positive lyrics. Finally, highly *neurotic* preferred sad, slow-paced songs with negative lyrics, whereas low-neurotic participants preferred happy songs with positive lyrics. Regarding the *activity*, we investigated the music type preferred by participants while working and chilling only as these two activities make up more than 65% of the responses, as shown in Fig. 2.

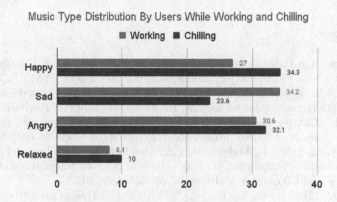

Fig. 2. Music Type Distribution By Users While Working and Chilling

7   Conclusion and Future Work

People and music are always connected. Each person has a unique taste in music, but have you ever wondered what factors cause this unique taste? In this paper, we first study the effect of the person's personality, situation, and person's affect on music listening behavior through data gathering and analysis. Following that, we use the extracted findings as the foundation for a character-based music recommendation explanation system. A web-based application was implemented based on the XReC module proposed by [9]. The aim of the application is to test the effect of adding character attributes to the recommendations and explanations using a three phases experiment which helps us answer our research questions. We have found that conscientiousness, neuroticism, and the situation have a significant effect on music-listening behavior. Additionally, the personalized playlist based on the significant character attributes studied was chosen by more than 50% more people than the non-personalized playlist, demonstrating that incorporating the character into the recommendation process outperforms non-personalized techniques and people preferred the playlist with a personalized explanation more than the playlist without an explanation. Moreover, using the users' mean values, we also looked at the song type, energy type, valence type, and sentiment of the lyrics most associated with each character trait.

For future work, we need to experiment on a larger scale. We can use a more extensive personality questionnaire, such as the BFI-44. Additionally, we could gather users' current affect using another emotional test and compare the results. One drawback of the sentiment analysis technique used on the lyrics is that it only works on English text, so we can apply different sentiment analysis techniques that can be applied to different languages to have a more diverse dataset and recommendations. Finally, we can consider the other features of the song, such as BPM and danceability, to study their relationship with the different character attributes.

References

1. El Bolock, A., Abdelrahman, Y., Abdennadher, S.: Character Computing. HIS, Springer, Cham (2020). https://doi.org/10.1007/978-3-030-15954-2
2. Bolock, A.E., Kady, A.E., Herbert, C., Abdennadher, S.: Towards a character-based meta recommender for movies. In: Alfred, R., Lim, Y., Haviluddin, H., On, C.K. (eds.) Computational Science and Technology. LNEE, vol. 603, pp. 627–638. Springer, Singapore (2020). https://doi.org/10.1007/978-981-15-0058-9_60
3. El Bolock, A., Salah, J., Abdennadher, S., Abdelrahman, Y.: Character computing: challenges and opportunities. In: Proceedings of the 16th International Conference on Mobile and Ubiquitous Multimedia, pp. 555–559(2017)
4. Breese, J.S., Heckerman, D., Kadie, C.: Empirical analysis of predictive algorithms for collaborative filtering. arXiv preprint arXiv:1301.7363 (2013)
5. Cherry, K.: The big five personality traits. Very Well Mind (2019). Accessed 23 May 2020
6. El Bolock, A.: What is character computing? In: El Bolock, A., Abdelrahman, Y., Abdennadher, S. (eds.) Character Computing. HIS, pp. 1–16. Springer, Cham (2020). https://doi.org/10.1007/978-3-030-15954-2_1
7. El Bolock, A., Herbert, C., Abdennadher, S.: CCOnto: towards an ontology-based model for character computing. In: Dalpiaz, F., Zdravkovic, J., Loucopoulos, P. (eds.) RCIS 2020. LNBIP, vol. 385, pp. 529–535. Springer, Cham (2020). https://doi.org/10.1007/978-3-030-50316-1_34
8. El Bolock, A., Salah, J., Abdelrahman, Y., Herbert, C., Abdennadher, S.: Character computing: computer science meets psychology. In: Proceedings of the 17th International Conference on Mobile and Ubiquitous Multimedia, pp. 557–562 (2018)
9. Elazab, F., El Bolock, A., Herbert, C., Abdennadher, S.: XReC: towards a generic module-based framework for explainable recommendation based on character. In: De La Prieta, F., El Bolock, A., Durães, D., Carneiro, J., Lopes, F., Julian, V. (eds.) PAAMS 2021. CCIS, vol. 1472, pp. 17–27. Springer, Cham (2021). https://doi.org/10.1007/978-3-030-85710-3_2
10. El Hefny, W., El Bolock, A., Herbert, C., Abdennadher, S.: Towards a generic framework for character-based chatbots. In: De La Prieta, F., et al. (eds.) PAAMS 2020. CCIS, vol. 1233, pp. 95–107. Springer, Cham (2020). https://doi.org/10.1007/978-3-030-51999-5_8
11. Helmholz, P., Meyer, M., Robra-Bissantz, S.: Feel the Moosic: emotion-based music selection and recommendation (2019)
12. John, O.P., Naumann, L.P., Soto, C.J.: Paradigm shift to the integrative big five trait taxonomy: History, measurement, and conceptual issues (2008)
13. Kumar, P., Thakur, R.S.: Recommendation system techniques and related issues: a survey. Int. J. Inf. Technol. **10**(4), 495–501 (2018). https://doi.org/10.1007/s41870-018-0138-8

14. Kumar, S., et al.: Survey on personalized web recommender system. Int. J. Inf. Eng. Elect. Bus. **10**(4), 1–8 (2018)

15. Merz, E.L., et al.: Psychometric properties of positive and negative affect schedule (PANAS) original and short forms in an African American community sample. J. Affect. Disorders **151**(3), 942–949 (2013)

16. Nalmpantis, O., Tjortjis, C.: The 50/50 recommender: a method incorporating personality into movie recommender systems. In: Boracchi, G., Iliadis, L., Jayne, C., Likas, A. (eds.) EANN 2017. CCIS, vol. 744, pp. 498–507. Springer, Cham (2017). https://doi.org/10.1007/978-3-319-65172-9_42

17. Paul, D., Kundu, S.: A survey of music recommendation systems with a proposed music recommendation system. In: Mandal, J.K., Bhattacharya, D. (eds.) Emerging Technology in Modelling and Graphics. AISC, vol. 937, pp. 279–285. Springer, Singapore (2020). https://doi.org/10.1007/978-981-13-7403-6_26

18. Pazzani, M.J., Billsus, D.: Content-based recommendation systems. In: Brusilovsky, P., Kobsa, A., Nejdl, W. (eds.) The Adaptive Web. LNCS, vol. 4321, pp. 325–341. Springer, Heidelberg (2007). https://doi.org/10.1007/978-3-540-72079-9_10

19. Rammstedt, B., John, O.P.: Measuring personality in one minute or less: a 10-item short version of the big five inventory in English and German. J. Res. Personal. **41**(1), 203–212 (2007)

20. Russell, J.A.: A circumplex model of affect. J. Personal. Soc. Psychol. **39**(6), 1161 (1980)

21. Shi, J., Yao, Y., Zhan, C., Mao, Z., Yin, F., Zhao, X.: The relationship between big five personality traits and psychotic experience in a large non-clinical youth sample: the mediating role of emotion regulation. Front. Psych. **9**, 648 (2018)

22. Song, Y., Dixon, S., Pearce, M.: A survey of music recommendation systems and future perspectives. In: 9th International Symposium on Computer Music Modeling and Retrieval, vol. 4, pp. 395–410. Citeseer (2012)

23. Soto, C.: Big Five personality traits, pp. 240–241 (2018)

24. Tkalcic, M., Chen, L.: Personality and recommender systems. In: Ricci, F., Rokach, L., Shapira, B. (eds.) Recommender Systems Handbook, pp. 715–739. Springer, Boston, MA (2015). https://doi.org/10.1007/978-1-4899-7637-6_21

25. Tran, V.: Positive affect negative affect scale (PANAS). In: Gellman, M.D., Turner, J.R. (eds) Encyclopedia of Behavioral Medicine, pp. 1508–1509. Springer, New York (2013). https://doi.org/10.1007/978-1-4419-1005-9_978

26. Van Meteren, R., Van Someren, M.: Using content-based filtering for recommendation. In: Proceedings of the Machine Learning in the New Information Age: MLnet/ECML2000 Workshop, vol. 30, pp. 47–56 (2000)

27. Watson, D., Clark, L.A., Tellegen, A.: Development and validation of brief measures of positive and negative affect: the PANAS scales. J. Personal. Soc. Psychol. **54**(6), 1063 (1988)

28. Zhang, Y., Chen, X.: Explainable recommendation: a survey and new perspectives. CoRR, abs/1804.11192 (2018)

29. Pytlik Zillig, L.M., Hemenover, S.H., Dienstbier, R.A.: What do we assess when we assess a big 5 trait? A content analysis of the affective, behavioral, and cognitive processes represented in big 5 personality inventories. Personal. Soc. Psychol. Bull. **28**(6), 847–858 (2002)

Character-Based Habit Recommender System

Kariman Eldeswky[1]([✉]), Fatma Elazab[1], Alia El Bolock[2],
and Slim Abdennadher[2]

[1] German University in Cairo, Cairo, Egypt
{kariman.elkassaby,fatma.hossam}@guc.edu.eg
[2] German International University, Cairo, Egypt
{alia.elbolock,slim.abdennadher}@giu-uni.de

Abstract. Habits play a significant role in an individual's life satisfaction and overall well-being. With the increased demand for health and wellness apps that track and help build healthy habits, there is a need for personalized recommendations that consider the user's character. Current habit-recommending apps lack personalization and only provide suggestions based on popularity. In this paper, we present CHabit, a habit recommendation system that adapts to the user's personality traits and gender to provide tailored recommendations. Our platform uses an architecture that considers the user's character to select the most suitable habit for them. We provide explanations for our recommendations to persuade users and improve their engagement. We investigated the correlation between habit preference, personality traits, and gender, using data from 103 participants to address the cold-start problem. Our web application allows users to contribute to the recommendation pool and receive tailored suggestions. The results obtained from this work were broken down into two partitions; one from the data gathered in the data-gathering phase, and the other from the testing phase highlighting the user preference. We report an accuracy of 71% for the system when considering the character as a whole and 75% when using gender and a subset of personality traits. Our work demonstrates the potential of personalized habit recommendation systems to improve user engagement and well-being.

Keywords: Recommender System · Character Computing · Habits

1 Introduction

Humans are creatures of habit, and these habits have a profound impact on our daily lives, either helping us move forward or hindering our success. As people become increasingly aware of the importance of habits, health and wellness applications and software are on the rise. However, the recommendations provided by these apps are often impersonal and fail to cater to individual preferences. This study aims to address this issue by using Character Computing to improve the selection process of recommender systems. Unlike previous research that focused solely on personality traits, we take a step further by including the user's gender and other character information to provide more personalized recommendations. By tailoring habits to each user's preferences and character, the user experience and recommendation accuracy are expected to increase. We also experiment with including explanations alongside the recommendations to enhance their effectiveness. This paper presents the related work, data handling, recommender system, testing, and results, with a final conclusion in the end. As habits are crucial to our overall quality of life, we chose them as our medium for testing the efficacy of our approach [1–3].

2   Related Work

To date, various recommendation systems have been proposed to address different research problem areas. These systems have attempted to overcome common limitations such as cold start, sparsity, and scalability problems. Cold start refers to difficulty of recommending items for new users or new items with no historical data. Sparsity refers to data that is missing or not available for a large number of users or items, making it difficult to build accurate models. Scalability refers to difficulty of processing and analyzing large datasets in a timely and efficient manner. The proposed system in this study addresses these limitations by utilizing the user's character to start the recommendation and beat the cold start problem as well as, collecting data from users before the experiment to beat the sparsity problem.

For example, Ifeoma Adaji et al. [4] used the Big Five personality test to recommend recipes to people based on their dominant personality trait. This study computed the personality of a user based on Linguistic Inquiry and Word Count (LIWC) analysis of a dataset produced by allrecipes.com. The study then built a network where the nodes were recipes and the edges were the reviews. The size of the node was proportional to its popularity, which helped eliminate the cold start problem. Recommendations were made based on the weight of the edges between nodes, which showed pairs of recipes that had commonly been reviewed by the same user. The study used collaborative filtering to recommend recipes to people with the same dominant personality trait.

In comparison, the current system recommends habits based on people's Big Five personality test results. The system uses a database of habits and their characteristics and matches them with the user's personality traits. The system then ranks the habits based on their suitability for the user's personality traits and recommends the top-ranked habits.

Another system proposed by Quan [5] uses user personality traits to address the sparsity and scalability problems of collaborative filtering. The system proposes two personality-based collaborative filtering recommendations: one is to compute user similarity from the user personality perspective and select the nearest neighbor to generate a recommendation. Another is based on the personality-item rating matrix, followed by making a recommendation to the target users. Quan also wrote another paper [6], which incorporates the whole user character instead of just the personality. The paper exploits the stability of people's character to make recommendations based on users' character as a whole.

In contrast, the current system focuses solely on the Big Five personality traits, age, and gender to recommend habits to users, similar to the second paper [6]. By using a comprehensive set of user characteristics, the system can provide more accurate and personalized recommendations for the user. Additionally, the current system proposes two types of recommendations: one based on the algorithm's output and one chosen at random. This highlights the importance of personalized recommendations, as the random recommendation is less likely to be suitable for the user's individual needs and preferences.

Finally, Elazab et al. proposed a framework called XReC for building character-based recommender systems [5]. It focuses on increasing the transparency, trustworthiness, persuasiveness, effectiveness, and user satisfaction of the recommendation system by making it explainable. The current system also incorporates some of these principles, by providing explanations for the recommendations.

3   Habit and Character Dataset

We conducted a survey and gathered character-habit data from 103 individuals prior to launching the web application. The data comprised BFI scores, user demographics (including age group, gender, and ethnicity), and their preferred habits across different categories, namely Productivity, Fitness, Personal Growth, and Eating habits. The habits were required to be in a similar format as one would advise someone to take on, with examples provided for clarity.

3.1   Data Collection

The survey collected character-habit data by asking users to complete the BFI-10 questionnaire [7] and provide their favorite habits for specific categories, namely Productivity, Fitness, Personal Growth, and Eating habits. To ensure consistency in the format of the data collected, participants were instructed to provide habits in the same manner they would recommend them to others. For instance, an example provided for the Eating habits category was "Drink a cup of green or white tea every day". In addition, users were asked for their age group, gender, and ethnicity. All participants were informed that their data would be used for research purposes and had to give their consent before submitting their data.

3.2   Data Pre-Processing

The scores for the Big Five personality traits (Extraversion, Agreeableness, Conscientiousness, Neuroticism, and Openness to Experience) were calculated based on the responses to the BFI-10 questionnaire. Each trait was assessed using two items from the questionnaire, one of which was reverse-scored (denoted by "R" in the formulas).

For Extraversion, the formula to calculate the score was $(6-Q1)+Q6$, where $Q1$ and $Q6$ are the responses to the two items measuring this trait. The reverse-scored item ($Q1R$) was subtracted from 6 to account for the fact that higher scores indicate higher levels of extraversion. The scores for the two items were then added together.

Similarly, for Agreeableness, Conscientiousness, Neuroticism, and Openness to Experience, the scores were calculated using similar formulas.

The habits that were similar but phrased differently were unified to avoid repetition and redundancies in the habits database. For example, "drink 3 liters of water every day" and "drink 3 liters of water daily" were both changed to "drink 3 liters of water daily". Only words that were synonyms and could be used interchangeably were exchanged.

The survey data were used to create a database with three collections. The first collection contained the user's data, including their age, gender, Big Five scores, ethnicity, and a unique user ID. The second collection was for the habits, their corresponding categories, any applicable attributes, and an ID. The third collection was a rating collection where each entry had a user ID, a habit ID, and a corresponding rating indicating how easy the habit was to pick up. The rating field added to the third collection would allow the system to gather feedback from users on how easy a habit was to pick up. This feedback could then be used in future recommendations, as the system could take into account the habits that were easier for users to adopt and suggest them more frequently. This would lead to more personalized and effective recommendations, tailored to the individual user's habits and preferences.

3.3 Data Analysis

The data was collected from a total of 103 people, out of which 93 people answered truthfully and seriously. The gender distribution was 68 females and 25 males. The collected habits from all 4 categories summed up to 170, with Personal Growth Habits having 57 entries, Eating Habits with 53, Fitness Habits with 31, and Productivity Habits with 28. The age distribution of the collected entries was 72 youths ranging from 14 to 24 years old and 21 adults ranging from 25 to 64 years old. The top 10 most entered habits were analyzed by calculating the mean value for each of the five personality domains and computing the percentages of each age group and gender. The habit factors were analyzed, and ethnicity was excluded due to Middle Easterns making up 93.5% of all users.

3.4 Character-habit Data Gathered Results and Discussion

We analyzed the character-habit data that was collected prior to the system implementation in order to form the basis for the system. Since 4 out of the 10 most rated habits had the same category, fitness habits, we looked further into the information on the users that submitted them. All four of them had a relatively high mean value of agreeableness compared to all other mean values of the rest of the domains. The standard deviation of all four agreeableness mean values was also very low (0.081) which leads us to believe that people high in agreeableness tend to be fitness-oriented. This follows the positive correlation between agreeableness and exercise behavior found in [8].

In addition, those who submitted walking as their most practiced habit scored a very high mean in conscientiousness, confirming the theory that highly conscientious people engaged in significantly more leisure walking, especially when motivated [9]. All other factors' means were also close in values but did not have significantly high or low values. The habit of 'Write a to-do list at the start of every day and sort them according to priority' had the highest mean value of conscientiousness compared to all other domains of that habit. This serves as a verification of the definition of conscientiousness as the "tendency to think, feel, and behave in a relatively enduring and consistent fashion across time in trait-affording situations." [10]. The reading habit scored the highest mean value in neuroticism which supports the correlation between high levels of neuroticism and reading explored in [11].

4   CHabit Recommendation System

We designed a web application called CHabit for habit recommendation based on the user's character to address the research topic of optimizing the recommendation quality of the preferred habit based on character.

The aim of the deployed version of CHabit was twofold: (1) to test the hypothesis of whether there is a correlation between habit preferences and character, and (2) to create a knowledge base consisting of characters and corresponding habits that are best suited for them. The idea was to create three modules: a character recognition module to obtain the user's character, a recommender module for getting recommendations, and another module for recommending a habit or adding a habit they already practice to the collection of habits.

The module for adding habits acts as a way of populating the habit pool for recommendations. To ensure that the habits the users are recommending to other users are valid, a human analyst continuously checks the habits collection to process the data, remove any ill-fitting habits, and tag the habits with appropriate attributes.

4.1   System Architecture

Before being able to use any of the system modules, the user has to sign up. The sign up process included the gathering of the user demographic information as well as the *BFI-10* personality questionnaire [12]. Once registered or logged in, the user has access to all modules of the system. Figure 1 shows an overview of the system.

4.2   Character Recognition Module

This module is responsible for querying similar users to the current user. It is triggered every time the user requests a recommendation and works as follows:

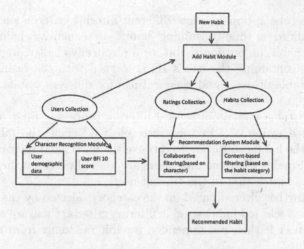

Fig. 1. CHabit System Architecture

1. Every time a user requests a recommendation, all users from the collection are queried, and the z-score[1] for each of the 5 personality domains is calculated.
2. Linear dimensionality reduction is performed using *svd* of the five z-score values to project them to a lower dimensional space of 2D using *PCA* [8][2]. The first vector maximizes the variance of the projected data, while the second maximizes the variance of what's left after the first projection.
3. The reduced data is then clustered to form k number of clusters, where k ranges from 2 to 8, using k-means[3]. Each time the data is clustered, the silhouette score [13][4] is calculated. The k value with the largest silhouette score is chosen to cluster the data.
4. The cluster containing the user's ID and all similar users is returned to the Recommender System Module.

4.3 Recommender System Module

The recommender module works as follows:

1. Whenever a user requests a recommendation, the Character Recognition Module is activated, and the cluster containing the user is returned.

---

[1] Z-score is a measure of how many standard deviations below or above the population mean a raw score is.
[2] *PCA* is a technique for reducing the dimensionality of large datasets, increasing interpretability while minimizing information loss.
[3] K-means clustering is a method of vector quantization that aims to partition n observations into k clusters in which each observation belongs to the cluster with the nearest mean, serving as a prototype of the cluster.
[4] Silhouette score is a metric used to calculate the goodness of a clustering technique. The higher the value, the better the clustering technique.

2. The user has the option to select different filtering criteria, such as whether they can afford a time-consuming habit, an expensive habit, a socially demanding habit, an outdoor habit, or a physically challenging habit.
3. The cluster containing the user's ID is merged with the ratings collection, creating a table of users and their ratings for different habits identified by habit ID.
4. The merged table undergoes several filtering processes. First, the top-rated habits with a rating of 4 or more are selected. Then, the table is merged again with the habits collection to retrieve the habits and their corresponding categories. Finally, the remaining users are filtered based on their gender and age group to match that of the current user.
5. Habits are further filtered based on the category selected by the user (if any). If the user has selected habit-specific filtering criteria, these are applied at this stage. The user is then recommended a habit randomly from the simplified table of habits.
6. Along with the habit, the user receives an explanation of why this habit is best suited for them. The explanation is generated by identifying the two domains with the most explained variance that were used in the user's clustering. The mean value for each domain is calculated, and the user's score in that domain is compared to the mean value to determine whether the user scores relatively high or low in that domain. The explanation is phrased as "Because you scored relatively high/low in this domain and relatively high/low in this other domain, we think this habit suits you best."
7. The user is prompted to rate the recommended habit on a scale of 1 to 5, indicating how likely they are to stick to it.

4.4 Habit Addition Module

The Habit Addition Module allows users to add habits that they like, so that we can use those habits as recommendations for similar users in the future. Here's how it works:

1. The user enters the habit definition and category.
2. The user then rates the habit according to the question, "How easy is this habit to stick to?" on a scale from 1 to 5.
3. An analyst behind the scenes approves the habit as being healthy and checks if it's in the correct category.
4. The analyst is also responsible for tagging the habit with appropriate attributes, such as time consumption, money exhaustion, social demand, outdoor requirements, and physical challenge.

4.5 Web Application Implementation

The data collected was stored in databases, which were uploaded to a web-based database (MongoDB). We used Flask to implement a system for user sign-up and registration. To sign up, users had to enter all the same data that was queried in the survey, as well as additional information such as their name, email, and password. If a user was new to the system, they were directed to a page containing the BFI-10 items version questionnaire to assess their personality trait domains. The habits that the user had rated before were stored in the database, and users could view all of their habits in their profiles. A simplified diagram of the user-system interaction can be seen in Fig. 2 below.

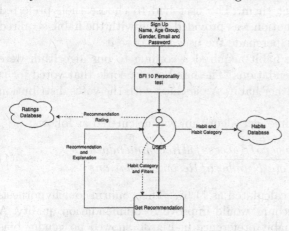

If a user was new to the system, they were directed to a page containing the BFI-10 items version questionnaire to assess their personality trait domains. The habits that the user had rated before were stored in the database, and users could view all of their habits in their profiles. A simplified diagram of the user-system interaction is drawn.

Fig. 2. User-System Interaction

5   Testing and Evaluation

The testing was conducted on a group of 81 people at the German University in Cairo campus, consisting of 42 females and 39 males. The age groups included 76 youths (14–24 years) and 5 adults (25–64 years). The users were first required to agree to the testing and the use of their data anonymously for research purposes. To access the system, users had to provide details about themselves such as their age group and gender, followed by completing the BFI-10 questionnaire.

A separate module was created for the testing phase, comprising two habits along with an explanation. The testing module worked as follows: the user could select the area from which to receive the recommended habit, followed by optional filters for the habit itself, including:

- Outdoors (I love the outdoors)
- Social (I want a social habit)
- Physically challenging (I want to be physically challenged)
- Expensive (Money is not a deciding factor for me)
- Time-consuming (I have a lot of time)

After the user selected the area and filters, our system recommended two habits: one using the approach described in our recommender system, and another from a different cluster than the user's, randomly chosen from any cluster other than the user's. Along with the recommendation, an explanation was provided for the recommended habit fetched using the recommender algorithm. The explanation stated, "Because you scored relatively high/low in this domain and relatively high/low in this other domain, we think this habit suits you best." The aim of the explanation was dual, with both focusing on persuasion. Firstly, we wanted to show the user that those who scored similarly in those two domains had the same habit, giving the user a push to try it. Secondly, if the user found the explanation convincing and relevant, they were more likely to believe that the recommended habit would suit them. The user had to choose their preferred habit and select it. The explanation was provided along with the habit acquired using our algorithm to further persuade the user to choose it.

The people who chose the habit acquired according to our algorithm were considered successful recommendations. The number of people that voted for it were 58 to 23 of votes to the other habit. A pie chart with the votes distribution can be seen in Fig. 3a.

The accuracy of the recommender algorithm was calculated as follows:

$$Accuracy = \frac{Number of Successful Recommendations}{Total Number of Recommendations} \tag{1}$$

The accuracy can then be calculated as 71.6%. This confirms our hypothesis that taking character into account would improve recommendation quality. A heatmap for gender against habit preference in Fig 3b showed no gender bias towards a particular habit.

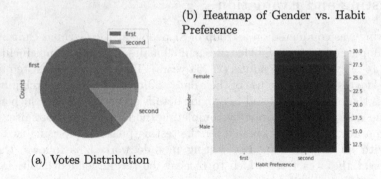

(b) Heatmap of Gender vs. Habit Preference

(a) Votes Distribution

Fig. 3. Statistics for habit preferences. In the following, the first habit is output from CHabit and the second is selected at random

During the final evaluation of the data including both data collected during data gathering phase as well as data collected during testing phase, we found that agreeableness and neuroticism had the highest explained variance of all five personality domains.

We conducted logistic regression[5] on the testing dataset we collected to predict the user's preferred recommender. Combining all 5 personality traits resulted in an accuracy of 56%. To improve the accuracy, we ran the regression on each of the big five personality traits separately. Openness to experience, conscientiousness, extraversion, and neuroticism all yielded 60% accuracy, whereas agreeableness produced no improvement at 56%.

To further enhance the results, we added gender to the machine learning process, resulting in a positive impact on all personality traits.

For females, the accuracy increased to 69% for openness to experience, agreeableness, extraversion, neuroticism, and conscientiousness. For males, the accuracy also increased, with openness to experience, agreeableness, neuroticism, and extraversion giving 67%. However, the accuracy for conscientiousness showed the least growth, with only a mere 58%.

To achieve even more accurate results, we went about solving the problem in a different way; we calculated the accuracy using two personality domains at the same time for each gender separately. The females did not have a difference in the accuracy whether it was an increase or a decrease but rather gave the same accuracy of each domain on its own when combined. The males on the other hand had significant differences in the accuracy with the addition of another trait to the equation as shown in Table 1. This technique considerably improved the accuracies of the results that were previously obtained. The most notable result obtained was an increase to 75% accuracy, which is the best result obtained with males. This result was obtained when combining extraversion with agreeableness, extraversion with neuroticism and conscientiousness with openness. We attempted to include three factors to furthermore improve the accuracy, however the results were disappointing and the accuracy was affected negatively.

Table 1. Table of the accuracy of intersecting 2 traits at once for males.

Personality	Extraversion	Agreeableness	Conscientiousness	Neuroticism	Openness
Extraversion	67%	75%	50%	75%	67%
Agreeableness	75%	67%	58%	67%	67%
Conscientiousness	50%	58%	58%	58%	75%
Neuroticism	75%	67%	58%	67%	67%
Openness	67%	67%	75%	67%	67%

6   Results and Discussion

Following the testing phase of our implementation, we can observe that including gender alongside the personality provides better predictions. We can also see that

---

[5] Logistic regression estimates the probability of an event occurring based on a given dataset of independent variables.

including all personality domains does not necessarily produce better results than each domain by itself, rather the opposite. We looked into the information of the people that voted for each habit to see if there existed a correlation between the choices made and the user making the choices. Table 2 gives a breakdown of the people who chose each habit and the average mean of their BFI-information.

Table 2. Choice and Character Analysis

BFI-10 mean	First Habit	Second Habit
Extraversion	6.48	6.87
Agreeableness	6.59	7.52
Conscientiousness	6.45	6.61
Neuroticism	6.21	6.65
Openness	7.12	6.96

Although, the mean values of the domains did not differ significantly in people that chose the first habit and those that chose the second, multiple things can still be observed.

To start off, the mean value for the people who chose the first habit, the one we recommended according to our algorithm, had a relatively high mean value of openness to experience. This aligns with the evidence found in [14] that suggests that openness is associated with broad persuasibility. We can then hypothesize that the explanation given with the first habit could have potentially persuaded people high in openness to choose it. On the other hand, people that scored relatively high in agreeableness were not as susceptible to persuasion applied by the explanation. The reason for that could be justified by [15] that argued that agreeable people tend to be persuaded by people they like, and no relation was cultivated between the testers and the system or the people conducting the test. In addition, this confirms the theory founded in [16] arguing that agreeableness does not always associate with one's susceptibility to persuasion.

7   Conclusion

In this work, we tackled the problem of refining recommender systems by using the character to produce a better-fitting recommendation. We used that technique to recommend habits to users using their characters. First, we collected data and formed a dataset of characters and their favored habits to find the correlation between characters and their habits. Following that, we experimented with a recommender system, CHabit, that exploits this correlation to recommend character-tailored habits. Experiments took place to evaluate CHabit and the results showed support for our thesis. In the future, we can use CHabit in persuasion systems for building habits, as well as, all sorts of different matters.

References

1. Fiorella, L.: The science of habit and its implications for student learning and well-being. Educ. Psychol. Rev. **32**(3), 603–625 (2020)
2. Verhoeven, A.A.C., Adriaanse, M.A., Evers, C., de Ridder, D.T.D.: The power of habits: unhealthy snacking behaviour is primarily predicted by habit strength. Br. J. Health Psychol. **17**(4), 758–770 (2012)

3. Orbell, S., Verplanken, B.: The strength of habit. Health Psychol. Rev. **9**(3), 311–317 (2015)

4. Adaji, I., Sharmaine, C., Debrowney, S., Oyibo, K., Vassileva, J.: Personality based recipe recommendation using recipe network graphs. In: Meiselwitz, G. (ed.) SCSM 2018. LNCS, vol. 10914, pp. 161–170. Springer, Cham (2018). https://doi.org/10.1007/978-3-319-91485-5_12

5. Quan, Z.: Collaborative filtering recommendation based on user personality. In: 2013 6th International Conference on Information Management, Innovation Management and Industrial Engineering, vol. 3, pp. 307–310. IEEE (2013)

6. Elazab, F., El Bolock, A., Herbert, C., Abdennadher, S.: XReC: towards a generic module-based framework for explainable recommendation based on character. In: De La Prieta, F., El Bolock, A., Durães, D., Carneiro, J., Lopes, F., Julian, V. (eds.) PAAMS 2021. CCIS, vol. 1472, pp. 17–27. Springer, Cham (2021). https://doi.org/10.1007/978-3-030-85710-3_2

7. Rammstedt, B., John, O.P.: Measuring personality in one minute or less: a 10-item short version of the big five inventory in English and German. J. Res. Personal. **41**(1), 203–212 (2007)

8. Hagan, A.L., Hausenblas, H.A.: Examination of personality correlates, exercise preferences, and exercise behavior. Malaysian J. Sport Sci. Recreat. **1**(1), 17–34 (2005)

9. Why, Y.P., Huang, R.Z., Sandhu, P.K.: Affective messages increase leisure walking only among conscientious individuals. Personal. Individ. Differ. **48**(6), 752–756 (2010)

10. Roberts, B.W., Jackson, J.J., Fayard, J.V., Edmonds, G., Meints, J.: Conscientiousness (2009)

11. Farley, F.H., Truog, A.L.: Individual differences in reading comprehension. J. Reading Behav. **3**(1), 29–35 (1970)

12. Maćkiewicz, A., Ratajczak, W.: Principal components analysis (PCA). Comput. Geosci. **19**(3), 303–342 (1993)

13. Shahapure, K.R., Nicholas, C.: Cluster quality analysis using silhouette score. In: 2020 IEEE 7th International Conference on Data Science and Advanced Analytics (DSAA), pp. 747–748. IEEE (2020)

14. Gerber, A.S., Huber, G.A., Doherty, D., Dowling, C.M., Panagopoulos, C.: Big five personality traits and responses to persuasive appeals: Results from voter turnout experiments. Polit. Behav. **35**(4), 687–728 (2012)

15. Wall, H.J., Campbell, C.C., Kaye, L.K., Levy, A., Bhullar, N.: Personality profiles and persuasion: an exploratory study investigating the role of the big-5, type d personality and the dark triad on susceptibility to persuasion. Personal. Individ. Differ. **139**, 69–76 (2019)

16. Lee, J., Albert, L.R.: Students' personality and susceptibility to persuasion during mathematics groupwork: an exploratory study. J. Pract. Stud. Educ. **2**(6), 10–22 (2021)

A Gamification of Psychological Tests for the Detection of Impaired Social Functioning

Nada Ibrahim[(✉)], Raneem Wael, Mai Gamal, and Slim Abdennadher

German University in Cairo, Cairo, Egypt
{nada.abdelfattah,raneem.wael,mai.tharwat}@guc.edu.eg,
slim.abdennadher@giu-uni.de

Abstract. An individual's ability to have regular everyday social interactions in addition to their usual behavior towards certain social situations can be impacted due to impaired social processing or social processing deficits that develop as a result of mental illnesses such depression. Although there are numerous verbal and written tests based on behavioral economics used to detect social processing deficits, little has been done to gamify those methods. This study explores the possibility of detecting social processing deficits in individuals through their participation in a story-driven serious game where the participant would interact with certain situations that are essentially gamified psychological tests. A questionnaire was filled by the participants to identify any deficits and the results were then compared to the findings obtained through gameplay. The results show that the detection of diminished cooperativeness, reduced empathy, trust processing and reaction processing were successfully gamified.

Keywords: Social Processing Impairments · Character Computing · Mental Health · Serious Games

1 Introduction

Humans have a fundamental need to have social interactions, which then help them form relationships with other individuals, enabling them to have a sense of belonging with others [1]. Not fulfilling this need can lead to loneliness, and later develop into depression [2], which then in turn can affect an individual's character, since to understand a person's character, all states, such as mental health and emotions, must be taken into consideration [3]. Detecting changes in mental health such as issues with social processing deficits, is vital since any changes in character will lead to changes in behavior, thus affecting the Character-Behavior-Situation Triad [3].

Impaired social functioning is defined as "an individual's ability to perform and fulfill normal social roles" [5], where social processing deficits develop thus affecting an individual's ability to interpret information through visual and

D. Durães et al. (Eds.): PAAMS 2023, CCIS 1838, pp. 116–127, 2023.
https://doi.org/10.1007/978-3-031-37593-4_10

auditory perception. This in turn affects their social interactions and participation [4]. Research done by Kupferberg, Bicks and Haslera [4] suggests that a social processing deficit can be classified under one of three categories; affiliation and attachment (social anhedonia, hyper-sensitivity, competitive avoidance and increases altruistic punishment), perception and understanding others (impaired emotion recognition and diminished cooperativeness), and social communication (reduced empathy and theory of mind).

Despite the availability and testing of various methods supported by research papers to detect such deficits, there have not been any attempts to gamify those techniques. Consequently, this research aims to explore the possibility of detecting an individual's social processing deficits through playing a game that focuses on detecting social anhedonia, increased altruistic punishment, diminished cooperativeness, reduced empathy and theory-of-mind. Consequently, this study aims to answer the following research question: can the concepts of behavioral economics be gamified to detect social processing deficits?

In order to further investigate this research question, 5 null hypotheses were developed:

1. H1: The social anhedonia score obtained from playing the game does not correlate with the social anhedonia score obtained from the questionnaire.
2. H2: The diminished cooperativeness score obtained from playing the game does not correlate with the diminished cooperativeness score obtained from the questionnaire.
3. H3: The reduced empathy score obtained from playing the game does not correlate with the reduced empathy score obtained from the questionnaire.
4. H4: The trust issues (theory of mind) score obtained from playing the game does not correlate with the trust issues score obtained from the questionnaire.
5. H5: The reaction (theory of mind) score obtained from playing the game does not correlate with the reaction score obtained from the questionnaire.

2 Related Work

2.1 Social Anhedonia

Social anhedonia is characterized by a lack of interest in social contact and a lack of pleasure in social situations, and is linked to lower social functioning and lower reward from social interactions [6]. This social characteristic creates a method for evaluating social reward responsiveness and determines how much people alter their actions in response to socially rewarding stimuli. People with high social anhedonia show minor changes in response bias in the social reward task compared to individuals with low social anhedonia [7]. Social anhedonia can be tested using the Effort-Expenditure for Rewards Task (EEFRT) [8], which is a multi-trial game in which participants are asked on each trial to choose between two different task difficulty levels in order to obtain monetary rewards [8]. Research has shown that there exists an inverse relationship between anhedonia and willingness to expend effort [8].

2.2   Increased Altruistic Punishment

An act, more specifically punishment, is altruistic if it is costly for the punisher and results in a change in the punished person's behavior. This is usually done to influence better actions from the punished individual in the future. Several different paradigms have been employed in altruism research, including the Ultimatum Game and the Public Goods Game [10].

The Ultimatum Game is an economic experiment which evaluates players' reactions to the fairness of offers of a share of money [11]. The first player suggests how to split a cash sum with a second player. If the second player rejects this division, nothing will be given to either. Logically, every offer ought to be accepted because no individual profits are made without an acceptance. However, if the division is considered unfair, Person B may punish their partner by denying the wrong offer [10].

The Public Goods Game (PGG) allows players to secretly choose how many tokens to put in the public pot in the game and the pot is divided evenly among the players. If either of the players does not contribute with their tokens, they retain them. The public goods game serves as a metaphor for modelling cooperative conduct, where those that contribute are said to be acting altruistically, while those that do not contribute are called "free riders". These "free riders" often incur altruistic punishment from others in attempts to force cooperation in the future [10].

These two paradigms were compared to the Altruistic Personality Scale and the Big Five Model of Personality Scale and were proven to accurately identify altruistic punishment in individuals.

2.3   Diminished Cooperativeness

Social cooperativeness is a concept developed from behavioral economics [4], where a person with diminished cooperativeness is less likely to exhibit the ability to cooperate with others, consider others' perspectives and enjoy working with others [4]. Diminished cooperativeness can be measured using two games, the Prisoner's Dilemma and the Dictator Game.

The Prisoner's Dilemma measures cooperation where the individual's self-interest conflicts with that of the partnership [12]. Two participants receive the same amount of money while deciding whether to cooperate (share) or defect (keep the money). If both defect or both cooperate, pay is the lowest. However, a participant can make the most if they defect while their partner cooperates [11].

The Dictator Game stems from the ultimatum game, where one player (the dictator) offers the other (the recipient) a one-time offer. The dictator's actions begin with giving nothing to the recipient or giving them all the funds. As the recipient plays a passive role, the dictator decides the final division of the money [11].

2.4 Reduced Empathy

Empathy is the ability to understand or feel what another person experiences, that is, the capacity to "put one's self into another person's shoes". This deficit is measured using two methods, the first one being basic empathy tasks such as making the player choose between helping other people or not [13]. Another symptom of reduced empathy is the inability to identify videos or audios depicting painful stimuli [4].

2.5 Theory of Mind

Having a theory of mind (ToM) is vital as it can predict and interpret other people's behaviour. It is an essential social-cognitive skill that involves thinking about mental states, both a person's own and others'. Deficiencies in this area were detected using situations that test for an individual's ability to correctly assess who of the other players to trust depending on how they have treated them before [14]. Testing for this ability is done by recording a player's repeated choices based on other characters' hints and their repeated reaction to them, which includes whether the participant trusts the character or not. As part of the theory of mind, empathy is often associated with the capacity to accurately gather the thoughts, intentions, and emotional states of others [13].

To ensure the success of the gamified tasks in measuring an imbalance in the theory of minds, the Multidimensional Mentalizing Questionnaire [15] (MMQ) was used to compare the game results to the actual ones from the questionnaire.

3 Methodology

3.1 Game Design and Characters

The game is set in a jungle where the player's aim is to reach their treehouse, and the psychological tasks were embedded into the game environment. The player was given the chance to play with a male or a female avatar.

At the beginning of the game, the participant is informed that they will be playing with three real players; however, that is not the case. The other players are Non-Player Characters (NPC) with all reactions and interactions which are hardcoded. This was done in an attempt to control the study. The participant believes that the other players are actual people to relate the game to real-life situations and act how they would with real people. The 3 main NPCs are an NPC that acts as a helpful person, an NPC that acts as a selfish and untrustworthy individual, and an NPC that acts generously.

The participants were not explicitly informed of the characteristics of each of the characters. Instead, the characters are portrayed through their interactions.

3.2   Social Anhedonia

Response Bias. A gamified experiment that was designed in one particular study [7] by Chevallier et al., consisted of showing a long then a short stick and then showing either of them one after the other, at each time asking whether it is long or short. A social reward in the form of a silent, full-color video clip of an actor offering approbation by simultaneously smiling, nodding, and showing a thumbs-up motion was shown after each successful answer. This was replicated in the serious game, the player is asked to decide whether the log shown is "long" or "short" in size, as shown in Fig. 1. The player must then mark a checkbox asking if they are sure of their answer as the difference in lengths of both branches was relatively unnoticeable to continuously test what the player is inclined to choose at times of uncertainty. The number of times this box was ticked with "long" as an answer (lean stimulus) is recorded along with the corresponding number of times it was ticked with "short" as an answer (rich stimulus). The lean stimulus was then subtracted from the rich stimulus and only added as a possibility of the individual having social anhedonia if it is greater than zero. A significant response bias indicates that an individual is more responsive to rewards [7]. The player was then shown a socially rewarding video but only to the rich stimuli. Response bias [7] was to be computed as :

$$log(b) = \frac{1}{2} * log[\frac{(Rich_correct * Lean_incorrect)}{(Rich_incorrect * Lean_correct)}] \qquad (1)$$

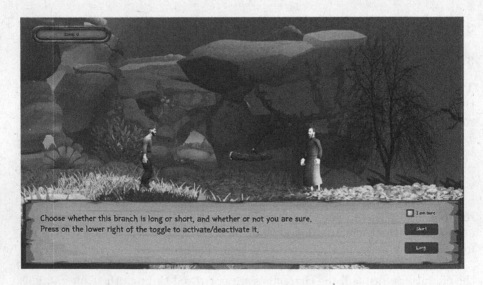

Fig. 1. Response Bias

This experiment suggests that players with low social anhedonia are more inclined to chose the rich stimulus when they are not sure as apposed to the lean stimulus [7] .

The research that carried this experiment suggested certain modifications to comply with the idea of "Corrections for Extreme Proportions" [7] . This idea implies that the previous question might present a 0 or 1 always if all the answers were respectively all correct or never correct. An extra question, along with a yes or no question, was added, and a new scale of measuring this deficit was used [16].

Effort-Expenditure for Rewards Task. In this part of the game, the player is offered a complex, highly rewarding task and an easy, less rewarding task and their choices are evaluated along with the gameplay.

As shown in Fig. 2 the helpful NPC approaches the player and hints to the player to dig in this area because he found some buried coins there before. After digging, the player is informed that they can earn more coins by digging some more. This is repeated three times after each dig. If the player chooses not to dig anymore at any given time despite the increased reward, it is hypothesized that this increases their possibility of exhibiting social anhedonia.

In another part of the game, the player comes across a treasure chest and in order to open it, the player is given a choice to play an immersive game of a sliding puzzle of three different difficulty levels, also shown in Fig. 2. The participant is told that the higher the difficulty, the higher the reward of opening the chest. Players that choose the easy game or choose to skip the task are deemed to have social anhedonia. Questions from the Self-Assessment Anhedonia Scale (SAAS) [9] were used when analyzing the game results.

3.3 Increased Altruistic Punishment

Two scenarios were added to test for increased altruistic punishment using the Ultimatum Game and the Public Goods Game. Questions from the Altruistic Personality Scale were added to the questionnaire to compare the answers to the game results.

Ultimatum Game: in the Ultimatum Game, shown in Fig. 3, the player comes across a treasure and is informed that somebody else has found this treasure first but is willing to share it with a 80–20 ratio in his favor. The player is also informed that if they reject this offer, neither one of them will get anything. If the player chooses to decline the offer, the player is then offered a more equitable divide. If the second offer is also rejected, the player is given a third offer. If all offers are rejected, the player is more likely to exhibit increased altruistic punishment.

Public Goods Game: in the Public Goods Game, shown in Fig. 4, the player and another NPC, that has been depicted as selfish and unhelpful, come across a magic well. It is explained that whatever amount of money put inside the well will be increased, then evenly distributed among them. The player is

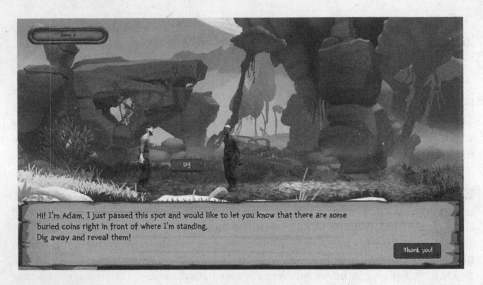

Fig. 2. EEFRT

Fig. 3. Ultimatum Game

told that the other NPC will not invest any of their money. It is then recorded whether the player invests or not.

3.4   Diminished Cooperativeness

Similar to affiliation and attachment, this class of social processing deficits also tackles the reward and evaluative brain systems [4], consequently, what is being

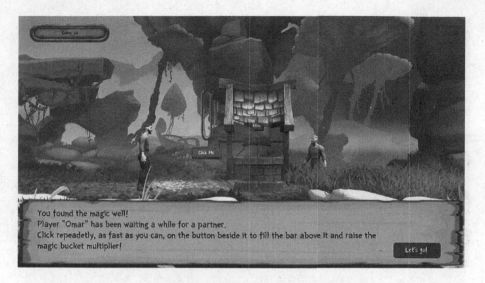

You found the magic well!
Player "Omar" has been waiting a while for a partner.
Click repeadetly, as fast as you can, on the button beside it to fill the bar above it and raise the magic bucket multiplier!

Let's go!

Fig. 4. Public Goods Game

observed is a pattern of behaviour. This is done using hints and through the Dictator Game. Questions from the Cooperative and Competitive Personality Scale (CCPS) [19] were used in the study questionnaire and the game results were compared to the questionnaire results.

Hints: The player comes across an NPC that has given them a hint before. This character will require information in the form of a hint that the player knows. Whether or not the player is willing to give them a hint as an act of cooperativeness is recorded. Along the way, the player was repeatedly asked if they would like to leave hints for other players to help them collect coins as well.

Dictator Game: The player is alerted by another NPC that there is a treasure up ahead. The player reaches the treasure first and is allowed to split it with the NPC if they want to. As the percentage of the treasure the player gives the NPC decreases, the player is expected to have a higher level of diminished cooperativeness.

3.5 Reduced Empathy

Reduced empathy depends on the brain's empathetic system [4], and two tasks were used to measure reduced empathy: the basic empathy accuracy task and evaluating audio excerpts depicting painful stimuli.

Basic Empathy Accuracy Task: the player comes across another NPC in need of help and is given the choice to help them or not. In the game, an old lady asks for help collecting the falling apples from the tree. If the player chooses to help her, they engage in a fast-paced mini-game where they move the basket below the tree to catch the falling apples as is illustrated in Fig. 5. The old lady proceeds to explain that her village has been raided, and they have not had food in a few days.

Fig. 5. Basic Empathy Accuracy Task

In another part of the game, the participant comes across a young boy asking for help fixing a water pipe to get water to his village from the river. If the player chooses to help him, they engage in an easy mini-game where they click on the pipe tiles to rotate them and get the water flowing.

Evaluating Audio Excerpts Depicting Painful Stimuli: the player crosses a cursed part of the jungle. During the crossing, the soundtrack switches to sad pleas and cries for help. Upon exit, the participant is then asked to rate the audio's disturbance, and their answers are recorded.

The players answered questions from the Basic Empathy Scale [17] (BES) in the study questionnaire to identify the effectiveness of the tasks in identifying the deficits they measure.

3.6   Theory of Mind (ToM)

The technique used to detect the theory of minds deficit was the second-order false belief test, which is a trust test. The player comes across a magic well and finds the untrustworthy NPC there. The NPC explains that he has just played this game and informs the player that to unlock it, they need to choose one of two mini-games. He hints to the player that the second mini-game is easier than the first. The player is first asked to rate their trust of this NPC on a scale of 0 to 10, 0 meaning the payer does not trust the NPC at all whereas 10 means they fully trust them. The player then chooses one of the mini-games to play and is later informed that the NPC has in fact lied and the second mini-game was not easier. The player is then asked if they were surprised by this revelation, considering that this specific NPC has been depicted as selfish throughout the game. If the player was surprised, this conveyed a deficit in trust processing.

Along with the previously mentioned cases, the player was asked questions from the Multidimensional Mentalizing Questionnaire (MMQ) to identify the effectiveness of the tasks in identifying the deficits they measure.

4   Results and Analysis

This study had 187 participants in total aged 18 to 28, where 54% were male (n=101) and 46% were female (n=86). The likelihood of a person having a specific shortage is measured on a spectrum or scale [18]. A Pearson correlation coefficient was computed to assess the linear relationship between each of the variable scores obtained by playing the game and their corresponding score obtained from the questionnaire. The goal was to find a positive, linear correlation between the gameplay data sets and questionnaire values to help find an answer to whether or not psychological tests can be gamified to detect social processing impairments. A summary of the results of each task can be seen in Table 1 below.

Table 1. Results Summary

Task	Correlation Coefficient	P-value	Hypothesis Result
Social Anhedonia	+0.84	P = 0.070	H1 Accepted
Diminished Cooperativeness	+0.82	P < 0.001	H2 Rejected
Reduced Empathy	+0.44	P < 0.001	H3 Rejected
Trust Processing (ToM)	+0.86	P < 0.001	H4 Rejected
Reaction Processing (ToM)	+0.50	P = 0.027	H5 Rejected

Social Anhedonia: the results showed there was a non-significant, strong, positive correlation between the social anhedonia score obtained by playing the game and the social anhedonia score obtained from the questionnaire, $r(185) = +.84$, $P = .070$. This means that the results reflected in the game are not strong enough to determine them to be statistically different from the results obtained from the questionnaire, given the sample size. Consequently, the null hypothesis H1 was accepted.

This failure to detect social anhedonia, despite the strong correlation, may have been due to people being able to lie about how they will act in social situations; however, this is not necessarily related to the gamification process of such tasks as they may lie if asked in person too. The sample size usually also has an effect on the result when too small in size and for this study it was large but perhaps not enough to show a significant difference between the results of the game and the results of the questionnaire for social anhedonia. It is also possible that social anhedonia cannot be properly detected using serious games.

Diminished Cooperativeness: the results showed there was a significant, strong, positive correlation between the diminished cooperativeness score obtained by playing the game and the diminished cooperativeness score obtained from the questionnaire, r(185)=+.82, $P < .001$. Consequently, the null hypothesis H2 was rejected.

Reduced Empathy: the results showed there was a significant, moderate, positive correlation between the reduced empathy score obtained by playing the game and the reduced empathy score obtained from the questionnaire, r(185) = +.44, $P < .001$. Consequently, the null hypothesis H3 was rejected.

Theory of Mind: for trust processing, the results showed there was a significant, strong, positive correlation between the trust processing score obtained by playing the game and the trust processing score obtained from the questionnaire, r(185) = +.86, $P<.001$. For reaction processing, the results showed there was a significant, moderate, positive correlation between the reaction processing score obtained by playing the game and the reaction processing score obtained from the questionnaire, r(185) = +.50, $P = .027$. Consequently, the null hypotheses H4 and H5 were rejected.

The moderate correlations for reduced empathy and reaction processing may have been due to the preferences of players in interacting with specific genders. Players were required to interact with NPCs that were mostly male and it may have affected the judgment of some players; however, this was not confirmed.

5   Conclusion and Future Work

A story-driven serious game with gamified psychological tests was developed in an attempt to detect the presence of social processing deficits in individuals. Throughout the gameplay, the results were collected and the participants were required to fill a questionnaire consisting of verified psychological questions that are used to detect social processing impairments. Four out of five null hypotheses were rejected, thus concluding that the detection of diminished cooperativeness, reduced empathy, trust processing and reaction processing is possible via gamification; however, the detection of social anhedonia was not successful.

Future work includes isolating each subcategory of impairments and testing it on its own. By incorporating more tests per individually tested impairment, the results may be improved further. This can also be done via virtual reality (VR) to emulate real-life scenarios, immersing the user in the game. It would also be highly beneficial if the game was used by participants with a confirmed diagnosis of social processing impairment to shed light on the accuracy of the game in testing for these impairments, since this was a major limitation to the study as none of the participants had a confirmed diagnosis of impacted social processing.

References

1. Taormina, R.J., Gao J.H.: Maslow and the motivation hierarchy: measuring satisfaction of the needs. Am. J. Psychol. (2013). https://doi.org/10.5406/amerjpsyc.126.2.0155

2. Erzen, E., Çikrikci, Ö.: The effect of loneliness on depression: a meta-analysis. Int. J. Soc. Psychiatry. Essential Facts. (2018). https://doi.org/10.1177/0020764018776349
3. El Bolock, A.: What is character computing? In: El Bolock, A., Abdelrahman, Y., Abdennadher, S. (eds.) Character Computing. HIS, pp. 1–16. Springer, Cham (2020). https://doi.org/10.1007/978-3-030-15954-2_1
4. Kupferberg, A., Bicks, L., Haslera, G.: Social functioning in major depressive disorder. Neurosci. Biobehav. Rev. **69**, 313–332 (2016)
5. Hirschfeld, R.M., et al.: Social functioning in depression: a review. J. Clin. Psychiatry **61**, 268–275 (2000)
6. Tan, M., Shallis, A., Barkus, E.: Social anhedonia and social functioning: loneliness as a mediator. PsyCh J. **9**(2), 280–289 (2020)
7. Chevallier, C., et al.: Measuring social motivation using signal detection and reward responsiveness. PLOS ONE **11**, e0167024 (2016)
8. Treadway, M.T., Buckholtz, J.W., Schwartzman, A.N., Lambert, W.E., Zald, D.H.: Worth the 'eefrt'? the effort expenditure for rewards task as an objective measure of motivation and anhedonia. PLoS ONE **4**, e6598 (2009)
9. Olivares, J.O., Berrios, G.E., Bousono, M.: The self-assessment anhedonia scale (SAAS). Neurol. Psychiatry Brain Res. **12**(3), 121–134 (2005)
10. Filkowski, M.M., Cochran, R.N., Haas, B.W.: Altruistic behavior: mapping responses in the brain. Neurosci. Neuroecon. **5**, 65 (2016)
11. Sian, R., Repetto, L., Gountouna, V., Nicodemus, K.K.: A review of neuroeconomic gameplay in psychiatric disorders. Mol. Psychiatry **25**(1), 67–81 (2019)
12. Tone, E.B., et al.: Social anxiety and social behavior: a test of predictions from an evolutionary model. Clin. Psychol. Sci. **7**(1), 110–126 (2018)
13. Morrison, J.: Understanding others by understanding the self: neurobiological models of empathy and their relevance to personality disorders. Can. Child Adolesc Psychiatr Rev. **13**, 68 (2004)
14. Lamba, A., Frank, M.J., FeldmanHall, O.: Anxiety impedes adaptive social learning under uncertainty. Psychol. Sci. **31**, 592–603 (2020)
15. Gori, A., Arcioni, A., Topino, E., Craparo, G., Grotto, R.L.: Development of a new measure for assessing mentalizing: the multidimensional mentalizing questionnaire (MMQ). Personalized Med. **11**, 305 (2021)
16. Hautus, M.J.: Corrections for extreme proportions and their biasing effects on estimated values of d'. Behav. Res. Methods Instrum. Comput. **27**, 46–51 (1995)
17. Carre, A., Stefaniak, N., D'Ambrosio, F., Bensalah, L., Besche-Richard, C.: The basic empathy scale in adults (BES-a): factor structure of a revised form. Psychol. Assess. **25**(3), 679 (2013)
18. Trevisan, D., Tafreshi, D., Slaney, K.L., Yager, J., Iarocci, G.: A psychometric evaluation of the multidimensional social competence scale (MSCS) for young adults. PLoS ONE **13**(11), e0206800 (2018)
19. Lu, S., Wing-Tung, A., Feng, J., Xiaofei, X., Paton, Y.: Cooperativeness and competitiveness as two distinct constructs: validating the cooperative and competitive personality scale in a social dilemma context. J. Int. Psychol. Int. J. Psychol. **48**(6), 1135–1147 (2012)

Workshop on Decision Support, Recommendation, and Persuasion in Artificial Intelligence (DeRePAI)

Workshop on Decision Support, Recommendation, and Persuasion in Artificial Intelligence (DeRePAI)

Decision support systems are applied in different fields to support individuals and groups, as well as to influence human behaviour and decision-making. Decision Support Systems are expected to facilitate decision-making while enhancing the quality of that decision, and Recommender Systems are expected to facilitate the choice process to maximize user satisfaction. In decision support and recommendation for groups, it is important to consider the heterogeneity and conflicting preferences of the participants. In addition, decision support and recommendation systems must have strategies for configuring preferences and acquiring user profiles in a nonintrusive (implicit) and time-consuming manner.

On the other hand, the acceptance and effectiveness of the hints and recommendations provided by the system depends on several factors. First, they must be appropriate for the objectives and profile of the user, but also, they must be understandable and supported by evidence (the user must understand why the recommendation is provided and why it is good for him/her). Thus, it is necessary to provide these systems with a mechanism that supports suggestions by means of artificial intelligence. In this way, computational argumentation is a technique that builds upon the natural way humans provide reasons (i.e., arguments) why a recommendation is suggested and should be accepted. Therefore, a system that uses these technologies must be persuasive to obtain the desired results by influencing human behaviour.

In this workshop, we explored the links between decision-support, recommendation, and persuasion to discuss strategies to facilitate the decision/choice process by individuals and groups. This workshop aimed to be a discussion forum on the latest trends and ongoing challenges in the application of artificial intelligence technologies in this area.

Topics that were relevant for this workshop included especially applications, but also theoretical approaches, based on:

- Decision Support Systems (DSS), Group Decision Support Systems (GDSS), and Recommender Systems (RS)
- Multi-Criteria Decision Analysis
- Context-Aware Recommendation
- Cognitive and Affective Aspects in Decision-Making and Recommendations (Emotions, Personality, Mood, Motivations, among others)
- Argumentation and Persuasion
- Natural Language Processing, Argument Mining
- Machine Learning and Deep Learning Algorithms in DSS/GDSS and RS
- Cognition and Persuasive Technology
- Human-Computer Interaction in Persuasive Technology
- Expert Systems, Knowledge-Based Systems and Information Systems
- Knowledge Representation
- User Modelling

- Interdisciplinary Applications: Online Trading, e-Health and Well-Being, Industry, Tourism and Leisure, Assisted Learning Environments, Sustainability, Energy Efficiency, Smart Cities and Dynamic Environments in general.

Organization

Organizing Committee

Jaume Jordán   Universitat Politècnica de València, Spain
João Carneiro   Polytechnic Institute of Porto, Portugal
Goreti Marreiros   Polytechnic Institute of Porto, Portugal
Stella Heras   Universitat Politècnica de València, Spain

Program Committee

Patrícia Alves   Polytechnic Institute of Porto, Portugal
Andreas Brännström   Umeå University, Sweden
Carlos Carrascosa   Universitat Politècnica de València, Spain
Vicente Julián   Universitat Politècnica de València, Spain
Diogo Martinho   Polytechnic Institute of Porto, Portugal
Jorge Meira   Polytechnic Institute of Porto, Portugal
Juan Carlos Nieves   Umeå University, Sweden
Paulo Novais   Universidade do Minho, Portugal
Víctor Sánchez-Anguix   Universitat Politècnica de València, Spain
Ichiro Satoh   National Institute of Informatics, Japan

Trust-based Negotiation in Multiagent Systems: A Systematic Review

Ricardo Barbosa[1,2]([✉]) [ID], Ricardo Santos[1] [ID], and Paulo Novais[2] [ID]

[1] CIICESI, Escola Superior de Tecnologia e Gestão, Politécnico do Porto, Porto, Portugal
{rmb,rjs}@estg.ipp.pt
[2] ALGORITMI Center, University of Minho, Braga, Portugal
pjon@di.uminho.pt

Abstract. In this work, we conducted a systematic review on trust-based negotiation in Multiagent Systems (MAS), through a bibliometric analysis over the past 25 years of research publications, on three of the most popular scientific databases (Google Scholar, Scopus, and Web of Science). Our analysis reveals that this research topic is regaining interest, after some oscillating years, and the impact of its contributions is equivalent to other equally important research variants like ontology and argumentation (in a negotiation scenario). Discarding the human-to-agent trust challenges, we only focus on agent-to-agent trust concepts, and we performed an analysis of the different types of trust dimensions, using the findings and concerns of past review works, as we identify and select the dimensions that, in our opinion, have the most potential to lead the research advances on the topic of trust in MAS. Furthermore, we discuss the current challenges and open issues associated with those trust dimensions, and how current advancements in the literature could provide insights for the solution of those challenges, or even the finding of new research paths.

Keywords: Trust · Negotiation · Multiagent Systems

1 Introduction

It is difficult to pinpoint the exact first negotiation in history, as negotiations have been a part of human interaction since the beginning of civilization, but we can assume that could be related to some form of basic transaction (an exchange of goods) between two actors. The question is, how did they trust each other without a previous history of interaction between them? How could they know that the other party would fulfil their part of the agreement? They simply trusted each other, as one should expect that trust (in a negotiation context) to be defined as the expectation that the other party will act in a way that is mutually beneficial and will not take any type of advantage. Some definitions of trust include keywords like positive expectations or willingness to be vulnerable, and

D. Durães et al. (Eds.): PAAMS 2023, CCIS 1838, pp. 133–144, 2023.
https://doi.org/10.1007/978-3-031-37593-4_11

even the Oxford Dictionary classifies trust as "to have confidence in somebody", perhaps the most commonly used definition is given by Rousseau et al. [22] that classifies trust between humans as "a psychological state comprising the intention to accept vulnerability based upon positive expectations of the intentions or behaviour of another". As for negotiation the most acceptable definition is given as "the process by which a joint decision is made by two or more parties. The parties first verbalize contradictory demands and then move towards agreement by a process of concession making or search for new alternative" [20].

Through the years, several authors have suggested different main types of trust, three to be specific [15]: (1) deterrence-based trust: the basic form of trust that states that actors must trust the other will follow through with promises made during the negotiation; (2) calculus-based-trust: where the trustor should rationally decide to trust the other party, not because of fear of negative consequences, but to achieve positive consequences; (3) knowledge-based trust: a form of trust beyond trusting that the other party will follow through with their promises, that resides in the ability that one actor could understand the others so well, to accurately predict their behaviour during a negotiation process.

With the emergence of autonomous agents, the capability to engage in a negotiation and argue about its outcome was quickly recognized as a challenge. As result, three broad topics for research on negotiation where defined: (1) negotiation protocols; (2) negotiation objects; (3) reasoning models [5,13,14]. An agent is described as an entity that senses the environment and acts on it, performing a task continuously, with a strong autonomy, in a shifting environment, while coexisting with other entities and processes. Multiagent Systems (MAS) aim to provide both principles for construction of complex systems involving multiple agents and mechanisms for coordination of independent agent behaviour [25]. MAS, which consists of multiple autonomous agents with distinct goals, that communicate with each other and with the environment with a focus on understanding the latter and reason upon intelligent models, coordinating their efforts to achieve their goals and the one of the ecosystem where they are inserted in, and negotiating their preferences [2,17]. To achieve that, each agent must be equipped with trust mechanisms, that can be based on mathematical principles or extracted from cognitive characteristics that mimic their human counterpart.

Intrigued by the current state of this research field, in this work we conduct a bibliometric analysis over three of the main research databases, looking to understand the evolution of research interest towards trust in negotiation-based scenarios in MAS. Additionally, we address past review works to discuss the different types of dimensions that can be associated with trust and the current challenges and open issues in modeling trust in a negotiation scenario. Despite trust having two meanings in this context, namely trust of humans in the agent that represent them, and agent trust in other agents, we will be focused on the latter.

The remainder of this work is structured as follows. In Sect. 2 we present an empirical quantitative analysis based on a bibliometric analysis to obtain insights regarding the research interest of the subject of trust in negotiation in MAS over the past 25 years; Sect. 3 contains an analysis of some review documents on this subject, with a focus on some mentioned trust dimensions, namely, paradigm type, information sources, trust semantics, trust preferences, initial trust, and open environments; Sect. 4 complements the previous section with an elaboration on the challenges and open issues associated with each trust dimension described previously, including the mentioning of some possible research paths. This work concludes (Sect. 5) with a discussion of the actual state of research regarding trust-based negotiation in MAS, its strengths, limitations, and a reflection over possible future research paths.

2 An Empirical Quantitative Analysis

To understand the research activity regarding the subject of trust in negotiation between agents in multiagent system, we conducted a bibliometric analysis, a quantitative method used to evaluate and measure scientific literature and research activity in a particular field or discipline.

Such quantitative analysis was conducted according to the guidelines presented by the work of Donthu et al. [7], that defines the required steps, namely: (1) define the scope; (2) choose the techniques; (3) collect the data; (4) run the bibliometric analysis and report the findings.

As the scope of this analysis, we have interest in examining the growth in publication rates (and impact of those publications) over time in this field, and analysing the evolution of research topics. We intend to obtain a general overview on the scientific interest for this field, and understand if that interest has shifted through the years.

For the techniques we have selected a combination of performance analysis and science mapping techniques, namely: publication-related metrics; citation-related metrics; citation-and-publication-related metrics; and co-word analysis. The performance analysis techniques are the most common type of analysis, with number of publications and citations per year being the most prominent measures. Regarding the science mapping analysis, a co-word analysis is focused on words and examines the actual content of the publication itself. Those words can be found in the title, abstract, author keywords, index keywords, or the full text.

The data collection set can be divided into subtasks. We first need to select the data sources (the scientific databases), then we need to define the queries to conduct such research, and finally we want to automate this data gathering process using external tools. For the scientific databases we have selected:

- Google Scholar[1]: being one of the most popular scientific databases, this platform provides a search across many disciplines and sources. Such characteristic means that the results present on this platform are often found in others, which can lead to the duplication of data;
- Scopus[2]: a widely used bibliographic database that indexes scientific research output from a broad range of disciplines. It provides a comprehensive platform

---

[1] https://www.scholar.google.com.
[2] https://www.elsevier.com/.

136   R. Barbosa et al.

for tracking citations and analysing research impact, as well as for identifying emerging trends and collaborations in specific fields of study;
- Web of Science[3]: this scientific database platform, now maintained by the Intellectual Property and Science business of Thomson Reuters, was originally produced by the Institute for Scientific Information as comprehensive citation search across multiple databases.

As for the search query, it is a combination of title keywords and co-word analysis. Each search result must contain the words 'negotiation' and 'agent' in the title of the document, and the keyword 'trust' must be present in the corpus. To better evaluate any existing trend, we selected a period of 25 years (from 1998 to 2023 (at the time of this publication)), divided into five-year intervals. To execute this search, and collect the data, we have selected the 'Publish or Perish' tool developed by Harzing [11]. This tool also provides key metrics that will be used on our analysis, namely:

- Total Publications (TP): total number of results returned by the search;
- Total Citations (TC): total number of citations returned by the search;
- Citation Years (CY): number of years from the earliest year found in the currently selected results to the year of the search. Is given by a subtraction of the current year (i.e. 2023) by the year of the older publication in the search result (e.g. 1998);
- Total Citations per Year (TC/Y): average number of citations per year, given by TC/CY;
- Total citations per Paper: the sum of the citation counts across all papers, divided by the total number of papers. Given by TC/TP.
- g-index: Egghe's g-index, returning the g number of publications receiving at least g^2 citations (measure of impact).

Finally, our findings (represented by Table 1) allow us to conclude that the topic of trust in negotiation between agents in a MAS has been losing quantitative interest along the years. By looking at the results obtained from the GS database, we can observe that the TP has peaked in the 2008–2013 year year interval, but the overall impact of those publications were more prominent in the 2003–2008 interval. Although the results obtained from the SC and WoS platform are expressive low for an efficient bibliometric analysis, they allow us to understand that such tendency is also replicated in those platforms. With an expectable decreasing tendency in the TC metric (because each consequent interval has less CY), we note a small inversion of this descending tendency in interest found in later years (namely the last year interval of the data) that contains a small increase in TP. However, such event cannot invert the decrease in impact of such publications, observable by the decreasing value of the *g-index* metric.

Curious about how this topic of research is comparable to others, we conducted another bibliometric analysis, following the same methods and sequence as before, with the following alterations: the query maintains the 'negotiation'

---

[3] https://apps.webofknowledge.com/.

Table 1. Bibliometric analysis result for publications with 'negotiation' and 'agent' keywords present in the title of the document, and the keyword 'trust' present on its corpus, across different scientific databases (GS - Google Scholar; SC - Scopus; WS - Web of Science), over the past 25 years, contextualized with specific year intervals.

Metrics	Year Interval														
	1998–2003			2003–2008			2008–2013			2013–2018			2018–2023		
	GS[a]	SC	WoS	GS[a]	SC	WoS	GS[a]	SC	WoS	GS[a]	SC	WoS	GS[a]	SC	WoS
TP	28	6	4	68	10	7	80	15	12	38	6	3	47	10	4
TC	1,251	135	86	1,344	51	115	909	41	69	464	53	23	166	27	9
CY	25	23	22	20	20	16	15	15	15	9	9	6	4	5	4
TC/Y	50.04	5.87	3.74	67.20	2.55	6.76	60.60	2.73	4.31	51.56	5.89	3.29	41.50	5.40	1.80
TC/P	44.68	22.50	21.5	19.76	5.10	16.43	11.36	2.73	5.75	12.21	8.83	7.67	3.53	2.70	2.25
g index	28	6	–	36	7	–	28	5	–	21	6	–	11	5	–

[a] The nature of this particular platform means that it can contain search results that are equally present on other platforms

and 'agent' keywords in the title of the document, but the co-word analysis is based on the keywords 'trust', 'protocol', 'ontology', and 'argumentation'; instead of getting five-year intervals result, we search for results in a single 25-year interval (from 1998–2023).

The findings reported on Table 2 allow us to understand that, contrarily to what could be anticipated, with an exception to the research performed on 'protocol', the research interest on 'trust' is comparable to other research topics. Despite a smaller TP count, the results on 'trust' show us a comparable TC values, and this tendency is also found in the TC/Y metric. More important, when excluding the 'protocol' results, we can observe a comparable overall impact measurement between results.

3   Types of Trust in Negotiation

Our analysis is initially based on the finds on the work of Granatyr et al. [8], which itself is a compilation and extension of previous reviews on this subject [1,6,9,12,16,19,21,23].

In their review work, authors define the trust and reputation models in a set of dimensions, which can have a set of values. Focusing on the existing dimensions presented by the Granatyr et al. work [8] we have selected six dimensions to be the focus of our analysis, and seven sub-dimensions. As for the dimensions we will address the paradigm type, information sources, trust semantics, trust preferences, initial trust, and open environment. For the sub dimensions we have select the sub-dimensions of the paradigm type: numeric; cognitive;

Table 2. Bibliometric analysis result for publications with 'negotiation' and 'agent' keywords present in the title of the document, and a specific keyword present on its corpus, across different scientific databases (GS - Google Scholar; SC - Scopus; WS - Web of Science), from 1998–2023 (25 years).

Metrics	Keyword											
	Trust			Protocol			Ontology			Argumentation		
	GS[a]	SC	WoS	GS[a]	SC	WoS	GS[a]	SC	WoS	GS[a]	SC	WoS
TP	65	41	30	882	200	211	248	78	53	322	53	43
TC	4,061	299	300	12,310	3,442	1,642	3,266	588	295	4,976	575	497
CY	25	23	25	25	25	25	25	22	25	25	22	21
TC/Y	162.44	13.00	10.07	492.40	137.68	79.42	130.64	26.73	15.05	199.04	26.14	23.67
TC/P	15.20	7.29	13.13	13.96	17.21	9.03	13.17	7.54	5.96	15.45	10.85	11.56
g index	57	16	–	83	49	–	49	21	–	60	23	–

[a]The nature of this particular platform means that it can contain search results that are equally present on other platforms

and hybrid. And four sub-dimensions of information sources: direct interaction; direct observation; witness information; and certified reputation. We have selected those dimensions, as we believe that they can be the most influential for future advances and development in this research path.

Paradigm Type.

This dimension, composed of numeric, cognitive, and hybrid sub-dimensions, is the most commonly found in literature. The numerical paradigm is vastly the most researched variant of this dimension, and the majority approaches are based on statistical methods to compute trust, including Bayesian probabilities, probability distribution, Dempster-Shafer functions, and machine learning. They are based on a numerical aggregation of past interactions, and produce a set of objective probabilities that agents will, correctly, execute a given task, and share close to none characteristics to human behaviour.

On the other hand, the cognitive paradigm is built to equip agents with human behaviours through the usage of cognitive processes to calculate trust. They are strongly related to beliefs and mental states that agents have, and trust is a measurement of these beliefs and the decision to trust, or not trust, another agent. Such characteristics link this approach to cognitive architectures, like BDI agents.

There is a possibility for both sub-dimensions to coexist in the same MAS, and this resulted in hybrid models based on beliefs (cognitive) and use numerical aggregations (numerical).

Information Sources.

Agents extract data from other agents, or environment, and use it to calculate trust and reputation values. Using the most simple form of transaction/negotiation as a global example, where A gives x to B, and B gives y to A in exchange (a simple trade of goods), there are several ways to extract data.

Direct interaction is considered the most relevant information source, requiring several interactions to be useful (which can be a challenge in MAS). Is one of the first computation trust models and occurs when A needs a historical set of interactions with B to evaluate the trust in the next transaction/negotiation process.

Direct observation removes the necessity for a history of past interactions between agents, since an agent can observe other agent behaviour in past or current interactions to decide about engaging with it (most applicable to MAS). Some observation characteristics include feedback provided by the agent, percentage of positive reviews, prior actions, and the results of contracts.

Witness information occurs when an agent does not own direct information, and have a necessity to 'ask' other agents. Agent A needs to interact with agent B, but query agent C to obtain its opinion about B. The trust (or reputation) value is then calculated through the aggregation of opinions who had some interaction with the trustee.

The usefulness of certified reputation is shown in first interaction scenarios between agents. To evaluate agent B, agent A will perform a direct query to B regarding his evaluations (a recommendation letter like behaviour). Sharing a similar concept to witness information, this approach can be an answer to its performance problems of due to a low computation cost to find witnesses, only if the model is able to deal with the dishonest manipulation of the list of witnesses.

Trust Semantics.

While most models measure trust in a single value, this dimension relies on ontologies to define trust as a composite measure. Instead of defining the outcome of a negotiation process as 'my trust in you is 0.7 on a 0–1 scale', we can specify their trust in the capability to deliver a product/service, and their trust in the (perceived) quality of such product/service. Meaning that instead of relying on a single generalist trust metric, each agent is capable of deciding which feature is the most important according to its needs, and even defining weights for each feature (e.g. a weight of 0.4 for product delivery and 0.6 for product quality) (i.e. trust preferences).

Initial Trust.

Like the first ever negotiation in history, a negotiation process can start without a previous definition of an initial trust. When a model assumes that trust is already present at any given, it is neglecting an important step in the initial set up of trust, and obstructing the entrance of new agents in the environment by mitigating their possibilities for success.

To address this major difficulty in building trust for newcomers, some authors have using machine learning models to predict trust values based on expectation, recommender systems, or alter the range of reputation values by including a negative dimension expanding its possibilities to any value between −1 and 1 where newcomers enter the network with an initial value of reputation set to zero.

Open Environments.
When agents are allowed to enter and leave a MAS environment as they please, this generates uncertainty about the environment, and the concept of trust becomes a greater challenge. Knowing that, authors [12] have stated relevant characteristics for a model to address this type of environments: information sources can be replaced, but their historical data must be persisted to avoid the comeback of an agent being mistaken by a newcomer and delete their past behaviour; must be decentralized to allow each agent to have its own evaluation mechanism; and be robust and secure against intrusive and cheater agents. Although many suggestions where made to solve those issues, the approach with most potential relies on the usage of digital certification to correctly recognize agents.

Granatyr et al. review over the most significant trust and reputation models published over the past two decades [8], concluded that the majority of the significant results (those with characteristics of MASs) are related to negotiation (51%), and the remaining are related to coalition, argumentation, and recommendation. The report addresses the increase in number of cognitive and hybrid models (16%), but the mathematical models are still predominant in the literature. A possible explanation for that growth tendency can be associated with a growth of the interest in applications closest to human behaviour, that consider cognitive aspects like argumentation or reasoning.

As for the information sources dimension, they concluded that most models employ direct interaction and witness information. This is explained by the necessities of the majority of scenarios where negotiation is used (e-commerce), and those models are the most common approaches to extract information from other agents, with direct interaction considered to be the most valuable information source. Nonetheless, they reported an increase in the number of models that employ different information sources, including certified reputation, which indicate a growing interest in finding new ways to extract information from agents and from an environment.

They also noted an increase in open environment dimension, that is motivated by the open characteristics of MAS models. Such growth can represent a direct proportionality between open MAS and trust and reputation models. If such argument is representative of the future reality, we can expect further developments in this dimension.

Regarding the trust semantics dimension, it shares a relationship with trust preferences, and this tendency would accompany further developments in this research subject. Contrary to previous reviews that report the lack of interest for further develop those dimensions [16], more recently several models are starting to incorporate them.

Finally, they conclude that despite the implementations of different dimensions in a single model is not common practice, this scenario only exists due to the efforts of contribution to a specific dimension rather than the trust concept as a whole. There is no correlation between the number of scenarios per model and the quality of it, meaning that the usage of fewer dimensions are not necessary worse than the inclusion of a wide variability of dimensions, and vice versa. This means that the identification of the best model or the best combination of dimensions is still an open question.

4 Challenges and Open Issues in Modeling Trust in Negotiation

While the representation of trust between agents in a MAS can be a simple concept to understand and apply (in its simple version is a numerical value between zero and one), further developments in trust-based negotiation in MAS, and its dimensions, are still facing some challenges. This is not a novel concern, since authors are notorious for indicate that user trust and trust between agents are essential for the success of MAS systems [3].

The fact that most trust and reputation models are domain and context specific, introduces an initial barrier to the development of MAS since it is not clear which model would be indicated for that environment, since most models often use particular variables. While noting the efforts related to the development of tools and frameworks regarding the selection and construction of a model for a MAS, there is still no framework capable of dealing with the most recent approaches to trust and reputation models [8]. This is also accompanied by a growth in open environments where agents can enter and leave an environment at any time, which represents a challenge for the initial trust dimensions. However, recent works have emerged with possible solutions to the problems identified by those dimensions through the usage and implementation of a blockchain [10,18,24].

While this challenges occur when addressing a simple negotiation scenario like a trade of goods between two agents, agent loses opportunities with other agents by interacting with just one agent at a time, cutting itself from information which it might have been generated during that negotiation. As result, such implementations become even more complex when the agent holds simultaneous negotiations, and could add an n-fold complexity in modeling trust in large-scale MAS [14].

While the developments in cognitive approaches diminish the virtual distance between humans and agents, such link to cognitive architectures can also inherit some existing problems regarding trust in negotiation between humans. As such, further developments could be slowed down by a lack of development regarding the subject of trust between humans and being limited by a close relationship and emulation of human to human negotiation.

As for other dimensions, they share a similar challenge: the need to trust a third party. Even direct interaction and observation still requires the existence of an enforcer that will guarantee the execution of the negotiation, which represents a recursive trust problem since, in most cases, each agent is always bound to trust a third-party entity (the enforcer). The same can be said for witness information dimension, where each agent needs to trust the opinion of other agents to even start to formulate their trust values regarding a specific agent that intends to negotiate with. However, some advances have been made in this direction with works trying to offer a solution to the need to trust third entities, by replacing them with more reliable and trustworthy environments [4].

5   Conclusion

Despite a recurrent lack of mentioning discussing the subject of negotiation in MAS, trust is an implicit constant that could dictate the success, or failure, of such models and implementations. This topic has accompanied the initial definitions of concepts needed to have a successful negotiation between agents in a MAS, alongside with negotiation protocols, negotiation objects, and reasoning models.

Although it had an oscillation in quantitative metrics through the research years, data suggests that this topic of research is currently on an ascending tendency and, overall, it has been on par with other fields of research like protocol, ontology, and argumentation, on impact metrics (*g-index*), number of total citations, total citations per year, and total citations per paper. This quantitative comparison suggests that, despite an apparent decrease in publications on the past decade, there is still significant research interest for this subject and new findings are emerging that could solve the challenges with current research (e.g. new machine learning models, or even the usage of blockchain to reinforce the concept of trust between agents, and removing recurrent trust challenges associated with the usage of third-party actors that enforce the outcome of a negotiation).

While we do believe that the dimensions of paradigm type, information sources, trust semantics, trust preferences, initial trust, and open environment (and some of its sub-dimensions) have the potential to lead the research advances in the future and change the tendency of single dimension scientific contributions even when the model contains more than one dimension (as we believe that the application of these dimensions can generate a solid base framework). However, even if those dimensions would be successfully applied in a single model, we would still not find a solution to some current challenges.

As we keep narrowing the gap between agent cognition and humans, and emulate and mimic human behaviour in agents, we are distancing ourselves from possible research paths that could offer more insights about the limits of trust-based negotiation in MAS. For example, by shifting the focus of trust from agent-to-agent to a trust in the environment, we could have potential solutions to the issues regarding open environments, or even the management of first interaction negotiation between new agents. We already have physical examples of this type of trust in the process, like the European Accident Report Form, that allow complete strangers to negotiate and reach an agreement without previous history of interaction between them, by having trust in the environment, that will enforce the outcome of the negotiation. As result, we strongly believe in a research path where the allocation of trust to the environment, instead of agents, can contribute to the success and advancements of this research subject, and offer some solutions to challenges that MAS are currently facing.

Acknowledgements. This work has been supported by national funds through FCT – Fundação para a Ciência e Tecnologia (Portuguese Foundation for Science and Technology) through the Projects UIDB/04728/2020, UIDP/04728/2020, and the Ricardo Barbosa doctoral Grant with the reference UI/BD/154187/2022.

References

1. Aljazzaf, Z.M., Perry, M., Capretz, M.A.: Online trust: definition and principles. In: 2010 Fifth International Multi-conference on Computing in the Global Information Technology, pp. 163–168, September 2010. https://doi.org/10.1109/iccgi.2010.17
2. Amato, A., Martino, B.D., Scialdone, M., Venticinque, S.: Multi-agent negotiation of decentralized energy production in smart micro-grid. In: IDC (2014)
3. Baarslag, T., Hendrikx, M.J.C., Hindriks, K.V., Jonker, C.M.: Learning about the opponent in automated bilateral negotiation: a comprehensive survey of opponent modeling techniques. Autonom. Agents Multi-Agent Syst. **30**(5), 849–898 (2016). https://doi.org/10.1007/s10458-015-9309-1
4. Barbosa, R., Santos, R., Novais, P.: Smart contracts based on multi-agent negotiation. In: De La Prieta, F., El Bolock, A., Durães, D., Carneiro, J., Lopes, F., Julian, V. (eds.) PAAMS 2021. CCIS, vol. 1472, pp. 104–114. Springer, Cham (2021). https://doi.org/10.1007/978-3-030-85710-3_9
5. Beer, M., d'Inverno, M., Luck, M., Jennings, N., Preist, C., Schroeder, M.: Negotiation in multi-agent systems. Knowl. Eng. Rev. **14**(3), 285–289 (1999). https://doi.org/10.1017/s0269888999003021
6. Carter, J., Bitting, E., Ghorbani, A.A.: Reputation formalization for an information-sharing multi-agent system. Comput. Intell. **18**(4), 515–534 (2002). https://doi.org/10.1111/1467-8640.t01-1-00201
7. Donthu, N., Kumar, S., Mukherjee, D., Pandey, N., Lim, W.M.: How to conduct a bibliometric analysis: an overview and guidelines. J. Bus. Res. **133**, 285–296 (2021). https://doi.org/10.1016/j.jbusres.2021.04.070
8. Granatyr, J., Botelho, V., Lessing, O.R., Scalabrin, E.E., Barthès, J.P., Enembreck, F.: Trust and reputation models for multiagent systems. ACM Comput. Surv. **48**(2), 1–42 (2015). https://doi.org/10.1145/2816826
9. Grandison, T., Sloman, M.: A survey of trust in internet applications. IEEE Commun. Surv. Tutorials **3**(4), 2–16 (2000). https://doi.org/10.1109/comst.2000.5340804
10. Grosse, N., Guerpinar, T., Henke, M.: Blockchain-enabled trust in intercompany networks applying the agency theory, July 2021. https://doi.org/10.1145/3475992.3475994
11. Harzing, A.W.: Publish or perish (2007). https://harzing.com/resources/publish-or-perish
12. Huynh, T.D., Jennings, N.R., Shadbolt, N.: FIRE: an integrated trust and reputation model for open multi-agent systems. In: European Conference on Artificial Intelligence, pp. 23–27, August 2004
13. Jennings, N.R., Faratin, P., Lomuscio, A., Parsons, S., Sierra, C., Wooldridge, M.: Automated negotiation: prospects, methods and challenges. Group Dec. Negot. **10**(2), 199–215 (2001). https://doi.org/10.1023/a:1008746126376
14. Kraus, S., Lehmann, D.: Designing and building a negotiating automated agent. Comput. Intell. **11**(1), 132–171 (1995). https://doi.org/10.1111/j.1467-8640.1995.tb00026.x

15. Lewicki, R.J., Polin, B.: Trust and negotiation, pp. 161–190, June 2013. https://doi.org/10.4337/9781781005903.00016
16. Lu, G., Lu, G., Lu, J., Yao, S., Yip, J.: A review on computational trust models for multi-agent systems. Open Inf. Sci. J. 325–331 (2009). https://doi.org/10.2174/1874947x00902010018
17. Okumura, M., Fujita, K., Ito, T.: An implementation of collective collaboration support system based on automated multi-agent negotiation. In: Complex Automated Negotiations (2013)
18. Pinheiro, P., Santos, R., Barbosa, R.: Improving collaboration in industry 4.0: the usage of blockchain for knowledge representation. In: De La Prieta, F., et al. (eds.) PAAMS 2020. CCIS, vol. 1233, pp. 226–237. Springer, Cham (2020). https://doi.org/10.1007/978-3-030-51999-5_19
19. Pinyol, I., Sabater-Mir, J.: Computational trust and reputation models for open multi-agent systems: a review. Artif. Intell. Rev. **40**(1), 1–25 (2013). https://doi.org/10.1007/s10462-011-9277-z
20. Pruitt, D.G.: Introduction: an overview of negotiation. In: Pruitt, D.G. (ed.) Negotiation Behavior, pp. 1–17. Academic Press (1981). https://doi.org/10.1016/B978-0-12-566250-5.50006-9
21. Ramchurn, S.D., Huynh, D., Jennings, N.R.: Trust in multi-agent systems. Knowl. Eng. Rev. **19**(1), 1–25 (2004). https://doi.org/10.1017/s0269888904000116
22. Rousseau, D.M., Sitkin, S.B., Burt, R.S., Camerer, C.: Not so different after all: a cross-discipline view of trust. Acad. Manag. Rev. **23**(3), 393–404 (1998). https://doi.org/10.5465/amr.1998.926617
23. Sabater, J., Sierra, C.: Review on computational trust and reputation models. Artif. Intell. Rev. **24**(1), 33–60 (2005). https://doi.org/10.1007/s10462-004-0041-5
24. Samuel, O., Javaid, N., Khalid, A., Imrarn, M., Nasser, N.: A trust management system for multi-agent system in smart grids using blockchain technology, December 2020. https://doi.org/10.1109/GLOBECOM42002.2020.9348231
25. Stone, P., Veloso, M.: Multiagent systems: a survey from a machine learning perspective:. autonomous Robots **8**, 345–383 (2000). https://doi.org/10.1023/a:1008942012299, http://www.dtic.mil/docs/citations/ADA333248

Negotiation Algorithm for Multi-agent Pickup and Delivery Tasks

Takumi Iida[1]([✉]), Itsuki Noda[2][ID], Toyohiro Kondo[3], Hiroki Soda[3],
Naoharu Ueda[3], Masamichi Nawa[3], and Norihiko Kato[3]

[1] Graduate School of Information Science and Technology, Hokkaido University,
Sapporo 060-0808, Japan
iida_t@eis.hokudai.ac.jp
[2] Faculty of Information Science and Technology, Hokkaido University,
Sapporo 060-0808, Japan
i.noda@ist.hokudai.ac.jp
[3] Toyota Industries Corporation, Aichi 474-8601, Japan
{toyohiro.kondo,hiroki.soda,naoharu.ueda,masamichi.nawa,
norihiko.kato}@mail.toyota-shokki.co.jp

Abstract. We propose a task-allocation procedure that includes pre-planning and a resource reallocation method using negotiation for the path management of multiple carry robots (agents) in automated warehouses. Task-allocation to agents and path-management as a resource allocation are key factors for determining the performance of a warehouse. We assumed these two factors as separated, independent problems, and applied the preplanning and negotiation method, respectively. The proposed methods were evaluated by simulation experiments with several problem settings. The results of the experiments show that the proposed method did improve the performance of the warehouse and the usage of agents with reasonable computational complexity.

Keywords: Multi-Agent Pickup and Delivery (MAPD) · Negotiation · Multi-Agent Path Finding (MAPF) · Task Assignment

1 Introduction

Multiagent pickup and delivery (MAPD) is a key problem in the application of multi-agent systems [4]. In a MAPD problem, a number of tasks, each of which consists of a pickup position, a good to deliver, and its destination, are given. These tasks are assigned to multiple mobile agents (robots). Generally, the main problem is to optimize the assignment of the tasks to agents and the application of certain restrictions, such as the avoidance of collisions between agents, the limitation of mobile spaces, and the task order.

Real-life applications of MAPD vary widely, including aircraft-towing vehicles [6], warehouse robots [1,9], and the behaviors of game characters in video games [8]. This work focuses on the application of MAPD to control shuttle robots in an automatic warehouse. Here, the most important issues are smooth performance and exclusive control to avoid collisions between the robots in a restricted network of warehouse corridors.

Online solution is also an important requirement for MAPD because, generally, the number of delivery tasks is large in a MAPD problem, making it hard to find an optimal solution offline before execution [5]. Therefore, in real applications, finding semi-optimal solutions online is necessary.

In this work, we establish an online procedure to assign given tasks to shuttle robots working in an automatic warehouse.

Section 2 describes previous related work on PAMD, Sect. 3 defines the problem addressed in this paper, Sect. 4 describes the new Rollong Horizon Negoriation proposed in this paper, Sect. 5 provides an overview and results of a simulation simulating a real warehouse, and Sect. 6 provides a summary and future perspectives.

2   Background and Related Work

Multi-agent path finding (MAPF) solutions are evaluated in terms of flowtime (total time taken for an agent to reach a goal) and makespan (maximum time taken for an agent to reach a goal). Finding an optimal solution to the MAPF problem is known to be NP-hard [5].

The optimal solution for MAPF is known to be a two-stage algorithm, CBS [7], comprising a high-level search for a conflict tree (CT), in which each node represents a constraint, and a low-level search for the shortest path within the constraints of the CT nodes. CA* [8], a suboptimal solution method, uses A* in a graph consisting of a time axis and two-dimensional single coordinates to plan, based on the priority of each agent, to avoid the agents in that order colliding. This is similar to the study of autonomous intersection management, which considers multi-agent path planning at intersections where many agents simultaneously enter the same location [2]. In this paper, the first come, first served scheme was used as the control policy in the horizontal aisle, introduced later in this paper, where agents can enter first if they reserve later and do not collide.

MAPF is often a "one-shot" problem, whereby, each agent is assigned only one starting point and one goal point, whereas in a real warehouse, tasks are assigned continuously. Therefore, lifelong MAPF, an extension of MAPF, has been proposed. Not all MAPD problems have solutions, but well-formed MAPD instances and their solutions have been proposed. Known MAPD solutions include TP, TPTS [4], and RHCR [3]. Basically, TP and TPTS are algorithms that execute tasks where the h-value between themselves and the task is small, without considering other agents. RHCR is an algorithm that divides the problem into problems of a defined window size and solves them as MAPF problems.

3   Problem Definition

We formalized MAPD as follows: Suppose a tupple $\langle \mathcal{E}, T \rangle$ is given, where $\mathcal{E}$ and T are a MAPD environment and a MAPD task set, respectively, as defined below. Then, MAPD is defined as the following optimization problem:

Find the optimum task allocation between agents and tasks that minimizes a certain objective criteria F

The MAPD environment $\mathcal{E}$ is defined by a tupple $\langle A, G \rangle$, where A is a set of m agents, $\{a_1, a_2...a_m\}$, and G is an undirected connected graph $G = (V, E)$, whose vertices V correspond to locations and whose edges E correspond to connections between locations that the agents can move along. Let $l_i(t) \in V$ denote the location of agent a_i in a discrete timestep t. Agent a_i starts in its initial location $l_i(0)$. In each timestep t, the agent either stays in its current location $l_i(t)$ or moves to an adjacent location, that is, $l_i(t + 1) = l_i(t)$ or $(l_i(t), l_i(t + 1)) \in E$. Agents need to avoid collisions with each other; therefore, 1) two agents cannot be in the same location in the same timestep; that is, for all agents a_i and $a_{i'}$ with $a_i \neq a_{i'}$ and for all timesteps $t : l_i(t) \neq l_{i'}(t)$; and 2) The location where one agent was located cannot be located by another agent at the next time step, that is, for all agents a_i and $a_{i'}$ with $a_i \neq a_{i'}$ and all timesteps t: $l_i(t) \neq l_{i'}(t+1)$ and $l_{i'}(t) \neq l_i(t+1)$. A path is a sequence of locations with associated timesteps, that is, mapping from an interval of timesteps to locations. Two paths collide if the two agents moving along them collide.

The MAPD task set T contains the set of unexecuted tasks. At each timestep, the system adds all new tasks to the task set. Each task $\tau_j \in T$ is characterized by a pickup location $s_j \in V$ and a delivery location $g_j \in V$. The vertices specified in s_j or g_j are called task endpoints, and their set is called V_{tsk}, and other vertices are called non-task end points. An agent that is not executing any task is called free, and an agent that is executing a task is called occupied. Any free agent can be assigned to any task in the task set T. To perform task t_j, the agent needs to move from its current location (where the previous job ended) to s_j and from s_j to g_j. When the two operations are named 'pickup job' and 'delivery job,' t_j is composed of a pickup job and a delivery job. However, if the current location and s_j are the same, a pickup job is not necessary. Each job has the restriction that it cannot be stopped once it has started executing. This limitation is based on the difficulty of bringing the robot to an abrupt stop when considering the execution of the algorithm in the real world.

A typical objective criteria F is the time taken to complete the execution of each task or all of the tasks. Therefore, makespan is evaluated for all agents at the time step at which they arrive at their destination and stop moving.

4 Rolling Horizon Negotiation

Most algorithms, such as TPTS [4], consider only cases where tasks are assigned to free agents. However, in this study, we consider cases where tasks are swapped between agents to optimize the objective criteria. To make such swapping efficient, we propose a negotiation procedure with planning in advance up to a predefined window size w. In this chapter, we first describe the negotiation algorithm and then describe an algorithm that applies the negotiation algorithm to preplanning using the rolling horizon concept.

4.1   Negotiation Algorithm

In this section, we introduce the negotiation algorithm.

First, Algorithm 1 shows the calculation of the cost to exchange temporal tasks between two agents. After *agent*, which is the first argument of the SwapLastJob function in Algorithm 1, reserves a pickup job, SwapLastJob is called in Algorithm 2.

All MAPD algorithms in this paper, as well as TP and TPTS [4], assume that an agent will remain stationary (i.e., stay forever) at the last location on its path when it reaches the end of the path. Therefore, to cancel the *lastJob*'s resource reservation with SwapLastTask, the starting point of the *lastJob* must have been reserved last by the agent canceling the *lastJob*. Moreover, the arrival point of the *lastJob* does not need to be accounted for because it is always reserved by the agent.

The cost calculation in line 8 of Algorithm 1 can specify any evaluation function, for example, the average or sum of the completion times of the last jobs of all agents.

Algorithm 1. Tentative calculation of costs between two agents

---

1: **procedure** SWAPLASTJOB(Agent: *agent*, Agent: *other*)
2:     All the following operations are performed in a temporary state (to be reverted later).
3:     Cancel resource reservation for *agent.lastJob*.
4:     Cancel resource reservation for *other.lastJob*.
5:     Swap *agent.lastJob* and *other.lastJob*.
6:     Reserves resources for *other.lastJob*.
7:     Reserves resources for *agent.lastJob*.
8:     *cost* ← Calculated cost.
9:     Restores the temporary state to the original state.
10:     return *cost*
11: **end procedure**

The negotiation algorithm is shown in Algorithm 2. The function is called after an agent has reserved a pickup job. Negotiations are made with agents that have reserved a pickup job as their last job and can cancel that reservation. The last job is tentatively exchanged with each agent by the SwapLastJob function (Algorithm 1), and the job is exchanged with the agent with the largest time step decrease.

The negotiation algorithm works as follow: First, memorize the initial settings, the pair that does not exchange the last job in bestSwapPair, and keep the current cost in bestSwapCost. The cost is calculated using the same cost function used in line 8 of Algorithm 1 [Line 2–3]. Next, consider negotiating with other designated agents [Line 4–12]. Check whether the negotiating party can delete the resource reservation for the last job, and if not, do not negotiate [Line 5]. If the last job can be deleted, the last job is exchanged, and the cost is calculated by the SwapLastJob function [Line 6]. If the cost is less than bestSwapCost, update bestSwapPair and bestSwapCost [Line 7–9]. Finally, the last job is exchanged with bestSwapPair [Line 13].

Algorithm 2. Negotiation Algorithm

1: **procedure** NEGOTIATE(Agent: *agent*, List<Agent>: *others*)
2:     *bestSwapPair* ← [*agent, agent*]
3:     *bestSwapCost* ← Cost of current plan
4:     **for all** *other* in *others* **do**
5:         **if** *lastJob*s of *agent* and *other* are swapable. **then**
6:             *cost* ← SWAPLASTJOB(*agent, other*)
7:             **if** *cost* < *bestSwapCost* **then**
8:                 *bestSwapPair* ← [*agent, other*]
9:                 *bestSwapCost* ← *cost*
10:            **end if**
11:        **end if**
12:    **end for**
13:    Swap the last job with *bestSwapPair*.
14: **end procedure**

4.2 Rolling Horizon Negotiation

The rolling horizon negotiation (RHN) algorithm is shown in Algorithm 3. The RHN algorithm reserves jobs up to a prespecified window size w steps ahead in advance. Unlike TPTS [4], there is no need to cancel a job in progress or consider the route from a non-task end point, and it is more realistic when used to plan and execute a route for an actual robot. Negotiation takes place when an agent executes a pickup job but not a delivery job. This is because the starting and ending points of the delivery job cannot be changed, while the starting point of a pickup job can be changed.

RHN works as follows. The start time step is stored in currentTime [Line 2], and the priority queue is prepared for a look-ahead reservation. The priority queue is used to make reservations in the order of the agent whose time step is earlier than the time step for when the job ends. The first of the tuples is the time to book the task, and the second is the agent. First, the reservation time for all agents is initialized to 0 [Line 3–6], and planning and implementation then begins [Line 7–43]. The fastest reservation start time is retrieved according to the priority queue [Line 9]. Since the priority queue plans from the current time step to w steps later, if the agent has already planned w steps later, it skips that agent [Line 10–12]. If a_i has already made a reservation, the time when the last job ends is assigned, or if not, the current time step to c_i is assigned [Line 13–17]. A reservable task set T' is then set [Line 18]. If T' is not empty, a job is created [Line 19–29]. The task with the lowest h value is then retrieved. At this time, the h value may be the precalculated travel distance, or it may be the time it takes to actually make a tentative reservation and then use the time it takes to travel [Line 20]. If the agent is at the starting point s_j of the selected task, a delivery job is reserved. At the same time as the reservation, the shortest route that does not conflict with the other agents is planned. With this planning, the time step at which the job will end can also be calculated. Based on the time step, a_i is again inserted into the priority queue [Line 21–24]. If an agent is not at the starting point s_j of the selected task, a pickup job is reserved. At the same time as the reservation, the shortest route that does not conflict with the other agents is planned. With this planning, the time step at which the job will end is also calculated. Based on the time step, a_i is again inserted into the priority queue [Line 25–28]. If there are no feasible tasks, then move or avoidance [Line 30–38]. If the position of a_i is not in the set of goal points of the unexecuted tasks, a_i does not move and waits as it is [Line 32–33]. If a_i's location is in the set of goal points of the unexecuted task and there is an avoidance point, a_i moves to the shortest avoidance point [Line 34–37]. Finally, the agent executes the job for one step and increases the count in currentTimestep [Line 41–42].

5   Experimental Evaluation

An experiment was conducted to see if the proposed method improves makespan using a warehouse as a subject.

5.1   Warehouse Overview

The target warehouse is a hierarchical structure comprising layered planar warehouses. An overhead view of one warehouse plane is shown in Fig. 1. The experiment was conducted using only one level of the planar warehouse. Due to the constraints of the warehouse, only one agent is allowed to enter the aisle of each unit (vertical aisle) at a time. However, the horizontal aisle can be entered by multiple agents at the same time as long as they do not collide with each other. The parameters of the number of units and the length of the vertical aisle of each unit can be changed.

The agent can move through the entrance, the horizontal aisle, and the vertical aisle of the unit. The range of movement is shown in Fig. 2.

The mapped warehouse area is shown as a graph in Fig. 3. Since only one agent can enter each unit at a time, each unit is considered to be a vertex and to be occupied when an agent is working in the unit.

5.2   Tasks

We conducted experiments using two types of tasks: a storage task, where luggage was brought into an empty warehouse until it was filled to 100 percent, and a retrieve task, where luggage was removed from a warehouse that had been filled to 100 percent.

Algorithm 3. Rolling Horizon Negotiation (RHN)

1: **procedure** ROLLINGHORIZONNEGOTIATION(Int: w)
2:     $currentTime \leftarrow 0$;
3:     $heap \leftarrow []$;
4:     **for** a_i in A **do**
5:         INSERT($heap, (0, a_i)$);
6:     **end for**
7:     **while** True **do**
8:         **while** $heap \neq \Phi$ **do**
9:             $t, a_i \leftarrow head.pop()$;
10:            **if** $currentTime + w > t$ **then**
11:                continue;
12:            **end if**
13:            **if** a_i has last job **then**
14:                $c_i \leftarrow$ end point of the last job;
15:            **else**
16:                $c_i \leftarrow$ the current point;
17:            **end if**
18:            $T' \leftarrow \{\tau_j \in T \mid$ The end location of the last job of another agent is not in s_j or $g_j\}$;
19:            **if** $T' \neq \Phi$ **then**
20:                $\tau \leftarrow \arg\min_{\tau_j \in T'} h(c_i, s_j)$;
21:                **if** s_j of $\tau = c_i$ **then**
22:                    Remove τ from T;
23:                    Add delivery job from s_j to g_j to job queue of a_i;
24:                    INSERT($heap$, (End time step of last job of $a_i + 1$, a_i));
25:                **else**
26:                    Add pickup job from c_i to s_j to job queue of a_i;
27:                    NEGOTIATE($a_i, A/a_i$);
28:                    INSERT($heap$, (End time step of last job of $a_i + 1$, a_i));
29:                **end if**
30:            **else**
31:                $V' \leftarrow$ the set of g_i in T;
32:                **if** (c_i not in V') or ($V_{ep}/V' = \Phi$) **then**
33:                    INSERT($heap, (t + 1, a_i)$);
34:                **else**
35:                    $v \leftarrow \arg\min_{v_k \in V'} h(c_i, v_k)$;
36:                    Add avoidance job from c_i to v job queue of a_i;
37:                    INSERT($heap$, (End time step of last job of $a_i + 1$, a_i));
38:                **end if**
39:            **end if**
40:        **end while**
41:        All agents move along their paths in first job of job queue for one timestep;
42:        $currentTime \leftarrow currentTime + 1$;
43:    **end while**
44: **end procedure**

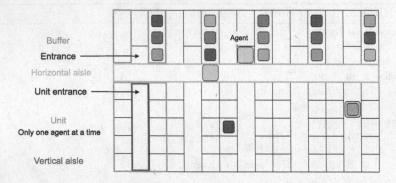

Fig. 1. Overhead view of one plane of the warehouse.

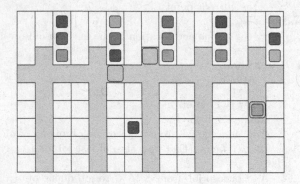

Fig. 2. Area the agents can move in shown in green. (Color figure online)

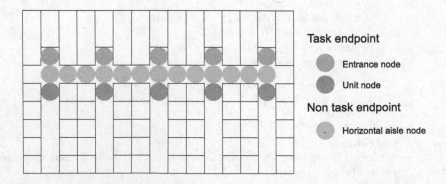

Fig. 3. Graphical representation of the warehouse.

For the storage task, the first load in each loading buffer was delivered to a randomly selected destination from a uniform distribution.

For the retrieve task, there were multiple tasks, with a destination specified for each retrieve buffer. The task was to retrieve a package from a randomly specified location and deliver it to a specified retrieve buffer.

5.3 Parameter Set

Experiments were performed with the parameters specified in Table 1. Each experiment was run 10 times with different random number seeds and evaluated.

Table 1. Parameter set

Variable	Value
Number of units	10
Vertical aisle length	50
Number of agents	$\{3, 4, ..., 10\}$
Number of look-ahead steps(w)	$\{0, 150\}$
Negotiation	$\{True, False\}$

5.4 Results

Table 2 shows the experimental results of the retrieve task for 10 units and a vertical corridor length of 50. Makespan is the maximum time taken by the agent to reach the goal point; the smaller the value, the faster the task was completed. Runtime is the computation time per step in ms. The smallest makespan was obtained when the negotiation algorithm was introduced. In this case, there was a slight increase in runtime, but a makespan reduction of about 4.5% to 12.7% was achieved by using RHN($w = 150$) compared to the case without look-ahead and negotiation.

Because we would like to take acceleration/deceleration into account in the future, we did not use the exact same algorithm as in the previous study. However, the algorithm when $w = 0$ is similar to TP in that it sequentially selects close tasks and generates routes. Therefore, we believe that it can be used as a reference as a base indicator.

Table 3 shows the experimental results of the retrieve task for 10 units and a vertical corridor length of 20. Basically the same trend was observed as the results for $w = 50$. Experiments show that increasing the number of agents too much decreases the capability. This is because increasing the number of agents too much decreases the mobility options. In the experiment, the number of agents was capped at half the number of nodes.

Figure 4 shows the makespan of the retrieve task at lengths of 20 and 50 vertical aisles (number of units: 10, w: $\{0, 150\}$, negotiation: $\{True, False\}$). The

Table 2. Experimental results for the retrieve task using 10 units and the length of the vertical aisle = 50

agents	w : 0		w : 150, negotiation: *False*		w : 150, negotiation: *True*	
	makespan	runtime	makespan	runtime	makespan	runtime
3	25, 928.1	1.068	24, 939.3	1.158	24, 207.6	1.298
4	19, 860.9	1.222	19, 427.7	1.331	18, 664.8	1.518
5	16, 442.1	1.373	16, 044.0	1.516	15, 694.5	1.750
6	14, 502.2	1.521	13, 943.0	1.684	13, 419.2	2.002
7	13, 100.5	1.672	12, 779.2	1.892	12, 057.9	2.320
8	12, 626.3	1.817	12, 093.0	2.079	11, 428.5	2.720
9	12, 414.4	1.990	11, 998.3	2.354	11, 089.0	3.137
10	12, 441.5	2.183	11, 736.7	2.625	10, 859.9	3.723

Table 3. Experimental results for the retrieve task using 10 units and the length of the vertical aisle = 20

agents	w : 0		w : 150, negotiation: *False*		w : 150, negotiation: *True*	
	makespan	runtime	makespan	runtime	makespan	runtime
3	6, 023.4	0.995	5, 920.0	1.110	5, 791.3	1.273
4	4, 784.0	1.182	4, 688.9	1.347	4, 553.3	1.589
5	4, 150.6	1.334	3, 920.0	1.565	3, 831.4	1.923
6	3, 705.1	1.477	3, 594.5	1.753	3, 393.8	2.231
7	3, 406.4	1.620	3, 319.3	1.966	3, 091.3	2.609
8	3, 334.3	1.777	3, 270.2	2.129	2, 970.3	2.911
9	3, 399.4	1.914	3, 218.3	2.322	2, 862.0	3.364
10	3, 465.3	2.012	3, 379.1	2.585	2, 942.8	3.827

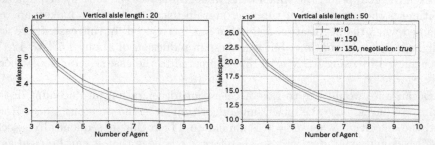

Fig. 4. Makespan of the retrieve task at lengths of 20 and 50 vertical aisles (number of units: 10, w : {0, 150}, negotiation: {*True, False*})

horizontal axis represents the number of agents, and the vertical axis represents the makespan, where the smaller this number is, the more efficiently the task was completed.

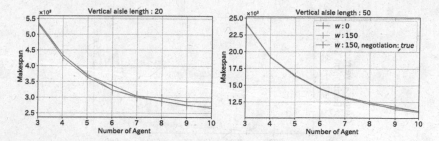

Fig. 5. Makespan of the storage task at lengths of 20 and 50 vertical aisles (number of units: 10, w: $\{0, 150\}$, negotiation: $\{True, False\}$)

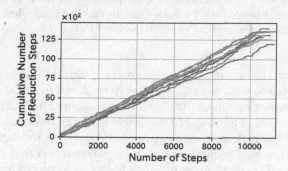

Fig. 6. Cumulative value of the number of steps decreased by the negotiation algorithm when executing the retrieve task for each random number seed when the number of units: 10, the length of the vertical aisle: 50, and w : 150.

Figure 5 shows the makespan of the storage task at lengths of 20 and 50 vertical aisles (number of units: 10, w: $\{0, 150\}$, negotiation: $\{True, False\}$). The storage task showed less reduction in the makespan compared to the retrieve task due to the negotiation algorithm. To investigate the cause of this, the cumulative number of reduction steps made by the negotiation algorithm is illustrated in Figs. 6 and 7.

Figure 6 shows the cumulative values of the number of steps decreased by the negotiation algorithm when the retrieve task was executed for each random number seed when the number of units was 10, the length of the vertical corridor was 50, and w was 150. The horizontal axis represents the number of steps when the negotiation algorithm is applied, and the vertical axis represents the cumulative value of the number of steps decreased by the negotiation algorithm. The larger the cumulative value, the more steps were reduced by the negotiation algorithm. Each line represents a trial for which the random number seed is changed. The step reduction by the negotiation algorithm was a constant occurrence. At the end of the simulation, the cumulative number of reduction steps stagnates. This is because there are no more tasks left and more agents are waiting and do not perform negotiation.

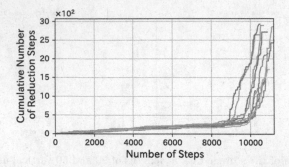

Fig. 7. Cumulative value of the number of steps decreased by the negotiation algorithm when executing the storage task for each random number seed when the number of units: 10, the length of the vertical aisle: 50, and w : 150.

Figure 7 shows the accumulation of decreasing steps by the negotiation algorithm for a warehouse with the same geometry as shown in Fig. 6 for the storage task. The step reduction due to the negotiation algorithm occurred mainly at the end of the process. The storage task differs from the retrieve task in that the starting point of the task is at each entrance and does not overlap. Therefore, it is thought that time step reductions due to negotiation occurred relatively infrequently. In the final stage, there were only a few tasks available for selection, and it is thought that the time step could have been reduced by exchanging tasks through negotiation.

6   Conclusions

We proposed a negotiation algorithm called rolling horizon negotiation (RHN) to solve a multi-agent pickup and delivery problem (MAPD). In the formalization, we considered an MAPD as a lifelong version of multi-agent path finding (MAPF) that requires proper task assignment and route planning to execute the MAPD tasks. We introduced a negotiation process among the agents to improve the total performance of the MAPD execution.

The simulated experimental results confirmed that the introduction of the RHN algorithm can improve makespan performance. When $w = 150$, the makespan decreased by about 4.5%–12.7%. In addition, the computation time was short enough to be applicable for use with real warehouse products. The increase in computation time was approximately $1.21 - 1.70$ times.

Future work will include simulations that take acceleration and deceleration into account, and a more realistic evaluation will be made. Further investigation of other methods and further improvements are also needed.

References

1. D'Andrea, R.: Guest editorial: a revolution in the warehouse: a retrospective on kiva systems and the grand challenges ahead. IEEE Trans. Autom. Sci. Eng. **9**(4), 638–639 (2012)
2. Dresner, K., Stone, P.: A multiagent approach to autonomous intersection management. J. Artif. Intell. Res. **31**, 591–656 (2008)
3. Li, J., Tinka, A., Kiesel, S., Durham, J.W., Kumar, T.S., Koenig, S.: Lifelong multiagent path finding in large-scale warehouses. In: Proceedings of the AAAI Conference on Artificial Intelligence, vol. 35, pp. 11272–11281 (2021)
4. Ma, H., Li, J., Kumar, T.K.S., Koenig, S.: Lifelong multi-agent path finding for online pickup and delivery tasks. In: Proceedings of the 16th International Conference Autonomous Agents and Multi-Agent Systems (AAMAS 2017) (2017). http://arxiv.org/abs/1705.10868
5. Ma, H., Tovey, C., Sharon, G., Kumar, T., Koenig, S.: Multi-agent path finding with payload transfers and the package-exchange robot-routing problem. In: Proceedings of the AAAI Conference on Artificial Intelligence, vol. 30 (2016)
6. Morris, R., et al.: Planning, scheduling and monitoring for airport surface operations. In: AAAI Workshop: Planning for Hybrid Systems, pp. 608–614 (2016)
7. Sharon, G., Stern, R., Felner, A., Sturtevant, N.R.: Conflict-based search for optimal multi-agent pathfinding. Artif. Intell. **219**, 40–66 (2015)
8. Silver, D.: Cooperative pathfinding. In: Proceedings of the AAAI Conference on Artificial Intelligence and Interactive Digital Entertainment, vol. 1, pp. 117–122 (2005)
9. Wurman, P.R., D'Andrea, R., Mountz, M.: Coordinating hundreds of cooperative, autonomous vehicles in warehouses. AI Mag. **29**(1), 9–9 (2008)

Validating State-Wide Charging Station Network Through Agent-Based Simulation

Pasqual Martí[1]([✉])(iD), Jaime Llopis[1], Vicente Julian[1,2](iD), Paulo Novais[3](iD), and Jaume Jordán[1](iD)

[1] Valencian Research Institute for Artificial Intelligence (VRAIN), Universitat Politècnica de València, Valencia, Spain
pasmargi@vrain.upv.es, jaillohe@ade.upv.es, vjulian@upv.es, jjordan@dsic.upv.es
[2] Valencian Graduate School and Research Network of Artificial Intelligence, Universitat Politècnica de València, Valencia, Spain
[3] ALGORITMI Centre, University of Minho, Braga, Portugal
pjon@di.uminho.pt

Abstract. The electric car market in Europe is growing due to climate change awareness, expectations of fossil fuel depletion, and cost savings. However, the limited number of low-powered public charging stations in the case of Spain impedes longer interurban trips, causing "range anxiety" in users. Currently, there are proposals using genetic algorithms to design an optimal electric charging station network that satisfies the needs of all citizens in any region. The work presented in this paper aims to design and develop a simulation environment to test the allocation results of a genetic algorithm and compare them with the only fast charging station network of Tesla and other possible station distributions.

Keywords: Agent-based Simulation · Electric Vehicles · Genetic Algorithms

1 Introduction

The European Union's 2030 agenda sets among its sustainable development goals access to clean energy as well as resource creation and consumption sustainability. In this line, adopting the electric vehicle (EV) as a generalized individual transport is crucial for reducing air and noise pollution in cities [9]. If we take this problem to the interurban level, a significant percentage of the transport of goods and people is currently carried out with gasoline vehicles. A well-planned charging station network for electric vehicles in interurban areas ensures high-quality service and efficient operations. Previous research studies such as [1] and [12] have emphasized the significance of charging station planning in cities. It is evident from the literature that the planning of charging stations is a complex issue that requires careful consideration. Various approaches have been proposed to address this challenge in recent years, as discussed in reviews presented in [13] and [5]. However, most of these proposals lack sufficient validation, making it

D. Durães et al. (Eds.): PAAMS 2023, CCIS 1838, pp. 158–169, 2023.
https://doi.org/10.1007/978-3-031-37593-4_13

difficult to determine their effectiveness in practice. Therefore, it is essential to have a well-designed and validated plan for charging station placement to ensure a smooth transition to electric vehicle usage in interurban areas.

In previous works [2,4], the installation of an electric grid with a statewide perspective was proposed to enable travel without EV drivers experiencing range anxiety [10,11]; i.e., the fear of their vehicle running out of charge away from any station. In that work, the studied variables were the number of deployed stations and their location, also considering the total cost of the final infrastructure. It is imperative to emphasize that the currently proposed algorithms remain purely theoretical and require validation through simulation in large-scale interurban vehicle movement scenarios, like in the analysis of the urban case in similar works [3]. This underscores the critical need to verify the efficacy of the proposed models. Intelligent methods for transportation infrastructure deployment would ideally be evaluated through the real-world implementation of their outputs. However, changes in these types of infrastructures tend to greatly impact citizen's life, even redefining previous displacement trends. Because of that, before its implementation, these changes must be validated through software simulations [6]. A general scope proposal such as the present one aims to serve as many users as possible, which implies different EV types. Different EVs vary in autonomy (the average distance that can be traveled when fully charged). Therefore, evaluating a charging network must consider interurban displacements of EVs with various autonomy ranges. In addition, the deployed network would enable en-route recharging of the vehicles' batteries, thus providing a reasonably fast charge, a closer experience to filling up the gasoline tank in a regular vehicle.

Working towards such goals, this paper proposes using multi-agent simulation to evaluate a state-wide network of fast charging stations. An informed genetic algorithm generates such a network. That network, in turn, is compared against other infrastructures built following different patterns. The multi-agent simulator SimFleet is adapted and used to compare and validate the various station distributions. Interurban trips across the territory where the network is deployed are generated. Those trips are to be completed by vehicles (simulated agents) with ranging battery power. Each distribution is evaluated according to specific metrics. The experimental results prove the potential multi-agent simulation has for infrastructure validation as well as the flexibility of the genetic algorithm's approach to station distribution.

The rest of the paper is structured as follows. Section 2 introduces the multi-agent simulator and the genetic algorithm, and afterward characterizes the experimental setup employed to validate the charging infrastructure. Then, Sect. 3 goes over the experimentation results, adding a discussion that compares them from a global perspective. Finally, Sect. 4 contains the conclusions drawn from this work and future lines of research.

2   Materials and Methods

This section summarizes the technologies employed to carry out the experimentation. That includes a multi-agent simulator, a genetic algorithm that distributes stations, and finally, the experimental setup used to validate the infrastructure.

2.1   SimFleet

SimFleet [8] is a powerful simulation tool that provides several advantages for testing different mobility strategies. It is based on SPADE [7], a multi-agent system development environment, and specializes in simulating transports and customers interactions for urban mobility solutions. One of the main advantages of SimFleet is its flexibility and ease of use in managing simulated transport fleets. The agent architecture provided by SPADE allows every actor in the simulation to be a proactive and independent agent with its strategy and behavior, which makes scaling the simulation a simple process. In this context, SimFleet greatly facilitates the scheduling of the agents' negotiations in a simulation by abstracting everything related to agent communication. Underneath the abstraction layer is an XMPP[1] server, which makes getting messages sent from one agent to another very simple. It supports asynchronous reception of messages for efficiency so that agents do not have to stop to receive and process them.

In addition, SimFleet uses the OSRM[2] routing software to locate the shortest routes in the road network for vehicle trips. A query to OSRM receives the origin and destination points and returns the shortest route between them. Overall, SimFleet 's flexibility and scalability, coupled with its integration with the OSRM routing software, make it a highly effective simulation tool for testing mobility strategies.

However, the tool has been slightly modified to be used in interurban environments like the one proposed in this paper. On the one hand, a new state ABORTED for transportation agents has been included to indicate a vehicle that aborted its current trip due to a lack of power, i.e., its electric battery ran out. On the other hand, by default, the simulator awaits for every transport agent to be at their destination to finish the simulation. Such a behavior has been modified so that the simulator understands vehicles that aborted their trip have finished their execution too. Finally, the necessary code has been developed to allow transport agents to check their autonomy level and the charging station distribution. With this, agents can choose the closest station to recharge their batteries, implying a lower deviation from their planned trip.

2.2   Genetic Algorithm

The distribution that generates a genetic algorithm (GA) is the one presented in the works [2,4]. This GA uses several datasets to evaluate the potential charging

---

[1] https://xmpp.org.
[2] http://project-osrm.org/.

station locations to determine the best locations for electric charging stations in an interurban environment.

The GA creates a population of possible charging station locations and uses a fitness function to assess each location based on the input data. The possible locations are the existing petrol stations to provide a large set of possibilities. The fitness function considers factors such as the population density in the area, the traffic density on nearby roads, and the activity on social networks. The algorithm then uses genetic operators such as mutation and crossover to create new distributions of charging stations and repeats the fitness evaluation. The process continues iteratively until a number of generations are completed to converge on a set of near-optimal charging station locations. The algorithm has been tested using real data from the USA, demonstrating promising results in identifying suitable locations for charging stations.

2.3   Experimental Setup

Following, the use case chosen to illustrate the operation of our approach is described. In addition, the distributions against which the system's output is compared and the simulation evaluation metrics are presented.

Use Case. The peninsular territory of Spain has been chosen to deploy an infrastructure of fast-charging stations with an interurban perspective. The network aims to allow EV drivers to travel between any two points of the territory. The main variables of the experimentation are the total number of stations in the network (50, 100, 250, 500, 750, or 1000) and the maximum autonomy of the EVs, expressed in kilometers (50, 100, 200, or 400 km).

Besides the specific charging infrastructure, each simulation contains 500 EVs that perform randomly generated interurban trips within the territory. Each trip has a destination at least 600 km away from its origin. With such a trip distance, and considering the tested EV autonomies, drivers are forced to look for a minimum of one station through their journey, and thus the simulation allows us to evaluate a specific distribution of stations.

Types of Distribution. The genetic algorithm's distribution of charging stations is compared against four different distribution patterns. From those four, three of them are based on the spatial distribution of the stations over the deployment area; meanwhile, the last one is simply a reproduction of Tesla's[3] network of fast electric charging stations; also known as "superchargers". Figure 1 shows a graphical representation of each distribution.

A *Random* distribution of stations (Fig. 1a) serves as a baseline for the experimentation. In this distribution, stations are allocated at any valid point within the road network of the deployment area.

---

[3] Tesla enterprise website: https://www.tesla.com/ (accessed on 11/04/2023).

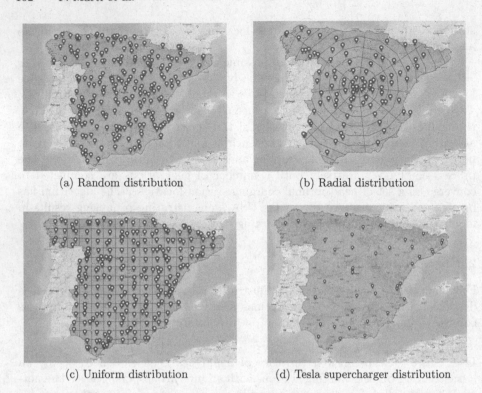

(a) Random distribution

(b) Radial distribution

(c) Uniform distribution

(d) Tesla supercharger distribution

Fig. 1. Visualization of station networks over the peninsular territory of Spain. Images (a) to (c) show the distribution of 250 charging stations following different patterns. Image (d) shows the distribution of Tesla's fast chargers. Each spot represents a charging station with a specific number of charging poles.

Following, a *Radial* distribution (Fig. 1b) is implemented, in which the territory is divided into several concentric circles, which in turn, get divided into a configurable number of sectors. Stations are allocated in the centroid of the resulting sectors, thus favoring a high density of stations towards the central point of the deployment area and a more dispersed, spider web-like distribution as the stations move away from the central point.

The last space-based distribution is the *Uniform* one (Fig. 1c), in which the deployment area is divided into a series of rows and columns, resulting in several square areas. Then, a station is allocated in the center of each square area until the total number of stations is reached. If there are more stations to allocate than square subareas, some areas are randomly chosen to have more than one station in them.

Finally, the Tesla's network of superchargers (Fig. 1d) is a real-life, implemented, state-wide network of charging stations that gives us a real infrastructure against which to compare the GA's output. By the time of writing this paper, the network is composed of 42 charging stations.

Evaluation Metrics. The charging station distributions are evaluated by the percentage of aborted trips and the vehicles' mean deviation. The aborted trips comprise the percentage of vehicles that cannot complete the planned trip. Regarding the simulation, this is flagged by the aborted trip state ABORTED of the vehicles, indicating the transport has been unable to complete its planned trip with the current station distribution due to not having proper access to autonomy recharge. For those journeys that can be completed, mean deviation refers to the average total detours, in kilometers, that drivers must perform over their planned path to travel to each of the used charging stations.

The aforementioned metrics are computed as follows. Let a simulation be configured to evaluate the charging station distribution X. Let i be one of the N vehicle agents in X, with a state S_i. Vehicle i has a planned trip with an estimated distance of eD_i km. Upon completing its journey, which may have included a detour to recharge its batteries, vehicle i has traveled a real distance of rD_i km. Eqs. 1 and 2 describe the computation of aborted trips and mean deviation, respectively.

$$Aborted\,trips(X) = \frac{|A|}{N};\ A = \{i \in N \mid S_i = ABORTED\} \tag{1}$$

$$Mean\,deviation(X) = \frac{\sum_{i \in F}(rD_i - eD_i)}{|F|};\ F = \{i \in N \mid S_i \neq ABORTED\} \tag{2}$$

3 Experimental Results

This section assesses the simulations that test the GA distribution against distributions with different spatial patterns (random, radial, uniform). In addition, the Tesla network is also tested according to the defined metrics (see Sect. 2.3). Figure 2 shows a visualization of the distributions that the GA obtains with a different number of stations.

3.1 Aborted Trips

Table 1 gathers the results of each simulation classified by vehicle autonomy, number of deployed stations, and type of distribution. The Tesla distribution is only assessed according to vehicle autonomy, as its number of stations is fixed.

The random distribution provides a baseline yet unrealistic network. On average, it performs worse than any other distribution. Allocating 750 stations, all trips are completed for vehicles with +100 km of autonomy. However, when 1000 stations are allocated, a few cars cannot complete their journey. This initially

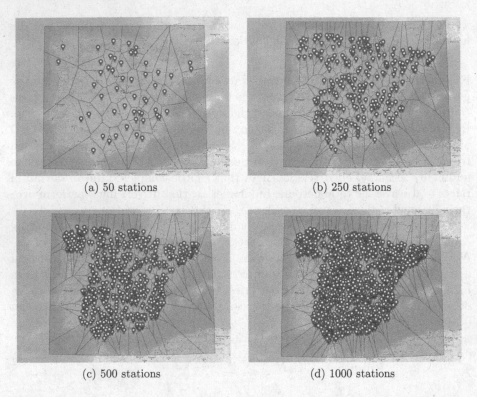

(a) 50 stations   (b) 250 stations

(c) 500 stations   (d) 1000 stations

Fig. 2. Visualization of the genetic algorithm's output for the allocation of the different number of charging stations. Each spot represents a charging station with a specific number of charging poles.

unexpected result is explained because no mathematical criteria are followed to allocate stations. Therefore, increasing the number of stations does not necessarily imply a decrease in aborted trips.

No trips can be completed for the radial distribution and 50 km autonomy vehicles with 100 or fewer stations. From 750 stations onward, the percentage of aborted journeys does not change significantly, reducing up to 65%. Then, with an autonomy of 100 km, we find significant improvements with 250 stations, as the number of aborted trips decreases to 19.4%. The best value is reached by deploying 750 stations, with only 2.6% of failed displacements. Finally, almost none of the vehicles with +200 km autonomy fail to reach their destination.

The uniform distribution performs well in terms of aborted trips. For low-autonomy vehicles, with 500 stations, just 15% of trips are uncompleted. Reaching up to 750 stations decreases the figure to 6.2%, or even 3%, if we locate all possible stations. Then, for the autonomy of 100 km, 250 stations are enough for all vehicles to travel freely around the area. Vehicles with +200 km autonomy can already travel anywhere with only 50 stations.

Table 1. Percentage of aborted trips for each autonomy of 50 km, 100 km, and 200 km (400 km is not shown as there are no aborted trips), each amount of stations (ranging from 50 to 1000), and the five presented distributions.

Autonomy	Stations	Aborted trips (%)				
		Random	Radial	Uniform	GA	Tesla
50 km	50 s	100	100	100	100	100
	100 s	100	100	100	100	
	250 s	100	96.8	100	100	
	500 s	77.8	80	14.8	80.6	
	750 s	42.6	66.8	6.2	33.2	
	1000 s	17.8	64.8	3	19	
100 km	50 s	99.6	95.4	100	99.8	100
	100 s	77	40.8	68.2	93.6	
	250 s	5	19.4	0	1.2	
	500 s	1.8	12.6	0	0	
	750 s	0	2.6	0	3.4	
	1000 s	2.2	4.6	0	1.4	
200 km	50 s	52	0.4	0	12.4	2.2
	100 s	0	1	0	0	
	250 s	0	0	0	0	
	500 s	0	0	0	0	
	750 s	0	0	0	0	
	1000 s	0	0	0	0	

Regarding the Tesla network, we can conclude that it is not possible to use its stations for long trips between municipalities with low (50–100 km) autonomy vehicles. However, for the autonomy of 200 km, the distribution serves practically the entire Spanish territory since only 2.2% of the transports could not reach their destination. Ultimately, vehicles can complete any journey with the highest autonomy of 400 km.

Finally, we assess the results of the GA's distribution, which, in turn, evaluates its capacity to allocate stations. With low autonomy and 250 stations or less, it is not possible to complete any of the trips in the sample. Adding more stations, the distribution efficiency highly increases, leaving about a fifth of the vehicles unable to travel when 1000 are deployed. Results for 100 km of autonomy are unfavorable in smaller deployments. However, with 250 stations, the aborted trips drastically decreased to 1%, and all journeys were completed with 500 stations. Note that the number of aborted trips increases again in tests with more than 500 stations. This is explained by the network saturation, i.e., with more than 500 stations, the same efficiency level can be maintained at most. A priori, the efficiency should have been kept at the maximum, but this can happen considering that the station location criteria (the result of the GA) are not additive. The stations do not follow a mathematical model as simple as in the uniform or radial distributions, nor are they additive to what already exists. Therefore, an increase in stations can completely change the location of previously existing stations. The GA's distribution allows vehicles to travel freely for the rest of the tests.

3.2 Trip Deviation

Figure 3, shows the average deviation of each simulation, in km, caused by vehicles moving out of their planned path to recharge their batteries. Results are plotted by vehicle autonomy, the number of deployed stations, and distribution type. Simulations with no associated value imply that none of the vehicles in them have been able to complete their journey (100% of aborted trips). Consequently, there is no average trip deviation to be computed.

The random distribution shows high deviation (335–250 km) for 50 and 100 km of autonomy and up to 500 stations when the value is reduced to 198 km. Such a value is improved for the autonomy of 200 km and 250 stations, decaying to 125 km. The least that can be achieved with this autonomy is 99 km. Finally, with the highest autonomy and number of stations, the deviation averages 47 km.

The radial distribution initially reports better results than its random counterpart regarding low-autonomy vehicles. However, the reduction in trip deviation evolves similarly to the random distribution one as more simulations are tested. With an autonomy of 200 km, the most balanced result is again found by placing 250 stations, leaving the total average deviation at 116 km. Then, with 400 km of autonomy, 50 stations would add an average of 87 km to a trip. Doubling the stations, the deviation drops to 59 km. From this point, the figure

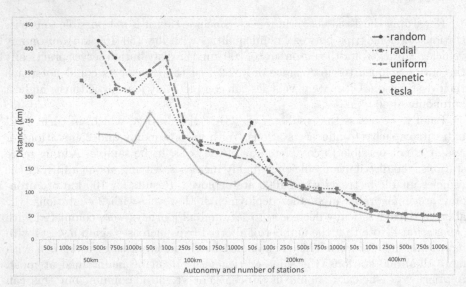

Fig. 3. Distance deviation from the optimal trip for the different distributions, number of stations, and levels of autonomy of the vehicles.

continues to drop asymptotically to 51 km, indicating it is not cost-effective to consider placing more than 100 stations.

The uniform distribution, with low-autonomy vehicles, performs slightly better than the random one and slightly worse than the radial. From 200 km autonomy upwards, it surpasses the radial, performing generally better and, at worse, similarly. This distribution achieves a deviation of 105 km with 500 stations and 200 km autonomy vehicles. Then, it improves to 47 km with 750–1000 stations and vehicles with the highest autonomy.

The Tesla distribution can only be tested with vehicles with +200 km autonomy. It yields excellent results with those with 400 km of autonomy, reducing deviations to 38 km.

Finally, the GA's distribution outperforms the random, radial, and uniform distributions while matching Tesla's results. For 50 km autonomy vehicles, all runs with the most stations on the map have a result that exceeds 200 km. Placing more stations has virtually no effect on efficiency. Then, with 100 km autonomy, the curve descends linearly as stations are added up to 750, where the average deviation is 120 km, less than half the value with which the series started. For cars with 200 km autonomy, deviation values show a similar progression according to the number of stations. With 750, the value decreases to 72 km. On the other hand, cars with 400 km autonomy have to deviate around 61 km with 50 stations. With 750 stations, the displacement is reduced to less than 40 km.

3.3 Discussion

Following, the results are assessed from a general perspective, comparing the types of station distributions used in the study and highlighting their strengths and weaknesses.

The experimentation with a random distribution proves that it is not strictly necessary to carry out an exhaustive study of the ideal location for the station network since just by placing them at any point on the map, acceptable results can be obtained, although only for the vehicles with a higher (+200 km) autonomy. A radial distribution pattern stands out since it quickly shortens the trip deviation with a relatively small number of stations. However, once again, this effect is mainly reflected in vehicles with high autonomy. Nevertheless, we could say the radial is a cheap distribution since it is unnecessary to invest excessive resources to achieve a satisfactory quality for travelers. Finally, the uniform distribution works well for high-autonomy vehicles, presenting lower deviations from the planned trip than the random and radial distributions. In addition, the uniform distribution of 500 stations is the first one in which 50 km range vehicles start to complete their journeys. This is a relevant feat, although it must be pointed out that EVs with such low autonomies are not designed for intercity travel. In conclusion, the explored spatial patterns can be acceptable for drivers with high autonomy EVs considering that it is both an expensive and naive deployment of resources.

When it comes to Tesla's network of fast chargers, results indicate that it is well tailored to the enterprise's purposes, allowing its direct customers to travel thanks to their vehicles' high autonomy. Trip deviations are low, as charging terminals are located adjacent to the country's main roads. Meanwhile, lower autonomy EVs that are not of its brand are disregarded. From a global perspective, it does not grant access to all types of EVs, creating an imbalance in the Spanish travelers' fair access to charging infrastructure. To improve this situation, future stations in Tesla could be placed in a greater variety of geographical points within the area, allowing more EVs to recharge batteries instead of accumulating many terminals in the same location.

Finally, the GA shows its best networks when distributing 750 stations, as those experiments present the lowest average deviations and very low instances of aborted trips. While it is true that so many stations involve a high outlay of resources, the algorithm outputs a concrete distribution that could be implemented over time. The trip deviation curves of this method are much more linear than in other distributions (see Fig. 3). This implies we can regulate and balance the investment in stations according to the desired effectiveness of the network. In this sense, the GA is a more flexible method for charging infrastructure allocation than its counterparts.

4   Conclusions

This paper focuses on designing and developing a simulation environment to test the allocation results of a genetic algorithm for an optimal electric charging station network in Spain. We propose using multi-agent simulation to evaluate a state-wide network of fast charging stations. Interurban trips with various lengths are generated across the territory where the network is deployed and then simulated with SimFleet to validate each station distribution. Simulations are run in scenarios with a different number of deployed charging stations as well as varying EV autonomy. The results show that the proposed genetic charging station distribution satisfies the needs of interurban travelers, providing more flexibility than Tesla's network and other possible station distributions.

A possible line of future work would be the improvement of the genetic algorithm based on the conclusions drawn from this work. For example, a refinement of the stations' distribution area could increase the algorithm's effectiveness. It has been observed that stations close to main travel routes help to reduce passenger diversion. Favoring the placement of stations on these roads would improve the final allocation of the algorithm.

Another improvement in charging infrastructure evaluation would be to inform the generated intercity trips using a dataset of real intercity displacement in Spain. Additionally, information on the most typically used routes can be employed to improve both station distribution and network evaluation.

Acknowledgements. This work is partially supported by grant PID2021-123673OB-C31 funded by MCIN/AEI/ 10.13039/501100011033 and by "ERDF A way of making Europe". Pasqual Martí is supported by grant ACIF/2021/259 funded by the "Conselleria de Innovación, Universidades, Ciencia y Sociedad Digital de la Generalitat Valenciana". Jaume Jordán is supported by grant IJC2020-045683-I funded by MCIN/AEI/ 10.13039/501100011033 and by "European Union NextGenerationEU/PRTR".

References

1. Brown, S., Pyke, D., Steenhof, P.: Electric vehicles: the role and importance of standards in an emerging market. Energy Policy **38**(7), 3797–3806 (2010). https:// doi.org/10.1016/j.enpol.2010.02.059
2. Jordán, J., Martí, P., Palanca, J., Julian, V., Botti, V.: Interurban electric vehicle charging stations through genetic algorithms. In: Sanjurjo González, H., Pastor López, I., García Bringas, P., Quintián, H., Corchado, E. (eds.) HAIS 2021. LNCS (LNAI), vol. 12886, pp. 101–112. Springer, Cham (2021). https://doi.org/10.1007/ 978-3-030-86271-8_9
3. Jordán, J., Palanca, J., Martí, P., Julian, V.: Electric vehicle charging stations emplacement using genetic algorithms and agent-based simulation. Expert Syst. Appl. **197**, 116739 (2022)
4. Jordán, J., Martí, P., Palanca, J., Julian, V., Botti, V.: Interurban charging station network: an evolutionary approach. Neurocomputing **529**, 214–221 (2023). https:// doi.org/10.1016/j.neucom.2023.01.068
5. Kchaou-Boujelben, M.: Charging station location problem: a comprehensive review on models and solution approaches. Transp. Res. Part C: Emerg. Technol. **132**, 103376 (2021)
6. Ouyang, M.: Review on modeling and simulation of interdependent critical infrastructure systems. Reliab. Eng. Syst. Safety **121**, 43–60 (2014)
7. Palanca, J., Terrasa, A., Julian, V., Carrascosa, C.: SPADE 3: supporting the new generation of multi-agent systems. IEEE Access **8**, 182537–182549 (2020)
8. Palanca, J., Terrasa, A., Carrascosa, C., Julián, V.: SimFleet: a new transport fleet simulator based on MAS. In: De La Prieta, F., et al. (eds.) PAAMS 2019. CCIS, vol. 1047, pp. 257–264. Springer, Cham (2019). https://doi.org/10.1007/ 978-3-030-24299-2_22
9. Pautasso, E., Osella, M., Caroleo, B.: Addressing the sustainability issue in smart cities: a comprehensive model for evaluating the impacts of electric vehicle diffusion. Systems **7**(2), 29 (2019)
10. Pevec, D., Babic, J., Carvalho, A., Ghiassi-Farrokhfal, Y., Ketter, W., Podobnik, V.: A survey-based assessment of how existing and potential electric vehicle owners perceive range anxiety. J. Clean. Prod. **276**, 122779 (2020)
11. Rauh, N., Franke, T., Krems, J.F.: Understanding the impact of electric vehicle driving experience on range anxiety. Hum. Factors **57**(1), 177–187 (2015)
12. Wood, E., Neubauer, J.S., Burton, E.: Measuring the benefits of public chargers and improving infrastructure deployments using advanced simulation tools. Technical report, SAE Technical Paper (2015)
13. Zhang, Yu., Liu, X., Zhang, T., Gu, Z.: Review of the electric vehicle charging station location problem. In: Wang, G., Bhuiyan, M.Z.A., De Capitani di Vimercati, S., Ren, Y. (eds.) DependSys 2019. CCIS, vol. 1123, pp. 435–445. Springer, Singapore (2019). https://doi.org/10.1007/978-981-15-1304-6_35

Challenges and Solutions in Large-Scale News Recommenders

Joel Pinho Lucas$^{(\boxtimes)}$ and Leticia Freire de Figueiredo

Globo, Pelotas, Brazil
{joel.pinho,leticia.figueiredo}@g.globo
http://www.globo.com

Abstract. This paper describes the main challenges and solutions adopted in large-scale production news recommenders in Grupo Globo, the biggest Latin American mass media group. Its vertical information portals reach 100 million unique daily users, playing an important role in content distribution in Brazil. News recommenders encompass additional challenges in comparison to recommenders from other domains, especially regarding recency and cold-start. In this context, recommendation metrics and quality are highly impacted by the short lifetime of new items. This work shares the main challenges we have been facing in providing news recommendations in large-scale production environments. We also discuss solutions we have been applying so far to deal with these scenarios as well as some case studies evaluating the proposed approaches, where online metrics are tracked by means of an in-house AB testing platform.

Keywords: Recommender Systems · News Recommenders · Cold-Start · Decision Support

1 Introduction

Recommendation engines currently play a crucial role in systems from many domains and areas. Correspondingly, news portals that encompass a large number of users and multiple articles published daily highly depend on recommender systems. In this sense, Globo web portals encompass multiple recommendation strategies in order to enhance user experience, personalization and even publishing revenue based on articles and video consumption. Globo's vertical information portals reach 100 million unique daily users, where each portal is subjected to a specific stakeholder responsible for a domain subject (i.e. sports, entertainment, news, etc.). In this scenario, recommender systems also play the role of decision support systems, where product managers and human editors can define, and track, content-delivery strategies according to diverse Key Performance Indicators (KPIs), domain specificities, and editorial guidelines.

In this paper, we describe the main challenges and solutions adopted in developing and maintaining news recommenders in Globo. According to Raza and Ding [15], news recommenders are developed to suggest articles to users based on their preferences and behavior, dealing with short-term and long-term users.

D. Durães et al. (Eds.): PAAMS 2023, CCIS 1838, pp. 170–181, 2023.
https://doi.org/10.1007/978-3-031-37593-4_14

Such systems may make editorial decisions for the front page of an online newspaper, decide which additional stories to suggest to a reader of a story, decide on the selection and order of stories in the consumption flow of the user, unlock the long tail, and increase coverage [2].

Besides addressing recommendations to millions of users encompassing diverse profiles in terms of engagement and the type of content they consume, providing fresh and context-aware recommendations is also challenging, since thousands of news articles and videos are published every day. News recommendation problems often have certain characteristics that are either not present at all or that are at least less pronounced in other domains [11]. The news domain is faced with certain challenges that are different from those of other application domains of recommender systems [16].

In the next section, we describe the main challenges news portals like Globo currently face in providing news recommendations. In Sect. 3 we share more in detail some strategies and approaches to potentially overcome such challenges, including experimentation and engineering aspects.

2 Challenges Faced in News Recommenders

In addition to classical challenges traditional recommender systems present, such as sparsity, grey-sheep, cold-start, and scalability [14], news recommenders face additional challenges. In contrast to other domains like movie recommendation [11], the relevance of news items can change very rapidly (i.e., decline or re-increase due to recent real-life events) [1,11,20]. According to Raza and Ding [15], the news domain scenario encompasses a highly dynamic user behavior, where news readers may have long-term or short-term preferences that evolve over time, either gradually or abruptly.

In the following subsections, we discuss three challenges (recency, item cold-start, and dynamic user preferences) continually debated in the news recommenders research domain [4,11,15,18,20], but focusing Globo's news portals scenarios, where 100M unique users are impacted daily by recommendations from diverse topics. It is important to highlight that misinformation and ethics concerns are currently critical challenges in news portals and, therefore, have a high priority in Globo. Since all news articles in Globo's portals are written exclusively by Globo's journalists, and also revised by internal editorial teams spread out around the country, such challenges are already mitigated.

2.1 Recency

According to Schedl et al. [16], the lifespan of news content typically has shorter shelf-lives as they expire quite soon (maybe minutes, hours, or barely a few days) compared to other products such as music, books, and movies that may span even several months or even years. Thus, in news recommender systems the magnitude of recent items' impact is way more challenging. Moreira et al. [18] also state the news domain poses some challenges for recommender systems due to the fast-growing number of items, accelerated decay of item's value, and user preferences shift. Therefore any model older than a few hours may no longer be of interest and partial updates will not work [3].

Observing specifically the scenario of G1, the Globo's journalism portal and the most popular news portal in Brazil, users' interest in articles lasts less than a day. Figure 1 depicts the total volume of page visits during February 2023, where the x-axis corresponds to the number of hours between the news publication and the page visit event. The histogram clearly shows that items (news pages) are consumed predominantly on the same day they become available. In this sense, recommendations must reflect relevant and recent content. The accelerated decay reflects not only content consumption in Globo's portals but also due to multiple sources of information users handle nowadays, including other portals and social media.

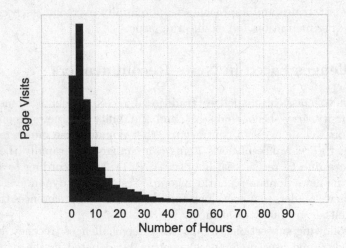

Fig. 1. Items age and their Page Visits.

2.2   Cold-Start

The requirement of providing recent content in news recommenders inevitably results in potential cold-start items. In such a scenario where user interest decays exponentially, new articles need to be published frequently in order to provide fresh content to users. This intensifies the cold-start problem, as for fresh items you cannot count on lots of interactions before starting to recommend them [4]. The cold-start problem arises when the user or item just arrived and the model does not have information, such as how many users viewed the item or what items the user liked [12,17].

Likewise, in Globo's portals, the high intensity of content publication implies challenges related to item cold-start, which, along with the massive volume of user events, are intrinsically related to software engineering. In 2022, G1 published more than 350k news content, which resulted in a daily average of almost 1k new items ingested in Globo's recommender system. This scenario poses scalability and personalization challenges due to the diversity of content segments and the intensity of user interests.

In Globo user interests are acquired mainly through records of their browsing history. In this scenario, where the most relevant items are recent, tracking user preferences is also challenging and cold-start reflects not only in items but also at the user level. Gharahighehi and Vens [8] highlight the user cold-start challenge in news recommenders that present many anonymous users, whose profiles and long-term interaction histories are not available. User cold-start refers to situations where little is known about the preferences of the user for which a recommendation is requested [11].

Due to the lack of prior data on user interactions and item correlations, our algorithms, inevitably, have to face the cold-start problem. As stated previously, the high volume of publications along with the user interest in recent content turns item cold start into an arduous challenge for portals. In this context, algorithms runtime plays a crucial role in processing as many fresh items as possible in order to keep user preferences up to date on recent consumption.

2.3 Dynamic Context

Besides taking into account factors such as the very short duration of news articles, news recommenders have to deal with more intangible challenges that inevitably emerge from the recency and cold-start scenarios described previously. In this sense, user preferences are highly dynamic and are also affected by different factors related to their contexts such as device type (desktop or mobile phone), time of the day, day of the week, or any other unexpected event. In addition, user preferences must also reflect the occurrence of breaking news, which results in drastic variations in the volume of pageviews. Figure 2 depicts the total volume of page visits during October 2022, where the x-axis corresponds to the day of the month and the y-axis to the volume of page visits. The plot clearly shows four days reflecting high peaks of page visits reflecting the effect of breaking news events. Such page visits come both from light users (who do not access Globo portals in a while) and from heavy users (who increase their time spent during such events). This kind of dynamic scenario results in severe data drifts to be handled by the models.

Breaking news scenarios are also challenging in terms of serendipity. Herlocker et al. [10] refer to serendipity as items that help users find surprising and interesting content in recommender systems, which they might not have noticed before. In this context, there is an intrinsic trade-off to deal with: surprise the user with serendipitous recommendations or continue recommending the same topic related to the breaking news. At the individual level, a news reader may get bored of reading similar types of news stories all the time [16]. This kind of decision must be addressed by the models, which must optimize metrics associated directly with business KPIs.

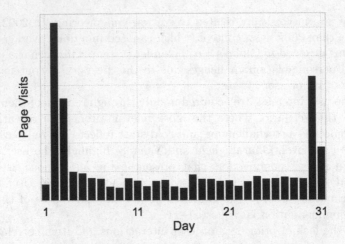

Fig. 2. Daily Volume of Page Visits.

3   Strategies to Overcome News Recommender Challenges

In order to deal with the challenges described in the previous section, experimentation plays a crucial role in facing trade-offs and verifying models' performance. Therefore, Globo has an internal AB testing platform in which updated versions of current models, or even new ones, can be run in production for only a small set of users. In Globo, every new recommendation is, mandatorily, an AB testing experiment. Therefore, we can easily track online metrics and communicate faster with stakeholders. Moreover, the AB testing platform turns all steps of decision-making processes faster as online metrics are directly associated with business KPIs. Garcin et al. [7] state that offline performance is not necessarily directly associated with online success. Frequently, models performing best offline not necessarily will perform the same way on online metrics in production. In this way, AB testing with online metrics is especially important with more sophisticated algorithms, since they are more subjected to overfitting or over-personalization. Typical accuracy-centric approaches may fail to consider other aspects of subjective user experiences (such as choice satisfaction, perceived system effectiveness, better recommendations, and exposure to different points of view) when evaluating the recommendation quality [16]. When developing a good News Recommender System, one must consider the beyond-accuracy aspects to evaluate the quality of news recommendations [16].

AB tests are also useful to face trade-offs like the ones described in Sect. 2 (such as recommending items related to breaking news x serendipitous content). In this type of scenario, tracking online metrics and constantly communicating them to stakeholders is crucial to promote collaboration among interdisciplinary teams in order to reach the company's KPIs. Subsequently, we propose and share some strategies that achieved successful AB testing results when adopted in Globo's portals to face the challenges described in the previous section.

3.1 Combining Recency with User Preferences

Traditional recommender systems depend on user ratings over items to learn user preferences. However, in the news recommenders' scenarios, such as the one described in [3] about Google News, explicit ratings are usually not available. Thus, we need to infer the personal interests of users from their implicit feedback like clicks [19]. Das et al. [3] proposed to define implicit binary item ratings, where a click on a story corresponds to a 1 and a non-click corresponds to a 0. Similarly, Lu et al. [13] propose to combine different forms of user behavior, context, and content features of the news items to find similar users in sparse-data situations considering the user's browsing, commenting, and publishing behavior as implicit feedback signals.

Nowadays users are exposed to multiple sources of information and their behavior in reading articles is highly diverse and solely clicks are not enough to effectively learn their preferences. Therefore, in Globo we also consider two additional events after the user clicks: the amount of time spent on the article and the percentage of the page scroll. Combining both events are more effective than considering them separately, otherwise, events such as a fast scroll to the end of the page or an inactive session on a single browser tab could be considered as high interest to an article. Equation 1 depicts how we calculate user preferences, where *s(scroll)* and *t(time)* are functions defining the percentage of page scroll and time spent on the article:

$$p(u,i) = \sqrt[3]{s(scroll) \times t(time) \times (s(scroll) + \frac{t(time)}{2})} \qquad (1)$$

The *p(u,i)* function will present a low value (or even equals zero) if either *s(scroll)* or *t(time)* is low. In this sense, *p(u,i)* may be interpreted as an average weight between *s(scroll)* e *t(time)*. This approach is employed both in collaborative filtering (CF) and knowledge-based models along the portals.

However, since news recommenders suffer from a severe cold-start scenario, where many new items emerge daily and old ones will expire fastly, considering only user preferences over an article is not enough because recency will directly impact an article's relevance. In this sense, recency must be addressed by recommendation models in addition to user preferences over articles. In this sense, we propose to apply the Min-Max normalization to estimate the recency relevance of an article. Equation 2 presents such intuition, where *a* refers to the publication date of an article and *A* is the set of all publication dates of the candidate articles respecting a determined recency rule defined previously with stakeholders. The recency rule includes the maximum number of hours that occurred between the current time and the article's publication event (in other words, the age of the article).

$$r(a, A) = \frac{a - min(A)}{max(A) - min(A)} \qquad (2)$$

It is important to highlight that every recommendation experiment is configured following a set of business rules (such as the recency rule), which will determine the candidate items. These rules also define the recency relevance in every recommended component within portals. At the end of the day, such relevance is subjected to multiple variables: the domain area, the region where the user is located (and the number of contextual articles available there), user engagement level, number of page visits during the day, etc. Finally, a model is responsible for learning the weights of such variables when combining $r(a,\ A$ and $p(u,i)$.

3.2   Session-Based Methods

According to Gulla et al. [9], some recommendation methods, such as CF, need to wait several hours to collect enough clicks to recommend incoming news stories to users, resulting in undesirable time lags between breaking news and recommendations. In news websites most of the users are anonymous and the only available data are sequences of items in anonymous sessions [8]. In Globo, the fraction of anonymous users, as well as the level of data available from users, varies according to seasonality and domain area of the portal. In any case, readers, including anonymous users, usually want to be updated about different news articles at a time, which results in more than a single page visit in the same session. Thus, models considering consumption sequences within a sole session, as also described in [16] and [8], are also employed to deal with the severe cold-start scenario.

The implementation of a session-bassed approach has been delivering promising results in certain scenarios in Globo, which will be described in more detail in the next section. This implementation uses two deep neural networks to predict the next item to be consumed by the user. In this way, two models are trained: one with a convolutional neural network (CNN) and another with a recurrent neural network (RNN). The first is responsible for generating embedding representations of the available candidates from features based on items' metadata. The second is responsible to learn consumption sequences within the same session and then predicting, for every user, the next embeddings, which ultimately represent the ranking items to be recommended. The biggest advantage of this method of recommending items to a specific user is that it is based on a single session, not requiring a large historical consumption like in CF methods. The focus on the session level, instead of on the sparse user-history level, turns this approach into a potential solution to deliver personalized content to light and even anonymous users.

Table 1 shows the case study 1, which refers to AB testing data tracked in March 2023, the session-based approach reached the greatest Click Through Rate (CTR) in the autonext video recommendation component in one of Globo's news portals. Even tiny variations in CTR (session-based outperformed CF by only 0.58%) result in significant business impact because of the large number of users and events.

Table 1. Case study 1 - Session-based approach in the autonext feature.

Strategy	CTR	LIFT
Most Recents (control)	12.25%	–
CF-Based	14.78%	21%
Session-Based	15.36%	25%

3.3 Fallback Models

Besides recommending items directly to the users (i.e. a user-based recommendation), recommendations can also focus on items. In item-based recommendations, a specific news article is taken as an anchor, or pivot, item instead of the user. In this case, recommendations are provided to the item, not to the user. In G1, for example, every news page encompasses a newsfeed component displaying other news related to the pivot article.

In addition to the recommendation approaches mentioned so far in this paper, content similarity approaches are also designed in Globo, mainly focusing on item-based scenarios. Ferreira at al. [6] describe one of these methods, which consists of a content-based approach based on multi-modal features such as visual characteristics and audio patterns found in video content. Nevertheless, CF is also employed for item-based recommendations, where they usually outperform content-based methods in terms of page visit metrics. Despite depending on a certain volume of items co-visitation, they are much simpler and faster to be applied in production because, in contrast to content-based methods, they are domain-independent and do not encompass a training model depending on content metadata.

As stated in Subsect. 3.1, every recommendation experiment in Globo is configured following a set of business rules. These rules are configured by means of an internal administrator system, which is also responsible for providing the appropriate metadata to be the respective input on every recommendation experiment. The type of experiment (item or user-based recommendation) is also configured within the administrator system. Afterward, recommendation models will process this input along with users' event data. Every model depends on specific time ranges for loading user events, as well as some (like CF) are more dependent on high volumes of data. As a consequence, for cold-start users and cold start-items (in the case of item-based recommendations) models will not provide any output. Besides affecting KPIs, this scenario could also result in a critical user experience problem since some of Globo's Web and mobile app components use the output of such models to render the component content. In this way, Globo's recommender systems architecture provides a fallback strategy, where a secondary, and typically more straightforward, model is requested for providing items to the recommendation list.

From a practical standpoint, multiple recommendation strategies are tested in production at the same time within independent AB testing experiments. Accordingly, every recommendation strategy contains a primary/preferred model, which has the highest priority on providing recommendations. In this context, in circumstances where the pivot item is a cold-start (item-based) or there are not sufficient events from the user receiving recommendation (user-based), a secondary, or even a tertiary model is achieved. Hence, fallback models can have different levels of priority, which are usually established according to their performance and complexity. In this sense, session-based and content-based methods are usually primary models. Conversely, CF-based methods are usually secondary models and top-based (i.e. most popular items in a given period of time) tertiary. At the end of the day, fallback models guarantee relevant recommendations even in cold-start scenarios.

3.4   Measuring Cold-Start in Item-Based Recommendations

Despite fallback models making sure relevant recommendations be provided, higher online metrics and quality would probably be achieved when the primary model is employed. In this way, model optimizations and engineering efforts should constantly be taken in order to increase the usage of priority models. Hence, measuring the impact of cold-start becomes a challenging but necessary task to be accomplished. Thus, we propose to measure the velocity news recommenders respond to new items. In item-based recommendation this translates into tracking algorithms' response time to a new pivot item might.

Therefore, we propose to track the difference of time (number of hours) between the news publication event and the first time the algorithm outputs similar items to the pivot, meaning that significant co-occurred items were able to be tracked. We defined an intuition for the algorithm's *Item-cold Start Responsiveness* (ICSR) as metric accounting for the mean number of hours between those two events in a given period of observation. Afterward, we compare the primary model's *coverage* against the fallback models in a given period of observation. Measuring the proportion of items, among all recommendations, were originated from the primary model might also determine the amount of effort spent on software engineering improvements.

Table 2 describes another case study, which makes a comparison between two versions of a CF model applied to recommendations in a newsfeed component: v.1 from March 2021 and v.2 from November 2021. The latter contains engineering improvements responsible for reducing the algorithm's processing time and, consequently, considering item interaction data earlier. Such engineering improvements consisted mainly of optimizations in our Hadoop cluster, which is beyond the scope of this study. Table 2's data consists of CTR, algorithms' coverage, and the item cold-start responsiveness (ICSR) measured in both versions.

Table 2. Case study 2 - measuring cold-start incidence.

	CTR	ICSR	Algorithm Coverage
CF v.1	4.14	4.47h	22.2%
CF v.2	4.57	3.01h	32.96%

Table 2 shows that CTR is directly proportional to CF coverage and inversely proportional to its responsiveness to item cold-start. This scenario demonstrates improvements in our recommender architecture resulted in higher CTR as a consequence of more responsiveness to item cold-start.

3.5 Reinforcement Learning-Based Approaches

In circumstances of severe impacts caused by breaking news, such as the ones in Fig. 2 and also for brand new items, employing the primary model is extremely unlikely, even with the best engineering effort to develop near real-time response models. In this sense, naive top-based algorithms will inevitably be requested. Even though these circumstances are infrequent, there is a significant volume of potential page visits to be accomplished with the help of top-based models. Thus, top-based algorithms must not be neglected but enhanced.

With the purpose of maximizing the performance of top-based algorithms, one straightforward strategy vastly employed in Globo is to create segments within top-based results. Thus, in item-based approaches, for example, the recommended items for a cold-start article in the economy topic could be the most popular articles within the economy domain. Similarly, in a user-based scenario, recommendations to a cold-start user could be the most popular items consumed within the region where this user is located, for example. This kind of segmentation is available for multiple variables related to both user and item metadata.

Besides segmentation, drastic variations in the volume of events are also an opportunity to be explored. In a nutshell, top-based algorithms count the number of page visits to every item during a given period of time and sort them in the end. We name as *input minutes* the variable referring to the period of time the page visits are counted. Depending on users' seasonal behavior and/or breaking news, the volume of page visits per minute changes accordingly. As a consequence, the top stories change more dynamically in certain circumstances such as the subsequent hour after a football game (in the sports domain), at the begging of the morning when users want to be updated about economy topics before starting to work (hard news domain), at early evening after work when users want to relax and check entertainment stories, etc. Ideally, the more dynamic the scenario, the lower

Despite being able to sometimes interpret and define rules to detect this type of scenario, it would not be feasible to define static heuristics due to the diversity of topics and unpredictability of users' behavior. Therefore, we propose to apply a multi-armed bandit (MAB) approach to dynamically determine the *input minutes*, where rewards are associated with the volume of page visits. In some aspects, this kind of strategy is also proposed by Felicio et al. [5] when applying MAB for model selection to face cold-start.

Table 3 shows the case study 3, which refers to AB testing data tracked in March 2023. The Top with dynamic input minutes algorithm outperformed the static top-based algorithm CTR in a newsfeed component of G1.

Table 3. Case study 3 - Session-based approach in the autonext feature.

Strategy	CTR	LIFT
Most Recent (control)	0.94%	–
Top in the last 24 h	1.26%	33.42%
Top with dynamic input minutes	1.31%	39.07%

4   Conclusion

The case studies described in Sect. 2 indicated that engineering and experimentation play crucial roles in large-scale recommender systems. News recommenders, in particular, bring up the content recency challenge as items' interest presents fast decay. As a consequence, the cold-start problem is even more critical in this scenario, which demands higher engineering efforts. In this context, creating segments (either user or item-based ones) and defining a concise fallback strategy have been demonstrated to be effective strategies for mitigating such drawbacks.

Moreover, performing granular AB testing favors product data-driven decisions and accelerates the learning of user behaviors. Since each recommendation component has its own specificities, such as position on the screen and type of content, experimentation results and decisions will depend on online metrics. In this sense, stakeholders' KPIs will drive the definition ad tracking of such metrics.

References

1. Ahn, J.W., Brusilovsky, P., Grady, J., He, D., Syn, S.Y.: Open user profiles for adaptive news systems: help or harm? pp. 11–20 (2007). https://doi.org/10.1145/1242572.1242575
2. Bernstein, A., et al.: Diversity in news recommendation **9** (2021). https://doi.org/10.4230/DagMan.9.1.43
3. Das, A., Datar, M., Garg, A., Rajaram, S.: Google news personalization: scalable online collaborative filtering, pp. 271–280 (2007). https://doi.org/10.1145/1242572.1242610
4. Díez Peláez, J., Martínez Rego, D., Alonso-Betanzos, A., Luaces Rodríguez, O., Bahamonde Rionda, A., et al.: Metrical representation of readers and articles in a digital newspaper. In: 10th ACM Conference on Recommender Systems (RecSys 2016). ACM (2016)
5. Felicio, C., Paixão, K., Barcelos, C., Preux, P.: Multi-armed bandits to recommend for cold-start user (2016)
6. Ferreira, F., Souza, D., Moura, I., Barbieri, M., Lopes, H.: Investigating multimodal features for video recommendations at globoplay (2020). https://doi.org/10.1145/3383313.3411553
7. Garcin, F., Faltings, B., Donatsch, O., Alazzawi, A., Bruttin, C., Huber, A.: Offline and online evaluation of news recommender systems at swissinfo.ch, pp. 169–176 (2014). https://doi.org/10.1145/2645710.2645745

8. Gharahighehi, A., Vens, C.: Making session-based news recommenders diversity-aware (2020)
9. Gulla, J., Svendsen, R., Zhang, L., Stenbom, A., Frøland, J.: Recommending news in traditional media companies. AI Mag. **42**, 55–69 (2022). https://doi.org/10.1609/aimag.v42i3.18146
10. Herlocker, J., Konstan, J., Terveen, L., Lui, J.C., Riedl, T.: Evaluating collaborative filtering recommender systems. ACM Trans. Inf. Syst. **22**, 5–53 (2004). https://doi.org/10.1145/963770.963772
11. Karimi, M., Jannach, D., Jugovac, M.: News recommender systems - survey and roads ahead. Inf. Process. Manage. **54**, 1203–1227 (2018). https://doi.org/10.1016/j.ipm.2018.04.008
12. Ricci, F., Rokach, L., Shapira, B., Kantor, P.B. (eds.): Recommender Systems Handbook. Springer, Boston, MA (2011). https://doi.org/10.1007/978-0-387-85820-3
13. Lu, M., Zhen, Q., Yiming, C., Zhichao, L., Mengxing, W.: Scalable news recommendation using multi-dimensional similarity and Jaccard-Kmeans clustering. J. Syst. Softw. **95** (2014). https://doi.org/10.1016/j.jss.2014.04.046
14. Pinho Lucas, J., Segrera, S., Moreno, M.N.: Making use of associative classifiers in order to alleviate typical drawbacks in recommender systems. Expert Syst. Appl. **39**(1), 1273–1283 (2012). https://doi.org/10.1016/j.eswa.2011.07.136
15. Raza, S., Ding, C.: A survey on news recommender system - dealing with timeliness, dynamic user interest and content quality, and effects of recommendation on news readers. arXiv preprint: arXiv:2009.04964 (2020)
16. Schedl, M., Zamani, H., Chen, C.-W., Deldjoo, Y., Elahi, M.: Current challenges and visions in music recommender systems research. Int. J. Multimedia Inf. Retrieval **7**(2), 95–116 (2018). https://doi.org/10.1007/s13735-018-0154-2
17. Schein, A.I., Popescul, A., Ungar, L.H., Pennock, D.M.: Methods and metrics for cold-start recommendations. In: Proceedings of the 25th Annual International ACM SIGIR Conference on Research and Development in Information Retrieval, pp. 253–260 (2002)
18. de Souza Pereira Moreira, G., Ferreira, F., Marques da Cunha, A.: News session-based recommendations using deep neural networks. In: Proceedings of the 3rd Workshop on Deep Learning for Recommender Systems. ACM (2018). https://doi.org/10.1145/3270323.3270328
19. Wu, C., Wu, F., Huang, Y., Xie, X.: Personalized news recommendation: methods and challenges. ACM Trans. Inf. Syst. **41** (2022). https://doi.org/10.1145/3530257
20. Özgöbek, O., Gulla, J., Erdur, C.: A survey on challenges and methods in news recommendation. In: WEBIST 2014 - Proceedings of the 10th International Conference on Web Information Systems and Technologies, no. 2, pp. 278–285 (2014)

Author Index

D. Durães et al. (Eds.): PAAMS 2023, CCIS 1838, pp. 183–184, 2023.
https://doi.org/10.1007/978-3-031-37593-4

Printed in the United States
by Baker & Taylor Publisher Services

Printed in the United States
by Baker & Taylor Publisher Services